BANK 3.0

Praise for Bank 2.0

"**BANK** 2.0 will change the way you think about banking in the future. Audacious, provocative and sometimes controversial, Brett King redefines the paradigm of consumer banking. This compelling book is guaranteed to send your pulse racing and your mind searching for a new strategy for your bank."

Suvo Sarkar,
Executive Vice-President, Emirates NBD

"**BANK** 2.0 represents a view of the future of bank retailing and channel strategies for the next decade. The fact that banks take so long to respond to these changes in the status quo means that any bank acting upon the key recommendations in this book will be a step ahead of the competition, and that surely is no bad thing. Now think what you could be if you acted upon all of the recommendations."

Chris Skinner,
Chairman, Financial Services Club

"**BANK** 2.0 is informed by Brett King's analysis of trends in banking over many years. Brett's work has led to significant performance improvements in some very large and well-respected financial institutions. I've worked with Brett and I have seen some of the results; they explain why Brett is highly sought after as an authority on banking and how the industry is likely to evolve into the future."

Dr Richard Petty,
President, CPA Australia

"On the Web and on Mobile the customer isn't king—he's dictator. Highly impatient, skeptical, cynical. Brett King understands deeply what drives this new hard-nosed customer. Banking professionals would do well to heed his advice."

Gerry McGovern,
author of *Killer Web Content*

Praise for Bank 2.0

"The impact of the Internet and mobile devices has made the rules in managing channels and how we reach customers a moving target. This book does something that no one I know has been able to do thus far—teach us to re-design our instincts first and then our knowledge about how this moving target will evolve. With the correct instinct, we will be able to respond correctly to the rules as they change. I am very grateful to Brett for putting down to paper the instincts that he has been able to hone over the years. Brett is a true international; he is probably one of the few I know who can draw from personal examples from across Asia, where as much and maybe more innovations are taking place in financial services, as anywhere else in the world."

Emmanuel Daniel,
Chairman, *The Asian Banker Journal*

"Creating more value for customers is a hallmark of successful and growing organisations. But the field of competitive battle has changed. What customers value today is different from what they appreciated years ago, and will be very different once again in the rapidly unfolding future. **BANK** 2.0 brings together Brett King's incomparable view of technology, strategy, customer value and delivering superior service. His insights are a "must read" for anyone who wants to attract and keep customers in the incredible years ahead. If you are a bank customer, you will find this a fascinating read that likely puts you ahead of your own bank in preparation, insight and understanding."

Ron Kaufman,
bestselling author of *Uplifting Service*

"**BANK** 2.0 is a very comprehensive and well-researched book that should be read by everyone responsible for—or interested in—innovation in banking."

BlueCoin

"Brett King raises the bar very high for this book. At 397 pages, he delivers."

ABA Banking Journal

BANK 3.0

BANK 3.0

WHY BANKING IS NO LONGER SOMEWHERE YOU GO, BUT SOMETHING YOU DO

BRETT KING

WILEY

John Wiley & Sons Singapore Pte. Ltd.

Other Wiley Editorial Offices
John Wiley & Sons, 111 River Street, Hoboken, NJ 07030, USA
John Wiley & Sons, The Atrium, Southern Gate, Chichester, West Sussex, P019 8SQ, United
    Kingdom
John Wiley& Sons (Canada) Ltd., 5353 Dundas Street West, Suite 400, Toronto, Ontario, M9B
    6HB, Canada
John Wiley& Sons Australia Ltd., 42 McDougall Street, Milton, Queensland 4064, Australia
Wiley-VCH, Boschstrasse 12, D-69469 Weinheim, Germany

ISBN 978-1-118-58963-2 (Hardcover)
ISBN 978-1-118-58968-7 (ePDF)
ISBN 978-1-118-58965-6 (Mobi)
ISBN 978-1-118-58964-9 (ePub)

Printed in the United States of America.
10 9 8 7 6 5 4 3

To my family,
my father, who is my biggest fan, and
my Movenbank buddies, who are changing the world
—one line of code and one customer at a time

Contents

PART THREE: The Road Ahead—Beyond Channel

Acknowledgements

I'D LIKE to pass on my thanks to the following people who assisted me in pulling together this book.

To the team at HSBC, including Louisa Cheung, Peter Brooks, Martin Rawling, Christina Yung. To Matthew Dooley, Tom Cannon and Michael Armstrong as HSBC Alumni. To Steve Townend at MoBank, Ron Kaufman at UpYourService College, Ben May and Grace Lee for their help with the blogsite.

To Chris Skinner, who is the most prolific blogger I know in the FS space and who always has advice to offer—a complete banker. To Sean Clifford who remains a great pal and constant balancing force when I'm thrashing out strategy.

To Alex Sion, Michael Degnan and the team at Sapient who helped me organise my thoughts on customer journeys and engagement banking, and to the teams at Innotribe and Anthemis, who provide the most amazing peer group opportunities in the space.

I would be remiss not to thank Geoff Bye (a fellow of the UK Chartered Institute of Marketing) and Scott Bales (Movenbank's Chief Mobile Officer) for their contributions to the book. Also to John Lambrides and the innovation team at NCR for their contributions and allowing me access to their top secret innovation centre somewhere near Area 51 (well, New York actually).

To my bloggers and tweeters in arms @rshevlin, @jmarous, @tek_fin, @visible_banking, @petervan, @thebankchannel, @leimer, @venessamiemis, @heathervescent, @Hleichsenring, @copernicc, and many more.

To the team at O2 and CMI Speakers who've become a major support team as I embarked on my *Bank 2.0* world tour to change the world of banking. It has been an extraordinary ride, I hope this is just the beginning.

To the team at Marshall Cavendish who had their own transition to make to Publishing 2.0 as we worked towards an e-book strategy and who stuck with me as the demand for *Bank 2.0* exceeded all expectations.

But most of all to my family who put up with me neglecting them as I spent time on the road preaching the mantra and writing.

Introduction

BANK 2.0 was written at the start of a time of great disruption in the banking and financial services space. We were in the midst of a "global financial crisis", second only to the Great Depression for many commentators. In the midst of this chaos, however, the retail banking space faced an entirely different challenge as the cracks in the façade that was the "secure banking system" appeared.

> "Global Central banks have pumped $8.7tn into the banking system to 'save the world'. Saving the banks has cost more money than it cost to fight WWII, the first Gulf War, put a man on the moon, clean up after last year's Japanese Tsunami, and the entire African aid budget for the last 20 years all put together."
>
> —David McWilliams, PunkEconomics

This was not just a crisis of identity, a challenge to the perception of banks as "secure" and "socially responsible" bastions of the community. It was a challenge to the very role of banks in an open, transparent society. This was more than just the "occupy" movement and a backlash against unreasonable bonuses—bankers suddenly found themselves having to answer to the public for their decisions that led to the crisis.

Bankers rallied in this environment to claim how unjust negative public opinion was, how they had the right to make a profit (thanks for that gem, Brian Moynihan), how bankers needed to get huge bonuses because otherwise they might leave their employers, and that they were sick of the sledging they were getting from customers who really had no idea how banks or the banking system worked. Now you might think that's unfair, but those are the comments that stuck with customers in the midst of all this backlash.

The problem, however, was not one solely of perception, but of relevance. In an age where I use my mobile phone and the Internet more than I watch TV, and where bookstores, video rental stores and other mainstays of the physical retail commerce are quickly morphing, banks just appeared old-fashioned and out of touch.

In a world where I'm more likely to text you, update my status, upload a photo or use an app, rather than visit a bank branch—the change that was being thrust on bankers was not just a crisis of identity, forced transparency, and a battle for public opinion, but a crisis of modality. Retail banking was fundamentally ready to change the way it worked at the consumer interface, but the overwhelming tone of the industry was both a rejection of that notion and a dismissal of changing consumer needs at the same time. Bankers dismissed the concept that digital interactions were overtaking the branch, and reinforced the need for face-to-face interactions as superior when all they were really doing was trying to justify their bloated, costly, physical infrastructure.

It was in this environment that a new reality of banking started to emerge. Banking was no longer defined or hemmed in by a physical distribution network, or physical artefacts. The banking system emerging out of the global crisis would be one that was highly utilitarian, pervasive, mobile, and seamlessly engineered to work when and where we needed it. While the "death of cash" will still take many years to become a reality, the effects of the mobile phone and Internet are causing a massive shift in bank practices, distribution models and competitive landscape.

In the end, many of the banks that were household names during the 20th century will simply cease to exist as they are displaced or consolidated in the system-wide disruption that is soon coming. New players are emerging now that are taking ownership of the customer experience through revolutionary new techniques that attack the fringes of "banking" and payments.

PayPal, perhaps the largest financial institution in the world (by number of active customers), flourished by filling a gap in payments experience born out of a lukewarm industry reception to e-commerce, to become easily the dominant online payment provider. Now 12 years old, PayPal is still considered by many banks to be a "new" player in the sector, but for start-ups now disrupting the industry, PayPal is an incumbent.

Square, a company founded by Jack Dorsey of Twitter fame, went from start-up to a $4-billion business in revenue in just under two years, showing banks first that a point-of-sale terminal wasn't necessary, and then that even cards weren't necessary.

Simple (formerly BankSimple) emerged as one of the first non-bank entities that truly attacked the very front end of banking. Others quickly followed. The success of these start-ups is not yet certain, but with more than 100,000 registered customers when Simple opened its doors, so to speak, success would appear a simple matter of execution.

In the midst of all of this, a new class of consumer emerged in developed economies such as the US. This new class of consumer no longer needed a bank account to live and work in the system. In fact, millions of them abandoned their traditional bank relationships in favour of prepaid debit cards, PayPal accounts, mobile payments, and other such workarounds to a system that was coming apart at the seams. With $200 billion in prepaid debit cards in the US alone in 2011, this was not a minor blip, this signalled a fundamental change—the rise of the "de-banked".[1]

It has become clear that Bill Gates' quote of old about us needing banking, but not banks, has never been more likely an outcome of the technology and behavioural-led disruption we find ourselves in today.

In this revised edition, *Bank 3.0*, the message I want you to take away is this: Banking is no longer somewhere you go, it's something you do.

By this new measure, a customer's assessment of a service provider in the retail banking or financial services space will not be capital adequacy, branch network, products or rates. It will be how simply and easily customers can access banking when they need it, and how much they trust the partner or service provider to execute.

So if you're a bank—what are you going to do? How are you going to make the transition? When will you need to start scaling back branches? How real is this shift and how quickly will it happen?

While *Bank 3.0* retains some of the great case studies and groundwork that was in *Bank 2.0*, I've tried to update this based on the rapidly changing environment we've found ourselves in over the last few years. It's incredible how much has changed and what this means for the future of banking, and, as such, I felt these changes added tremendous value to the discussion. Much of the original content is gone, making way for a more relevant and up-to-date discussion.

For those of you who previously read *Bank 2.0*, this is an update that includes insight on the acceleration of mobile deployments, including detailed discussion on wallets and cardless solutions. We'll look at the differences between technologies such as NFC and Virtual Wallets, and what is the likely outcome for payments over the next decade, including how long before plastic cards are really on the decline. We'll look at what is happening in the web space as a result of our moving away from the PC browser to "screens", along with the death of Adobe Flash and the emergence of HTML 5. We're taking a much more detailed look at the implications of social media on your brand, how you engage customers and how this impacts organisation structure. We'll look into the emergence of journeys at the point of impact, and we'll look at the need for ever more pervasive banking solutions enabled through smart data and collaboration across disciplines and industries (e.g. mobile network operators and institutions.)

Be assured this is disruptive and controversial. This is about as exciting as banking gets. Everything from this point on is changing. What you used to consider as banking historically is about to get, not just a makeover, but a complete reboot.

If you're in retail banking, the future starts now and it's called **BANK** 3.0. Jump in, or get disrupted.

Endnotes

1   Ron Shevlin from Aité Group was the first to coin this word.

Part 01

Changes in Customer Behaviour

1 The Demands of the Hyperconnected Consumer

In 2011 the Internet surpassed television and newspapers as the primary news source for the Y-Gen demographic in the US.[1] In 2011 the average time spent daily using mobile phone apps surpassed the time people spent surfing the web on their PC.[2] In the US, approximately 25 per cent of all US households have no or very limited access to financial services,[3] while there is a 103 per cent adoption rate of mobile phones and a 76 per cent adoption of the Internet.[4] In Asia, there are 1.6 billion people without a basic bank account,[5] while in the same geography there are 2.6 billion mobile phones.[6]

In June 2011, the United Nations declared Internet access a basic human right.[7] By 2016 more than half the planet will own a smartphone with Internet access, and Internet access will basically come free with your monthly contract.[8] Today more people access the Internet via a mobile device than a PC. Tablets alone will pass PC sales in the next few years.[9]

We live in a world where being connected is not only a basic right, but an expectation, a simple foundation of our day-to-day lives. Today it's not enough to just be connected. Many of us live with multiple devices simultaneously. A smartphone or two, a tablet, a PC, a gaming device connected to the Internet, a web-enabled TV to stream content, and more. We live in a hyperconnected world.

My kids who are three, nine and twelve (at time of press) will never live in a world without a mobile phone or an Internet connection. They won't be able to conceptualise a world that never had "always on" messaging, social networks, multitouch tablets and other such technologies. They won't perceive of these technologies as unique, new, advanced or "alternative" channels. They'll simply expect the world to work in that context. If you don't—you're irrelevant.

With Facebook set to exceed one billion connected individuals in 2012,[10] it's likely that we'll soon have trouble finding even one of our friends who isn't on Facebook. Remember those holdouts who said they'd never ever use an ATM, have an email account, or use a mobile phone? There are those same responses to Facebook today, too. Now admittedly, Facebook might run out of steam (in terms of adoption) somewhere north of one billion users, but fewer than the estimated two billion users who already have an Internet connection—but that hardly makes Facebook a demonstrable failure, now, does it?

The fact is that the Internet, mobile apps, social media and other such innovations of the last 20 years are not special anymore. They might have been in 1999 to those of us who remember a time without them, but they are not new to anyone born after 2000. They just are part of the fabric of everyday life.

So when you are looking at your strategy for your bank and figuring out how quickly or holistically to integrate these technologies into your channel strategy, think about this. *This is the way banking will be done from this day forward, without exception. We're never going back to a world without internet banking access, mobile phones, social media and multitouch.* Thus, it just doesn't make sense to put off investment in these most basic of technologies that lay the foundation for the very future of banking. It's not like you can avoid the investment sometime in the future, or that you shouldn't take every opportunity to learn about them now, because they're absolutely critical for future revenue and engagement.

Now some might argue that it's not going to make that much of a difference delaying investment in digital. They'd be dead wrong. If the sceptics looked at every major industry that has been massively disrupted in recent times (books, music, newspapers, etc.), they would be certain to see that the businesses that believed in the status quo or didn't invest fast enough were the first casualties in the digital shift.

Clearly the expectation of the average consumer today is that you will simply provide access via this technology, just as you did via an ATM or a branch. You *have* to do this, you have no choice. As you'll see from this book, there's not even a choice of *when* you invest anymore—if you're not already heavily investing in all these technologies, you are well behind the behaviour and expectation curve, and you will be disrupted. In all likelihood, banks will be predominantly IT or technology companies in the near future, with banking simply the utility provided through that technology.

The average individual is spending 94 minutes or so a day using apps, checking emails and texting up to 100 times per day.[11] We're logging on to mobile banking 20–30 times per month[12] and internet banking around 7–10 times per month,[13] but visiting a branch only a few times a year.[14] We're shopping online and via mobile with increasing voracity, and we're even using our phone in-store to check prices of comparative goods we see on the shelf with others available online or around the corner. Amazon has even used this behavioural strategy specifically against the likes of Best Buy in the US. These are not novel experiences for the average consumer anymore, they are just the way we live our lives in the 21st century.

Being "always on" or hyperconnected presents its own challenges. Many users of such pervasive technologies are finding it increasingly difficult to detach themselves from such "always on" access and service, either because of demands from their employers/clients for uninterrupted access, or worse, because of addictions to connectivity. This almost compulsive need to stay connected is just one of the side effects of the Information Age.[15]

The customers of the Information Age have been empowered by greater choice, greater access, and better, faster, more efficient modes of delivery and service. To understand why resistance to technology investment is futile, we must recognise the underlying forces at work.

There are two major factors creating behavioural change, namely the ***psychological impact*** of the Information Age and the associated innovations, and the ***process of diffusion*** (of innovations). Each of these factors contributes to create a paradigm shift in the way financial institutions need to think about service and engagement of customers. There are ***four phases of disruption*** that constitute this behavioural paradigm shift with respect to consumers. These have serious long-term implications for banks and financial institutions.

Psychological impact

To understand the core psychological drivers at work in the modern, hyperconnected consumer, we need to revisit one of the foundational pieces of work in respect of the theory of motivation—that of Maslow's hierarchy of needs.[16] Abraham Maslow studied exemplary people of his era such as Albert Einstein, Jane Addams, Eleanor Roosevelt, and Frederick Douglass, and determined the hierarchical progression of the individual—essentially what amounts to a theory of positive motivation and personal development.

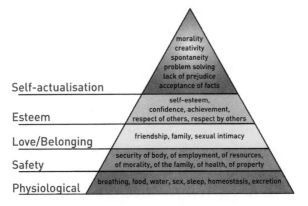

Figure 1.1: Maslow's hierarchy of needs (c. 1943)
(Credit: Wikipedia Creative Commons)

The growth of technology and more efficient service paths and ways to meet our self-actualisation needs have shifted the way we value our time, set expectations and perceive ourselves in our environment. For example, we understand through the introduction of new communications channels that if we can do something via phone or online, we are essentially wasting our time by persisting with a traditional interaction that is far less time-efficient. This, in turn, increases our self-esteem because we are using our time more wisely. Secondly, the execution of a transaction or a purchase *without* the assistance of a person, as long as it works well, gives us a feeling of control and self-achievement that cannot be achieved in a traditional interaction. Let me illustrate…

Take a mortgage proposition from the 1970s in middle America. Let's say I wanted to purchase a family home, but needed a mortgage from the bank to accomplish that. In those days, I would need to drive down to the local bank, make an appointment with the manager, and then prepare myself for an intense grovelling session to see if I could possibly convince the bank manager to give me his approval. If the bank manager liked me, or knew my family, or my business was strategic to the bank, then I might get an offer, but I had zero control of rates, fees and such, as the bank was totally in control. This might have led me as a customer to feel helpless, especially if the application was rejected.

Banks at the time began to believe it was ok to reject their customers and effectively started saying to them: "If you're lucky, if we approve your application, we might just let you be our customer." These days, the customer has much greater control over this type of interaction and is not dependent on a limited set of providers, and so he is empowered.

In 2008 the biggest seller of home loans in the United States was Countrywide, acquired by Bank of America in 2009 for US$4.1 billion in stock. Now before you start with the fact that the Department of Justice went after Countrywide, and they had massive losses associated with subprime, remember that none of this has anything at all to do with the fact that Countrywide proved repeatedly that you could sell a complex mortgage product online, that you didn't need a face-to-face interaction. I hear time and again from supporters of the branch that you need branches to sell mortgages, but that is simply not correct. Countrywide had more than nine million home mortgages on its books which originated online[17] at the time of the sale.

This is not specific behaviour for a younger demographic of first home buyers either. Generation X (born 1964–75) and baby boomers (born 1946–63) are the most likely candidates to research mortgages online.[18] Savings from online mortgage offerings also abound.[19] MyRate, a successful Australian online mortgage provider backed by ING, claims it can save borrowers about A$80,000 on a A$300,000, 30-year loan because of the savings the online channel produces. Mortgagebot reported in 2010 that 88 per cent of people who completed online mortgage applications were between 19 and 59 years of age.[20]

Google Finance Australia reported that 88 per cent of Internet users in Australia start their search looking for a mortgage online, and spend between six and 11 hours researching the mortgage before they select a potential provider and reach out to them.[21] When they do contact a mortgage provider, increasingly it will be via the website, rather than by walking into a branch or phoning the call centre. In the UK and the US results parallel this behaviourally. The myth that customers require a branch to buy a mortgage is just that, a myth. It is more than likely that the majority of mortgages sold today were actually selected by the customer online, and the branch was just a step in the application process.

Rather than feel threatened by this, traditional lenders should be buoyed by the fact that one of their most profitable products is so easily enabled through low-cost, digital channels. In fact, in the US alone, close to 50 per cent of lenders take 25 per cent or more of their mortgage applications online, and 61 per cent of all the loans that were submitted through third-party underwriting engines were approved online, according to the Mortgagebot study mentioned earlier. This is simply mainstream behaviour now. It's not new, it's not emerging—it's how the mass market behaves.

So let's get back to the psychological influences that these technology and competitive choices give me as an individual. **I am in control** and if the mortgage provider's offer doesn't meet my expectations—I walk away. I have an abundance of choices, and **I am better informed** because of access to extensive informational resources. **I get better deals** because service providers have to work harder to get my business, and **I save money** because the margins have been squeezed through better delivery methods and more competition. **I get a better-quality solution** because mortgage products fit my needs much more precisely than the one-size-fits-all solutions that I was restricted to previously.

How do I feel about this environment as a consumer, compared with the consumer of the 1970s example? In terms of Maslow's hierarchy, I associate these positive changes as personal development and an improvement in the perception of self. I am more motivated and feel better about myself, I am happier and **in control**.

Over time my overall expectations of my service providers in the finance sector have been lifted to where I now *expect* an element of self-control, efficiency and choice that I didn't have available to me previously. This then moves from being a nice *change of pace* to becoming a *driver of choice and selection*, and I penalise providers who aren't able to offer me this flexibility and level of control/empowerment.

Process of diffusion

We'll talk more about this in later chapters, but the other key factor in the shifting behaviour of customers is the increasing acceptance of technology and innovation in our daily lives. At the start of the 20th century, several fundamental new technologies were coming or had recently emerged onto the scene, namely the automobile (1886), electricity (1873), radio (1906), the telephone, and, in 1903, the aeroplane. This was the dawn of a new age in industrialisation and innovation that caused leaders of the world to claim these improvements would usher in a new age of peace and prosperity. However, we do share in common with our brothers of the 19th century the inevitable sceptics who could not envisage a world that was changing as a result of technological improvement:

> "Lee DeForest has said in many newspapers and over his signature that it would be possible to transmit the human voice across the Atlantic before many years. Based on these absurd and deliberately misleading statements, the misguided public ... has been persuaded to purchase stock in his company..."
>
> — A US District Attorney, prosecuting DeForest
> for selling stock fraudulently via US Mail for his
> Radio Telephone Company in 1913

New technologies that emerged in one geography took a lot longer to cross the seas in those days. Mass production was only just starting at the turn of the 20th century so getting products out of the factory and into the hands of distributors was a lot more difficult. There were not the large, mass retail brands and businesses that we have today; retail was often limited to the independently owned corner store or high street location. All these factors limited distribution and mass adoption.

By the late 1960s, Moore's Law had kicked into gear, and miniaturisation and the "'tronics" fad were leading to an increasing appetite for new gadgets and devices. In the late 60s, TV commercials and print advertisements often touted a science fiction-like future for consumers that was just decades away. Technology and innovation were capturing the imagination of society.

> *"I think there is a world market for maybe five computers."* Thomas Watson, IBM Chairman, 1943

In 1975 IBM invented the personal computer. It wouldn't be launched until a few years later, but it just showed how far technology had come in the three decades since 1943 when the chairman of IBM had envisaged that there would be a total market globally for only five computers.

Introduced in 1977, the Apple II[22] became one of the most successful mass-produced microcomputer products of all time, based on market share. The Apple II line continued to be sold until 1993.

Within 10 years of the launch of the IBM PC and the Apple II, terms such as DOS, mouse, keyboard, disk drive and dot matrix were in the common vernacular. By 1995, when Microsoft launched Windows 95, the desktop computer was already a global phenomenon accessible to more than 90 per cent of the world's population and with adoption rates of more than 25 per cent in most of the developed economies of the world. The launch of the cellphone in 1983 by Motorola set the pace at which consumers were being bombarded with new and revolutionary technologies.

Then in 1991 the Internet burst onto the world scene. The web was commercialised by 1994 and reached the dizzy heights of the dot-com bubble in 1999. I say dizzy heights, but the fact is that Internet adoption actually accelerated after the dot-com period, and did not slow down until around 2006 in most developed economies. History bears witness that the dot-com bubble collapse was not a collapse in Internet or technology adoption by any measure.

The rate of diffusion is the speed at which a new idea spreads from one consumer to the next. Adoption is similar to diffusion except that it also deals with the psychological processes an individual goes through, rather than an aggregate market process. What has been steadily happening

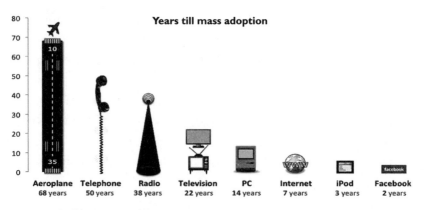

Figure 1.2: Technology adoption rates over the last 100 years

since the late 1800s is that the rates of technology adoption and diffusion into society have both been getting faster. While the telephone took approximately 50 years to reach critical mass,[23] television took just half that (around 22–25 years), mobile or cellular phones and PCs about 12–14 years (half again), and then the Internet took just seven years (half again).

Ultimately new technologies and initiatives such as the iPod and Facebook are now being adopted by consumers *en masse* in a period measuring months, not years. To illustrate this shift, Apple sold more iOS devices in 2011 alone than all the Macs it had ever sold in the 28 years prior.

> *"This 55m [iPads sold to-date] is something no one would have guessed. Including us. To put it in context, it took us 22 years to sell 55 million Macs. It took us about 5 years to sell 22 million iPods, and it took us about 3 years to sell that many iPhones. And so, this thing is, as you said, it's on a trajectory that's off the charts…"*
> —Tim Cook, Apple CEO during February 2012 reporting call

Apple then sold more iPhone 4S devices in fiscal Q1 of 2012 than in the preceding 12 months.

As we become more used to technology and innovation, it is taking us less time to adopt these technologies in our lives, and this further encourages innovation and thus increases the impact on business (which has less time to adapt).

Simply put: If you aren't introducing innovations into the customer experience at the same rate at which customers are adopting these new technologies, you are at a considerable disadvantage and risk losing your customers as more agile intermediaries and third parties capture the benefit of the innovation. Justifying your slow innovation because you are "the Bank", "we're a heavily regulated industry", or your legacy system/processes won't allow it just doesn't cut it anymore.

The core problem is that consumer behaviour is shifting with technology at the centre of that shift, but largely the "bank" is staying the same in respect of behaviour around onboarding, application processes and channel biases. This creates a significant behavioural gap between the consumer and the institution—one that is now being filled rapidly by better-positioned non-bank competitors like PayPal, Square, Apple, Starbucks, P2P lenders and many more.

For those of you who are thinking your organisation needs to watch for ROI (Return on Investment) to be demonstrated first or that maybe you'll be a fast follower, think of this. If it takes just months now for new emergent technologies to insert themselves into the mainstream and change behaviour, and if you've got a 12–24 month development and deployment cycle (typical of most banks' IT departments)—you'll be at least three to four years behind if you wait to see someone else's ROI demonstrated before you commit. Three to four years is the time it took Facebook to go from nowhere to half a billion users.

Here's how Jeff Bezos puts it:

> "I am emphasizing the self-service nature of these platforms because it's important for a reason I think is somewhat non-obvious: even well-meaning gatekeepers slow innovation. When a platform is self-service, even the improbable ideas can get tried, because there's no expert gatekeeper ready to say "that will never work!" And guess what—many of those improbable ideas do work, and society is the beneficiary of that diversity."
>
> —Amazon Form 8-K filing,
> Amazon.com Inc, 13 April 2012

You could be dead in three years with a fast-follower approach. That's more than enough time for a disruptive business to take a big chunk of your customers, for your revenue to disappear, or for the remaining margin you have to be hammered into non-existence.

If you're not constantly adapting and moving, you may as well just resign now, because you're already a dinosaur, and someone is trying to disrupt your ar… architecture?

The four phases of behavioural disruption

There are four stages or phases to the disruption occurring within retail financial services and each stage is disruptive enough to be a "game changer". However, by the time the third phase impacts retail banking, the changes will be complete and irreversible, resulting in a fracturing of the commercial banking business as we know it today.

The *first phase* occurred with the **arrival of the Internet**, and was amplified by social media. While many banks denied it at the time of the dot-com bubble, the Internet changed forever the way customers accessed their bank and their money. As we discussed in the psychology of customer behaviour, this gave them *control* and *choice* that were not available previously. Suddenly, customers were thrust into an environment where they could access their money as they wished, when they wished. As internet banking capability improved, the drive to visit the branch started to diminish, and customers began to rely on the new channel as their *primary* access point with the bank for day-to-day transactions. Within just 10 short years, we've gone from 50–60 per cent of transactions done over the counter at the branch to 95 per cent of our day-to-day transactions now going through the mobile, Internet, call centre and ATM.[24] Game changing…

In the later part of this first phase, in parallel to the start of the second phase, was the emergence of social media. Social media is a sort of theme running contiguously throughout each of the four phases, but it was enabled by the Internet (obviously). The key to understanding the disruption of social media can be seen not only in base crusades such as the Occupy Movement, but in the fundamental shift in power within the customer value exchange (see Chapter 5).

In retail banking previously, banks had the enviable position of being able to "reject" customers because they were too risky, or not profitable enough. Customers would come to the bank, jump through all these hoops called "KYC" (Know-Your-Customer), and if the bank didn't like them, sorry—they didn't qualify. Some of my banker friends refer to this as the "lucky to be a customer" philosophy. Banks got complacent enough to think that they could summarily reject customers on the basis of risk because that would lead to better profitability. This, of course, flies in the face of the perceived role of banks in society, where they are seen to provide a basic social right. In turn, over time this has led to a very cynical view by the public of the inequality of the bank-customer relationship.

The flip side of this in the social media age is that today, customers are assessing bank brands with a social lens that now lets them reject stupid bank policies, or the entire brand, based on recommendations from the "crowd". Essentially, the power of my friends and network is such that if the crowd tells me your bank sucks, there is no amount of advertising spend you can leverage that will bring me back to your brand. In the age of social media, the balance of "value" has tipped back in favour of the consumer, and has weakened the value proposition of the average bank brand.

No longer do banks have the luxury of being able to deal with customers unilaterally and without respect for the crowd, as Bank of America recently found out when it raised basic checking account fees as a result of the Durbin Amendment. It took just weeks of public pressure via social media to push them to reverse this decision. Trust is no longer a given in the social exposed world. I'll trust your brand when you engage with me openly and honestly, with a real commitment to service.

The *second phase* is occurring right now. The emergence of the **smart device** or **app phone,** such as the iPhone and Google Android-enabled phone, is a driver for portable or mobile banking. This has extended into the world of tablets and generic device "screens" that enable web or app access. While there's debate over the security and ROI (Return on Investment) of these screens, customers don't make that distinction—they just adopt. Already many banks are deploying what amounts to a cashless

Figure 1.3: Four phases of behavioural disruption (Illustration: Sebastian Gard)

ATM on a mobile application platform—yes, you can do everything on a mobile phone that you can do on an ATM, *except* withdraw or deposit cash. You can even deposit cheques via remote deposit capture technology.

Here are a few statistics that support the second-phase disruptive model:

- The US has a more than 100 per cent adoption rate of mobile phones (some people have more than one), and one-third of households are mobile-only now.[25]
- China has more than 950 million mobile users, almost three times that of the US,[26] and the number is growing at the rate of 20 per cent annually over the last decade. It has over 500 million Internet users—that's twice what the US has.
- China Mobile is deploying one million WiFi hot spots around China for ad-supported, free wireless access.
- The US population sends over two trillion text messages annually. It's estimated that more than 15 billion text messages were sent in China in just the first two days of Chinese New Year, contributing to the three trillion text messages expected in 2012.
- As of December 2011, smartphone users spend on average 94 minutes a day using apps, compared with 72 minutes using the web on browsers.[27]

- 99 per cent of mobile banking users view balances, 90 per cent view transaction details; about $10 billion of funds have been moved via mobile transfers/bill pay; 15 million location-based searches are being performed (annual run rate).
- More than 50 per cent of iPhone users have used mobile banking in the past 30 days, according to Javelin Strategy; 32 million Americans access mobile banking on their smartphone as of June 2011—a 45 per cent increase since 2010.
- 33 per cent of mobile banking users monitor accounts daily, 80 per cent weekly, also according to Javelin Strategy.

So if we didn't need physical cash or a plastic card, what would happen then? This is the *third phase*—when we move to **mobile payments** on a broad scale. NFC-based (Near-Field Contactless) mobile wallets and stored value card micropayments are already here, but more is to come. The third phase also involves the convergence of our mobile phone and our credit/debit card, which is a logical technical step in the next five years. When these changes occur, our need for cash will reduce rapidly, and the disruption will be far-reaching.

In the UK 43 per cent of payments is done by debit card, and 23 per cent by credit card.[28] Cash still makes up 32 per cent of retail payments, but as a percentage of the whole, it is expected to reduce by a further 20 per cent over the next five years. Cheques make up just over two per cent of payments these days, so it is not hard to see these disappear entirely in the UK within three to five years. As the growth of debit cards swells further and other mobile payments such person-to-person (P2P) are enabled on our phones, this will further reduce legacy payment methods.

It is not unimaginable to see 85–90 per cent of UK retail payments done by mobile/card in the next five years. In markets such as Japan, Korea, and Hong Kong, the requirement for cash may be even less compared with mobile payments.

While cash is not going to disappear overnight like cheques are, the fact is that mobile payments will accelerate the already declining use of hard currency. Between 2007 and 2010 in Australia, cash as a payment method at the retail point of sale declined from 40 per cent to 30 per cent,[29] the fastest decline in cash use we've ever seen anywhere. US consumers' use of cash is predicted to decline by 17 per cent between 2010 and 2015.[30] In the UK, cash was seen in 73 per cent of retail transactions in 2000, but will be a fraction of that by 2018.[31]

US Forecast Decline in Cash Use

US consumers' use of cash will decline by a total of 17%, or by 4% annually, between 2010 and 2015

Figure 1.4: Decline in Cash Use—US Forecast (Source: Aité Group)

There are the great unbanked who don't yet have a bank account and who currently rely heavily on cash and prepaid debit cards, but as we will see with M-Pesa and G-Cash (Chapter 6), this is hardly a hurdle for mobile cash and payments. The success of the Octopus card in Hong Kong, T-money in Korea, Edy and Suica in Japan, and other emerging technologies already prove the concept. What would quickly kill the need for cash in its entirety is a technical standard for mobile money that could be adopted globally by network operators and device manufacturers.

Even if only 50 per cent of cash transactions are replaced by electronic stored value cards, debit cards and mobile wallets in the next five to ten years, the current ATM and branch infrastructure that supports cash becomes untenable from a cost-burden perspective. If we no longer need to go to the ATM to withdraw physical cash or currency, then pretty much everything we do on the ATM today can be done on our mobile app phones. If branches no longer need to deal with cash, then a large part of the reason for their existence disappears.

In 2000, 59.5 per cent of retail payments in the United States were made via cheque. **That number plummeted to just 4.3 per cent in 2010.**[32] In Australia this decline has been even more severe. In 1995, 80 per cent of non-cash retail payments were made by cheque. **That number was just 3.3 per cent in 2010.**[33] In 1990, 11 million cheques a day were written in Britain. This number ballooned to 36 million cheques a day by 2003. According to the UK Payments Council report mentioned earlier, **fewer than one million cheques per day** will pass through the system in the UK **in 2012**, but more significantly, **by 2018 cheques will make up less than 0.8 per cent of personal payments.**[34] Regardless of UK Payments Council edicts, this translates to the death of cheques in short order.

Traditionalists might argue that the value of cheques still in the system is high, and thus more likely a part of business transactions and other such payments that are unlikely to shift to cards or other mechanisms in the near term. To balance out this claim, bear in mind this simple and undeniable fact. There is not a single economy or banking system in the world today where cheque usage is trending against a decline—not one. There is no use talking about saving cheques—these antiquated artefacts are in their death throes. The mobile wallet and person-to-person payments will simply accelerate the demise.

As we'll see in Chapter 12, every man and his dog wants a part of the mobile wallet—from Google, PayPal, mobile operators, handset manufacturers, mobile OS creators, app developers, start-ups, and banks. Phase Three is not just about the death of cheques and cash, it is about the loss of physicality. It is where we no longer need physical interactions with a bank for basic, day-to-day banking.

So what happens when Phase Three hits? From that point on the battle for the basic bank account will be on. The likely outcome is that for the great unbanked (approximately 61–64 per cent of the planet[35]), the phone will become the day-to-day bank account of the near future. While the average banker might dismiss this as immaterial to his traditional business, the unhinging of the bank account from the bank spells massive disruption for the financial services industry. It means that eventually the bank account will just be a value store commodity. While some form of e-money licensing, such as that in the UK, is likely to regulate and protect consumers, the taking of a deposit will no longer require a full banking licence.

Think of this. What's the difference between a balance on an Oyster, Octopus or a prepaid MetroCard, and a deposit in a CASA (Checking Account/Savings Account) account? How would we explain the difference in deposit taking mechanisms for a basic bank account, prepaid debit card and a prepaid telephone contract? What if our prepaid telephone account allowed us to pay at a point of sale using an NFC-enabled phone?

This is where the *fourth phase* emerges. If you think a banking licence restricts everyone except banks from taking deposits, you just haven't been paying very much attention, have you? When banks lose the basic day-to-day bank account to the mobile phone or commodity value store, the rest of banking is down to specialist banking products, investment management, and the movement of funds.

Phase Four is about banking no longer being somewhere we go, but something we just do. It is the realisation that the best way to deliver banking products and services is *pervasively*, wherever and whenever a customer needs the utility of a bank. The fact that banks simply don't have the ubiquitous coverage to deliver these products and services in the new world, and that a whole slew of partnerships will be required to ensure the product or service gets to the customer at the point he needs that banking utility will be a revelation to many. This is where retail distribution becomes unhinged from product manufacturing and risk mitigation. It's a time when you won't need to be a bank at all to provide what we've traditionally called banking, and it's already happening.

Customers will go about their daily lives with banking embedded into processes that require financial products or transactional support. The home-buying experience will integrate the mortgage sale, and we won't need to see a mortgage officer. Travel websites will not only integrate products such as travel insurance but will allow us to take a loan for our trip instead of using a debit card or credit card to pay for the flight. A car dealer sells us a leasing deal for that new car we bought. A retailer gives us a line of credit for that furniture we bought using our mobile wallet. Someone else owns the customer, banks become the manufacturers, networks and processes that support the utility of banking.

Phase Four will produce a fundamental split between banking as a distribution business and banking as a product-manufacturing or credit-provisioning capability, with banking never to be the same again. Banks can either own the product, transaction and payment platforms, integrate the technology, and embrace broad partnerships OR protest with their last dying gasp of breath that things are not really going to change. "The branch is back", "Cash is king", "Cheques will bounce back"—yeah, ok, and let's bring back vinyl records, telexes, VCRs and cassette tapes while we're at it!

Retail banking disruption and the de-banked

These changes, both in r of psychology and consumer adoption cycles, have empowered and liberated customers, but represent a real threat to the industry. As Evans and Wurster first posited in their book, *Blown to Bits* (2000), the threat for traditional intermediaries is that their business faces potential deconstruction if they cannot encapsulate their place in the value chain in new ways by utilising technology and innovation. This is increasingly why traditional intermediaries such as travel agents and stockbrokers are facing an impossible task of maintaining margins and restricting churn[36] or loss.

Online stock trading, first embraced by Charles Schwab and the likes of E*Trade, was phenomenally successful in the early days of the commercial World Wide Web, and still is. But there was significant resistance from the likes of traditional players such as Merrill Lynch, which regarded e-trading as a threat to its traditional brokerage model.

The difference in approach between the Charles Schwabs of the world and the Merrills of the world is perhaps the essence in identifying how an organisation copes with challenges presented by innovative technologies in the customer experience.

> "The do-it-yourself model of investing, centered on Internet trading, should be regarded as a serious threat to Americans' financial lives."
> —John "Launny" Steffens,
> Merrill Lynch vice-chairman, September 1998[37]

One reaction is to resist the change because it is uncomfortable and potentially "breaks" your traditional view of the world, while the alternative reaction is to realise that this is simply the inevitability of momentum and you need to figure out how to capitaliseon it, or benefit from it. Occasionally such new technologies turn out to be failures (not fads), like 8-Track, BETA video and WAP. This is due to the fact that, more often than not, the new technology is surpassed by something better. The lessons we learn in the first generation of the technology, however, are typically invaluable for future applications.

Today the Korean Stock Exchange owes 90 per cent[38] of its volume to internet trades, NASDAQ sees more than 60 per cent of its daily trading volume come from ECN (Electronic Communications Networks), and regional exchanges such as the CME (Chicago Mercantile Exchange) achieve more than 80 per cent of their volume from electronic trades. Between 2006 and 2007 the New York Mercantile Exchange observed an increase in electronic trading volume of 86 per cent,[39] leading to an overall increase in trading volume of 38 per cent. Today that figure is well above 70 per cent. It would appear by any measure that the online trading experience has been successful.

In Hong Kong, HSBC launched its online trading platform in 2001. Today, more than one million trades each month are completed on that platform. If this facility were to be shut down, there is no way the traditional channels of HSBC could cope with even half of this volume of transactions. Meanwhile, the more than 280 brokerage firms that were present in Hong Kong during the late 90s have dwindled to fewer than 80 players.[40] Indeed, internet trading was a *serious threat*—but not to consumers, only to traditional brokerage firms that weren't ready to adapt.

The more advantageous of these transformations have empowered customers in ways that a 1950s bank manager could only have had nightmares about. To illustrate, below is a list of retail banking products and the average approval times for applications, comparing 1980 and 2008.

Table 1.1: Comparison of Product Application Approval Times

Product	1980	2008
Credit Card	14 days	Instant approval
Personal Loan	7–14 days	Pre-approved, or 24 hours
Home Mortgage	30 days+	24 hours[41]

These product application approval times are indicative of the pressure on financial service providers to adapt to the changing expectations of customers, and the need to stay competitive. Barriers to entry are lowering, and new innovations in business models are creating pseudo banking services streamed right to our desktop, supermarket or corner 7-Eleven store.

Here's how I articulated this disruption for bankers in my last book, *Branch Today, Gone Tomorrow*:

> "Everything about retail financial services that relies on outmoded physical artefacts, proprietary and outdated networks, and processes that are complex and unwieldy—all lend themselves to disruption. If you can think of a better way to do your banking, then you already realize that the current status quo is not sustainable. In today's environment, if you can imagine it, then someone is probably building it.
>
> "If you are an incumbent player you might argue, for example, that NFC requires critical mass to reach adoption, but so did the Internet, so did music downloads, so did Wikipedia and electronic stock trading. The question is, do you wait until the disruption takes place to start planning for the new reality?"

The new value is not being a "bank". The new value is understanding the context banking products and services play in the life of the consumer, and delivering those products and services on that basis. The customer will expect and demand this type of integration. He will have no patience for a bank that insists he comes to its "place" before he can have access to banking.

There are two big threats to retail financial services distribution strategies today. The first is simply changing behaviour with respect to where and how the consumer shops for financial service products. The second is the proliferation of alternatives to traditional financial service organisations.

There's a growing group of consumers in the United States who have no checking/current or savings account, and they number in the tens of millions.[42] This group of unbanked or underbanked is increasing in size instead of decreasing, as conventional wisdom would dictate. Ron Shevlin from Aité Research Group aptly coined the word "de-banked" to describe the behaviour of this growing group of hyperconnected consumers who are abandoning traditional banking relationships. So how can they survive without a bank account?

This is where the fastest growing form of payments in the US comes into play today, namely prepaid debit cards. As an industry, this business has grown from $2.7 billion in 2005 to $202 billion in 2012. In November 2011, the Center for Financial Services Innovation (CFSI) released new data about the 2010 underbanked market. The research found that:

- Underbanked consumers in the US generated approximately $45 billion in fee and interest revenue for financial services providers in 2010.
- The total dollar volume of the underbanked marketplace in 2010 was approximately $455 billion in principal borrowed, dollars transacted, and deposits held.
- The market has shown strong growth in certain segments: payment services grew by six per cent from 2009 to 2010; credit services grew by two per cent in the same period.
- Approximately half of this group have college education, and close to 25 per cent of the underbanked segment are prime credit rated.

Several individual products witnessed very high revenue growth rates between 2009 and 2010: Internet-based payday lending (35 per cent), general purpose reloadable (GPR) prepaid cards (33 per cent), and payroll cards (25 per cent).

This appears to be a global phenomenon too. In China the prepaid debit card market came very close to $250 billion in 2011, and is growing at close to 30 per cent per year. Programme managers of prepaid debit cards can be any organisation—supermarket chains, private companies, telecoms companies, retailers, sporting clubs and memberships. There's a whole lot of non-bank organisations providing basic bank accounts today.

Niche payment solutions such as iTunes and other loyalty cards are also becoming increasingly commonplace for day-to-day transactions. *The Wall Street Journal* reports that the Starbucks Card sees more transaction volume than any in-store loyalty card of its kind.[43] A total of $2.2 billion was loaded onto Starbucks Cards in the year through to September 2011, up 151 per cent from the same period of 2006. Reportedly 25 per cent of in-store purchases at Starbucks are now made via their Starbucks Card Mobile App, accounting for 27 per cent of US domestic retail revenue.[44]

The bank account is becoming unhinged from the bank. Mobile is the ultimate disruptor in this shift. Once we can pay with our phone, and it is connected to a value store—this is a far better banking utility than a basic current/checking account. A bank still issuing cheque books simply doesn't provide a competitive platform to compete with a mobile wallet, and as we've already seen, businesses don't need a banking licence to power a value store on a wallet.

So how does this affect the future of banking? As value stores begin to abound and the mobile wallet gets hooked into everything from the iTunes store to Facebook credits, to loyalty cards, transport systems, and beyond, the basic bank account becomes impossible to differentiate, and will be the ultimate commodity. In the UK and markets such as Hong Kong, the regulators have responded to this increasing pressure by creating a sort of subsidiary banking structure for "e-money" or, in the case of Hong Kong, for basic deposit taking.

The problem for banks is that the ability to store a balance or take deposits is no longer the sole domain of "banks" that have a full-blown banking licence. The cost of this is significant. In 2011 almost $40 billion in deposits was freed from traditional banks to credit unions and the like, along with an additional $200 billion in prepaid cards, resulting in the loss of approximately $12 billion in revenue (including overdraft fees, monthly fees, lending fees, and interchange) for the incumbents. Again, look to de-banked consumers as an emerging group effecting this change.

The problem for banks is that increasingly this group of de-banked customers who use non-bank value stores for power purchasing are not the poor underprivileged struggling with unemployment and with dismal credit ratings (as banks imagine they might be). Increasingly these are technology-enabled professionals, university graduates with prime credit ratings. Valuable future customers for sure, but hardly unattractive today either.

You might argue that the most profitable high-net-worth customers or mortgage holders are hardly going to unhinge themselves entirely from the banking system. You'd be correct. But the problem with the unhinging of the bank account is not that you'll lose the high-end, investment-class business. The problem is that you lose the day-to-day connection with the customer.

The key to really understanding the fourth phase of disruption is that we all need the utility of banking, but increasingly we don't need a bank to provide that utility. Understanding that utility is the core value of a banked relationship, and not the "bank" itself, is a harsh realisation that most bankers will not be able to deal with philosophically. Those bankers are the targets for disruptors, as the bookstore was for Amazon.

The disruption that is occurring in the customer experience is all about removing friction in outmoded or outdated processes for customers. Whenever you tell a customer he needs to fill out manual paperwork, or visit a physical location, you're increasingly going to get kickback from a growing segment of the market. While many will argue passionately for the role of a face-to-face interaction and the "richness" of the branch experience, the reality is that there are two reasons most customers will baulk at that.

Firstly, they don't have the time or they perceive it is faster to go an alternative route—convenience was always a key driver for disruptors such as Amazon and iTunes. Secondly, we're being trained that we can open pretty much any non-bank relationship completely digitally today—so KYC (Know-Your-Customer) issues aside, the push is for rapid, digital onboarding of customers. In usability terms we call the latter a design pattern and it ends up driving consumer's expectations because it is an entrenched behavioural expectation.

Digital natives won't be able to figure out why they can sign up for Facebook, iTunes, PayPal and other relationships completely electronically, but your bank still requires a signature. It defies logic for the modern consumer, and no amount of arguing regulation will overcome that basic expectation. This is also why this generation is getting de-banked.

The end result of this is that banks, being the slow, calculated, and risk-averse organisations they are, will likely allow disruptors the opportunity to come into the space between the bank and the consumer as a "friction-eliminator".

Utility and service are the new differentiators

As the four phases of disruption occur, the old differentiators of banks evaporate.

In the past, retail financial institutions held that **Product, Rate** and **Location/Network** were the mechanisms by which they competed. But in a transparent, open world where information flows freely—products are just a commodity. In a low-interest-rate environment, a 25-basis-point differential is hardly something to write home about. And if I never visit your branch except once or twice a year, it's hardly going to be the linchpin in my choosing your bank over a competitor.

It's far more likely that your mobile capability, your internet banking support, and the ease of use in onboarding and day-to-day problem resolution will drive my decision to commit to your bank. Ultimately, I'm not going to stay your customer in the hyperconnected age unless you provide me with great total-channel service.

Think of it this way. If you're dependent on me visiting a physical location to get a great customer experience or service from your brand, you're seriously disadvantaged against a brand that has contact with me 10 times a week through a digital channel. If you are relying on the branch to keep me happy, you've already lost the battle for the customer of today.

What all this is teaching customers is that they can have control, and they have choice. No longer will customers stay with a bank just because it is the first bank they ever took a deposit account with, or because it appears too hard to change. Those protections will no longer be afforded to a service organisation that doesn't *serve* its customers.

As I move my day-to-day relationship to a mobile wallet hinged to a bunch of value stores that give me the functionality of a basic bank account—but none of the KYC hassles—the banking sector loses a vital platform for relationship development. As a consumer I get all the utility of payments, and basic banking (cash withdrawal, online payment, bill payment, etc.) without the need for a specific banking relationship.

Why do I go to a bank ultimately? There are three core expectations—my money is safe, and I get access when/where I need it, and, as my financial behaviour becomes more sophisticated, the bank can facilitate my financial life through access to credit and advisory services.

I want to be in control, and when I need it, I expect rapid and seamless delivery. Don't ask me to fill out an application form with all the same details you've already asked from me four times in the past three years—I am not here to work for you, you are here to work for me. Don't ask me to wait, I am impatient. Don't dictate to me that I have to go to the branch to do this because I now know that is simply not necessary for a progressive financial services provider with the right systems in place. Understand me, so that you will know what I need before I do—you're the experts—you tell me. When you recommend a solution to me, don't treat me like a novice—be prepared for me to be well-informed and know more about the alternatives than your staff. Tell me why you are recommending this product, and how it fits my needs.

Deliver to my criteria. I'm the customer. It's my total *experience* that matters.

KEY LESSONS

Customer behaviour is rapidly changing due to two key factors, namely the psychology of self-actualisation, and technology innovation and adoption—otherwise known as diffusion.

Banks can either try to reinforce traditional mechanisms and behaviour, or they can anticipate changing behaviour and build accordingly.

The pace and rate of behavioural change is speeding up, not slowing down. Thus institutions get less time to react and anticipate the impact of such changes on their business. The longer institutions wait, the bigger the gap between customer expectations and service capability becomes.

There are four key phases to these behavioural changes and we are already at the third phase, and it is the game changer—the loss of physicality and the mobilisation of payments. The fourth phase, the unhinging of the basic bank account from the bank, will occur gradually over the next decade, and banking will never be the same again because banking will be everywhere, and anyone can provide the utility of a bank. The rise of the "de-banked" is evidence of the growing trend of consumers who value the utility of banking over banks themselves.

When the world's bank account is a mobile phone—who exactly is the bank?

Keywords: Countrywide, MyRate, Merrill Lynch, Charles Schwab, Lead Generation, Psychology, Customer Experience, Unbanked, Underbanked

Endnotes

1   Pew Research Centre figures show the internet has surpassed television as the main news source for US adults under 30 (http://www.lostremote.com/2011/01/04/internet-surpasses-tv-for-news-among-18-29s/). 2009 comScore data shows globally that online news sources trump both TV and newspapers (http://techcrunch.com/2009/12/23/google-news-cnn/). Internet Advertising Bureau European research shows 91% of European Internet Users visit news websites weekly (http://blog.hi-media.com/426-9m-europeans-go-online-every-week/)

2   Flurry, http://blog.flurry.com/bid/63907/Mobile-Apps-Put-the-Web-in-Their-Rear-view-Mirror

3   FDIC Press Release 2 December 2009 (http://www.fdic.gov/news/news/press/2009/pr09216.html)

4   CTIA The Wireless Association, http://files.ctia.org/pdf/CTIA_Survey_MY_2011_Graphics.pdf

5   World Bank, http://www.cgap.org/gm/document-1.9.49435/Access_to_Financial_ Services_and_the_Financial_Inclusion_Agenda_Around_the_World.pdf

6   List of Mobile Operators in the Asia Pacific Region—Wikipedia, http:// en.wikipedia.org/wiki/List_of_mobile_network_operators_of_the_Asia_Pacific_ region

7   Wired, http://www.wired.com/threatlevel/2011/06/internet-a-human-right/

8   Author's own estimate based on following sources (http://thenextweb.com/ insider/2012/01/30/study-says-web-economy-to-nearly-double-by-2016- driven-by-mobile-growth/, http://articles.businessinsider.com/2012-02-29/ research/31109566_1_smartphones-pc-sales-mobile-phone-sales/2)

9   NPD Survey—http://techcrunch.com/2012/07/03/npd-tablets-to-overtake- notebooks-by-2016-as-the-most-popular-mobile-pc/

10 iCrossing (http://connect.icrossing.co.uk/facebook-hit-billion-users- summer_7709)

11 The average American teenager texts 3364 times per month (Nielsen: How the class of 2011 Engages with Media)

12 Monetise, Forrester and mFoundry usage data. Statistics show average users tend to use mobile banking once every day or so. Peak usage is as high as 60 times per month. See https://blogs.akamai.com/2012/06/making-up-for-lost-ground-in- mobile-banking.html

13 Author's own research

14 Author's own research via various US, Australia, Japanese and UK banks. See also (http://www.businesswire.com/news/home/20111102005712/en/Phone-Bank, http://whatjapanthinks.com/2010/03/20/almost-two-thirds-use-net-banking-in- japan/)

15 For a definition of the Information Age, see http://en.wikipedia.org/wiki/ Information_Age

16 A.H. Maslow, "A Theory of Human Motivation", *Psychological Review* 50 (1943): 370–96.

17 Countrywide.com

18 Matt Coffin, "The next generation of mortgage lead generation", LowerMyBills. com. Additional sources: Forrester Research Inc, Federal Trade Commission

19 "Online mortgage sites offer net gains", *Australasian Business Intelligence*, 18 September 2006

20 Mortgagebot's *Benchmarks 2011 Report*

21 Google Finance Australia

22 See http://en.wikipedia.org/wiki/Apple_II

23 The likes of Forbes have measured mass market adoption or critical mass by the benchmark of 25 per cent of the population for developed economies such as the United States, the United Kingdom, France, Germany, Australia, etc. or 100 million persons globally (See also http://photos1.blogger.com/ blogger/4015/329/1600/technology_adoption_11.jpg). The study of sociodynamics measures Critical Mass as "a sufficient amount of adopters of an innovation in a social system such that the rate of adoption becomes self- sustaining and creates further growth" (Wikipedia)

24 Gemalto (http://www.ebankingsecurity.net/stats/). In fact, as far back as 2004/2005 banking authorities stated 95 per cent of transactions were conducted electronically in markets like US, UK, Australia and Canada (http://thebankwatch. com/2005/01/09/banking-on-technology/)

25 CTIA Advocacy Research, http://www.ctia.org/advocacy/research/index.cfm/ aid/10323

26 Wikipedia: List of countries by number of mobile phones in use

27 TechCrunch, Flurry Analytics, comScore, Alexa

28 APACS (UK Payments Council), *The Way We Pay* Report, April 2010

29 Reserve Bank of Australia

30 Aité Group (http://www.aitegroup.com/Reports/ReportDetail. aspx?recordItemID=745)

31 APACS (UK Payments Council), *The Way We Pay* Report, April 2010

32 Federal Reserve, NACHA, National Retail Federation

33 School of Accounting and Law—RMIT University

34 APACS (UK Payments Council), *The Way We Pay* Report, April 2010

35 "The World's Unbanked Poor", *New York Times*, 30 April 30 2012 (http:// economix.blogs.nytimes.com/2012/04/30/the-worlds-unbanked-poor/)

36 Churn refers to customers moving from a service provider within one specific product category to another, based on price, value or some other factor

37 "Financial Services Monster Mash", *Wired* May 2000 (http://www.wired.com/ wired/archive/8.05/newmoney.html)

38 KOSDAQ statistics, February 2007

39 Press release, PRNewswire, New York, 14 Dec. 2007—NYMEX Holdings, Inc. (NYSE: NMX)

40 Hong Kong Securities and Futures Commission

41 UBS Wealth Management division now has mortgage approvals for clients down to minutes, and they're seeking instant approval capability in the near term

42 Estimates range from close to 30 million (8 million unbanked and 18 million underbanked) from census and FDIC data (http://www.fdic.gov/ householdsurvey/), to estimates from the *Financial Times* and Lexis Nexis which put the numbers closer to 70 million (http://insights.lexisnexis.com/ creditrisk/2012/04/16/the-population-dynamics-and-credit-quality-of-the-underbanked-market/)

43 *Wall Street Journal*, 17 January, 2012, "Starbucks Sees New Growth on the Card"—http://online.wsj.com/article/SB10001424052970203735304577165001 653083914.html

44 Starbucks

2 The ROI of Great Customer Experience

As we've already identified, we're seeing a sea-change shift in banking behaviour. Behaviour that will flip on its head, change typical interactions and channel preferences of the day-to-day bank relationship. Behaviour that will render irrelevant many of the processes, constructs, business rules, metrics and systems of the current retail bank. Behaviour that will redefine what it means to be a bank and to provide banking services. Big statements? Yes, but simply consider behaviour around day-to-day banking experiences.

By 2016, the average retail banking customer in the developed world will interact with a bank as follows[1]:

Retail Banking Channel Interactions 2016 Est

Mobile — 20-30 Times per month

Web/Tablet "Screens" — 7-10 Times per month

ATM — 3-5 Times per month

Call Centre, IVR & Voice Response — 5-10 Times per month

Branch — 1-2 Times per year

Figure 2.1: Customer experience is primarily a digital endeavour from this point forward

This means your customer experience—the way your brand interacts with your customers—is primarily defined not by an investment in people, but by an investment in technology.

It is conceivable that as a customer I could interact with you 500 times a year via mobile, web, tablet and ATM, and that I could actually speak to someone from your bank fewer than five times in an entire year. The average retail banking customer will visit your branch maybe twice a year, or, as an outlier, perhaps three to four times a year.

Back in the 1970s, as the customer, I had just one channel to interact with—the branch. Even when I called the bank, I called my branch manager. Then along came the call centre and ATM machines in the 80s and early 90s. Banks tacked on call centres to enable me to talk to someone, and answer simple questions. The ATM allowed me to get cash without a teller. Then in the late 90s the Internet arrived and changed things radically—I could do much of what banks did in-branch, online. The only things that perhaps prevented more widespread use of the Internet were system limitations, process and compliance rules, not necessarily adoption.

Throughout all of this, banks have maintained that the branch is central to banking, but in the face of the above projected mix of interactions in the next few years, that position not only isn't logical, it is a recipe for economic disaster. In fact, it doesn't make sense at all. There can be no metrics or data that can possibly substantiate a branch-led view for retail banking in light of such radically different day-to-day banking behaviour.

If as a bank you are hoping that one or two visits to your branch network are enough to hinge the entire customer experience, loyalty and relationship on… you're absolutely screwed.

Firstly, if I'm your competitor and I've got a superior messaging strategy via digital channels, you can't even come close to competing with me on a relationship basis with your face-to-face channels. You might argue that those two visits are critical, that the face-to-face visit could very well be the foundation of the relationship the customer has with the bank. That sounds a lot like justifying the existence of the branch network instead of trying to build a great overall customer experience. If you were totally customer focused, then you simply wouldn't care which channel the customer chooses, you'd make sure it was the best experience every time, regardless. So how do you measure, and thus improve, a total customer experience for the brand, across a channel mix that is largely digital?

In the past, when banks measured customer satisfaction, they'd do so by taking a customer survey in the branch. Later banks started *mystery shopping* the competition to see if their competitors' sales processes were superior to their own within the branch. Later, customer surveys were added via the call centre or snail mail to try to get more of a feel for the brand's performance. Then management tied in KPIs[2] to the customer survey—hoping for minor gains in the metrics of customer satisfaction.

Over the last few years, the industry has responded to this pressure by taking another look at channels and the way performance is measured—are customers waiting too long to have their calls answered? Would IVR systems lower the load for high-frequency enquiries? Are ATMs located in the right places? Will customers find them? Who is using the Internet, and what do they want to do online with the bank? Do you need to provide product applications online? Do you need apps?

Can retail banks integrate the banking experience better into customers' daily lives, for example by allowing them to sign up for car financing at the dealer, rather than having to come into a branch and insisting they treat it as a separate transaction? Could mini-branches or sales offices be positioned at locations and open at times more appropriate for different customer groups? Some of this analysis was cost-driven; other initiatives were marketing-driven. These piecemeal changes have only served to create some isolated improvements in the overall customer experience. Let's examine why.

Firstly, the **channels are still in silos** that discourage sharing of customer learning and, as a result, some of the most remarkable service opportunities go missing. Secondly, the **organisation structure and traditional business models frustrate change**. The most significant problem, however, is that all these changes are happening in isolation of the customer in most cases. **Customers are rarely involved** in the proposed solutions put forward internally within the institution. Let's discuss these three areas.

Channel silos

Customers don't use channels or products in isolation of one another. Every day customers will interact with financial institutions in various ways. They might wire money to a third party, visit an ATM to withdraw cash, go online to check if their salary has been deposited, pay a utility bill, use their credit card to purchase some goods from a retailer, fill out a personal loan application online, ring up the call centre to see what their credit card balance is, or report a lost card. If they are sophisticated customers or clients, they may also trade some stocks, transfer some cash from their Euro forex account to their US dollar account, put a lump sum in a mutual fund, or sign up for a home insurance policy online.

In the early days of the Internet and call centre, it was not uncommon to find that the call centre and internet banking were 24 hours behind the in-bank systems because the "batch" processes that updated the alternate channel databases/logs ran overnight. Thus, if I made a transaction via an ATM or through the branch, it wouldn't show on my online statement or could not be verified via the call centre until the next morning.

Today, my internet banking account view can show me that my available credit card balance is US$10,000, but because of transactions that don't yet appear on my statement, my actual available balance could be $250. When I try to get a bank to explain this discrepancy, they'll try to argue that those other charges are "pending" processing by the merchant or card issuer. For me as the customer, the problem is that I can't use more than $250 before my card acts as if it is maxed out.

The technical challenges to creating an integrated channel infrastructure from a transactional perspective are largely due to the fact that new channels have been added onto mainframe legacy systems that were simply not designed to work in real time, across a distributed architecture.

The more significant problem is that the owners of these disparate channels rarely, if ever, talk to one another. In fact, in most instances, the different channel owners view the others as competitors for budget dollars, customer mindshare and share-of-wallet. This spills over to product teams, where teams regularly compete against one another for customer attention.

There are rarely metrics or incentives that encourage silo owners to promote their internal competition, or to serve the customer ahead of revenue.

To illustrate the silo problem, I'd like to share an experience I had as a customer of a retail bank in Hong Kong a few years ago. At the time I held a Gold Visa credit card, but had recently been sent an invitation to upgrade to its Platinum Visa credit card product, along with a "pre-approved" application form. I was happy with this and was ready to sign up, but hadn't had the time to fax off the application form (why couldn't I do this online, I thought?).

About 10 days later I was in a retail shop purchasing a Persian rug for our apartment, and I got a call from the bank. They were querying the purchase, the equivalent of about US$5000, because it was an unusual one-off purchase for me to make. I confirmed the purchase over the phone, the transaction was authorised, and I was then told by the CSR[3] that the reason they were calling was that some Gold Visa cards had recently been compromised. They then suggested that just to be safe, they could reissue me with a new Gold Visa credit card to ensure I was properly protected. I could pick it up from my branch in two to three days' time.

I agreed to their suggestion and thought it was proactively a positive move, but I asked them to reissue me with a Platinum Visa card instead as the bank had sent me the pre-approval offer just a few days earlier. There was silence at the end of the line, followed by the CSR telling me, "I'm very sorry sir, the Platinum Visa Credit Card department is a separate profit centre within the bank—we are not related." I suggested that maybe the CSR could call the Platinum department and explain the situation and ask them to issue the card, and I would fax the application form to them as soon as I returned to the office. The answer was, "I'm sorry, sir. I wouldn't even know who to call. I don't even know if they are in our building…"

From a customer experience point of view, this was a total, unmitigated disaster. As a customer if I wanted a solution to this problem, my *only* choice at this point was to do all the work resolving it myself. I would have to ring the Platinum credit card department and explain the issue, fax through the form and wait for the new card to be delivered. In the meantime I would have to cancel the Gold card myself, and work out how to transfer the balance from the Gold card to the Platinum card. This would probably mean at least one but probably a couple of trips to the branch. Why?

The problem with this structure is that the primary measure for these business units or profit centres remains the acquisition of new customers and the retention of existing customers. The Gold Card team would actually be penalised on a performance measurement basis by recommending I take the new Platinum card. There was no incentive to transfer me over to the new product because their numbers would take a hit. It was in their interest only to do everything possible to retain my account within their product silo, regardless of whether this was best for me or not. The business rewards such profit centres for isolating customers, and categorises activities that holistically provide a better all-round service as inefficient, or worse, irrelevant.

The same thing happens frequently with customer channels. Although those teams mostly do not actively set out to isolate customers, they end up ignoring the rest of channel activity as irrelevant to their part of the world. Call centre teams don't talk to Internet teams, branch teams don't talk to call centre teams. IT, PR and marketing teams frequently battle it out for control of the web channel. Email marketing and push-mobile services are handled on an ad hoc basis, resulting in no one taking control of messages that ultimately reach the customer. Legal and compliance teams frequently hinder channel teams from simplifying application processes through new channels because of a conventional view of the world. It's a mess.

If the institution were to step back from the day-to-day operations and actually look at how a customer interacts with them, they'd realise that from a product, process and channel perspective, the customer is totally agnostic. They just want to get their banking task done...

Customers choose the right channel at the right time for them, depending on a number of factors, such as time constraints, availability, complexity and the availability of a "deal".

What customers *don't* do is think, "I think I'd like to go to the branch today to process that travel insurance application..." They think, "Hey, I forgot to renew my travel insurance and I'm travelling on Friday. Where am

I going to get this done before I have to travel?" If they are comfortable with the web, they might log on right there and then and apply. Alternatively, they might ring the call centre and see if they can sign up over the phone. Or they might call their travel agent or visit their airline's website and see if the airline/hotel package they have has some travel insurance deal linked to it. In the world of banking as a utility, however, they'll have the option to bundle travel insurance with their trip they purchase, or they'll receive a geolocation- and time-sensitive notification via their phone as they walk into the airport ready to depart on their trip.

So why aren't institutions taking a customer behavioural approach to this instead of building silos in isolation? The main issue is an organisational structure that is still built on the concept of branch-based transactional banking at the core, rather than a multichannel or a customer-led approach.

HOT TIP: Guaranteed to reduce your call centre and IVR load by at least 15 per cent this year…for the average bank more than US$1m in savings…

Channel silos cost banks money because they duplicate functionality and services around customer interactions. If you were a customer and you needed an answer from your bank, how likely would you be seeking assistance today? Most customers will fire up their browser on their office or home computer, go to the bank's website, and try to find the correct phone number to answer their query. If you're a bank, here are a few tips to reduce costs and improve customer satisfaction, based on better understanding customer behaviour.

- Don't discourage customers from calling you. You might think by hiding phone numbers on your website you save costs by reducing call centre load. Research shows, however, that if you can direct customers to the correct call centre number quickly, you reduce traffic and costs—rather than leave customers to experiment by calling many different numbers.

- On every product or transaction page on your website, list the specific call centre number for that type of product/service. This can direct customers to an Interactive Voice Response menu specifically designed for that query, which will reduce call centre load and ensure CSR (customer service representatives) are appropriately equipped to answer specific questions.
- Even better, put a Skype calling button on the website where they can contact someone from the bank as they have a question, rather than waiting for them to find the correct number and call you separately. UBank™ in Australia used this methodology with great success.
- Customers are already coming to your website to find the solution, so why not put a list of the most frequent call types, issues or questions in the same area of the site where customers look up the telephone number? Even better, why not put the same list on the homepage!
- Compile this list of these "top" service enquiries by checking call centre data for the most frequent call types over the last six months. By simply putting the answers of these frequent issues on the site, you can reduce call centre traffic by 10–20 per cent.
- Keep in mind you would actually have to provide a solution on the site, and not just some FAQs. There may have to be some process intelligence. But get this right and those customers *already* going to your website to solve this problem will not ring your call centre. Thus, immediate load reduction...
- Remind customers when they withdraw cash from an ATM that their credit card payment is due.
- Ask customers if they'd like their account balance sent by SMS to their mobile phone. By SMS-ing customers their account balance, you reduce transaction load on the ATM network for customers who withdraw cash and then recheck their account balance. With 20 per cent of call centre enquiries typically related to account balance, imagine what reduction in call centre load would be possible with SMS and mobile apps providing the balance.

Banks should not so much be looking for channel migration opportunities as simply looking at which types of transactions work best on which channel, given a set of circumstances customers might find themselves in. Doing this in an integrated fashion so the customer gets an overall view of the institution is far more important than just blasting individual offers down a new pipeline because the technology allows you to do so.

While revenues, application numbers and transaction activity help compare performance year-on-year and against competitors on a balance sheet basis, aggressive, non-traditional competitors are entering the financial services arena without these preconceived notions. As early as 1994, Bill Gates made the statement that "Banking is necessary, but banks are not."

"Banking is necessary, but banks are not." Bill Gates, *Microsoft chairman, 1994*

Institutions will need to adapt and change and find new ways of working, or give up market share. Yes, many of the traditional "functions" of the bank are now being handled by intermediaries, specialist providers and non-bank institutions. Within the Bank 3.0 paradigm, this disruption to the traditional model of banking is only set to accelerate.

Organisation structure

By examining the behaviour of customers, the glaring realisation is that institutions are essentially assuming that customers only ever use one channel at a time to interact with them. Hence, it is not unusual to find a web team that believes that it can take 30–40 per cent of branch traffic and service it online. Likewise it is not unusual to hear proponents of branch banking telling you "the branch is back" and that the winning strategy is to be investing in more real estate and variations of the branch to retain customers. It's also not unusual for customers to receive dozens of direct mail offers, email marketing offers or SMS promotions from different "revenue centres" within the bank, independent of one another.

Today, 95 per cent of daily transactions are done electronically[4] and, in most cases, most of the transaction volume comes through direct channels, namely the ATM, call centre, mobile and the Internet. By February 2007, HSBC in Hong Kong had reported in the *South China Morning Post*[5] that 90 per cent of its daily transactions were through the phone, the Internet or ATM, leaving the rest to branch. RaboBank, FirstDirect, INGDirect, UBank and others have been able to operate successfully without any reliance on branch structures. This is not a criticism of branches, because I believe that branches will remain an essential part of the future of banking. However, look at the organisation structure of most banks today and you'll see a complete and total lack of understanding of customer behaviour inherent within the organisation chart. It's really quite appalling that the organisation structure of most banks has not caught up with this reality of consumer behaviour.

When we examine the organisation structure of most retail banks, the Head of Branch Network is second only to the Head of Retail and, in many cases, is a direct report to the CEO. In contrast, the manager responsible for the Internet often sits under the IT or marketing department, three or four levels below the organisational equivalent of the branch business unit head. So let's get this straight. Ninety per cent of the transactions go through channels that are managed by managers who have only a modicum

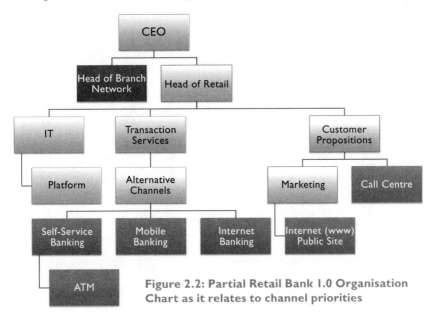

Figure 2.2: Partial Retail Bank 1.0 Organisation Chart as it relates to channel priorities

of influence within the organisation structure, while the head of branches has the ear of the CEO yet looks after just 5–10 per cent of the daily transaction traffic within the bank.

That doesn't even start to address the fact that mobile will be your number one day-to-day banking channel in just four years and you probably don't even have a separate Head of Mobile function, or the fact that 50 per cent of your customers are on Facebook and Twitter and you still don't have a Head of Social Media. That shows organisational priorities that don't relate to consumer behaviour.

"Ah, but the branch generates all the revenue…" we've heard it argued. This is a really good justification for keeping traditional structures in place. Well let us examine if that is really the case.

Let us take credit card acquisitions as an example. How do you market credit cards? Currently you might use direct mail, newspaper advertisements, web and possibly promotional marketing offering a "free gift" if clients sign up for a new Visa card or MasterCard. Customers are then faced with probably two or three choices on how to apply. The first option is that they can phone the call centre, but the call centre refers them to the branch because they need to present proof of income and proof of identity to an officer of the bank. The same might be the case for the Internet, where the application form can be filled online, but you then call them and ask them to come into the branch to complete the application.

Who gets to record the revenue for the credit card application? Not the call centre, or the internet channel, but the physical branch that executes the final signature on the application form and the Know-Your-Customer compliance check on the proof of income. Yet the branch actually has had practically zero involvement in the sale and is simply just a "step" in a required adherence to an outmoded compliance process. So does the branch actually generate the revenue, or does it merely handle the accounting?

The attitude of many retail banking senior executives seems to be that the branch is a serious banking channel, whereas the remainder of "alternative" channels are just that—alternatives to the "real thing". The problem is that customers simply don't think like this.

If as a bank you separate digital channels from other distribution channels today by calling them "alternative channels" or e-channels, then you don't understand that these are your primary channels today, and you are already out of touch with your customer base. Your organisation doesn't match the behaviour of your customers.

Customers simply don't assign a higher value or priority to the branch; they just see it as one of the many channels they can choose to effect their need for banking. In fact, many customers these days choose specifically not to go to the branch because they don't want to stand in line, or they find it troublesome to get to the branch at times when they are open. Admittedly the branch is a premium service channel, but it is not the *only* channel. In addition, how do I measure premium service? If you built internet and mobile channels really well, customers may even pay for the use of those channels in return for the time and service benefits. Why the growing gap in understanding?

Widespread dissatisfaction signals the need for change

One of the key problems that obfuscate the ability of the organisation to serve customers is the increasing adoption of bank policy in the name of risk mitigation or reduction. No greater an opportunity has there been to see this conflict of organisation and purposes than during the recent global financial crisis.

Bailout funds were an issue hotly contested and argued in the US, UK, EU, Australia and elsewhere as very expensive mechanisms for preventing a 1929-type global depression. There were consistently two arguments given for injecting capital into the ailing banking system. The first was that the asset-backed securities underlying the subprime bubble had become "toxic" and only by purchasing these toxic assets could the market come to terms with the ongoing factoring in of these assets. The second was that the crisis had created a liquidity and capital adequacy crisis for banks and that they could only free up funds for the general public if their liquidity was improved.

The first goal may have been accomplished although the long tail may yet still appear. The second goal was a failure with respect to customer expectations, however.

While banks achieved a welcome top-up that reduced their cash-flow problems, internal risk strategy dictated that in an economy in trouble, all but the very best customers represented too great a credit risk to chance lending them money. So banks started to freeze loan books, aggressively pursue those accounts that were having problems meeting their repayment schedules, and basically stopped all lending to those that needed it—small businesses and individuals. Small business activity and retail consumption are two critical levers in kick-starting an economy after a recession, thus bank policy on credit adversely affected the recovery cycle. In the meantime, as regulators got tougher on banks and investment firms, institutions sought to maximise fee and margin on lending products out of fear that regulation would restrict future options in this regard.

There was another significant factor here, though. In taking government money, many banks suddenly found themselves, within the space of a few months, cashed up. As they weren't lending to customers, what could they do with all this money? They invested it, of course. Based on the Warren Buffet school of successful investing, we all know that *reversion to the mean* was guaranteed to restore value to the markets once economic figures started to turn around, if only back to the historical averages. Most consumers weren't that confident—but the bankers know a good trading bet when they see one.

Margin-trading off government bailout funds, basically free money, created some healthy returns in the space of just six to nine months. So instead of using bailout cash to bolster lending to those that most needed it, banks used the funds to generate profit for the bank. Now, if this resulted in more dividends for shareholders and the relaxation of some of the bank policies on lending for consumers, then it would be a fair result. But instead bankers decided that as they had all done so well in investing this cash, that they deserved a hefty bonus for their hard work.

Customers understandably have not been impressed by such a brutal, net-margin-led approach to policy and bank strategy. Customers rightly expect the bank to act as a service organisation and to look at even more opportunities to provide support for customers during a period of economic instability. The customer response to the industry approach was overwhelming.

Since 2008 it is estimated that blogs extolling the negatives of banking have increased by more than 400 per cent. A specific campaign in the US, first covered by *Huffington Post* and then supported by major networks such as ABC, encouraged consumers to move their money out of big banks and into credit unions.[6] Customers angered by opportunistic credit card rate hikes and overdraft fees flocked to YouTube to tell others of their treatment. Obama, Cameron, Sarkozy, and other leaders criticised the "fat cat" bankers and their bonus schemes, even slapping heavy tax penalties on future windfall gains.

Things haven't subsided for distraught bankers more recently. In 2011, Kristen Christian, an art gallery owner in Los Angeles, California, said she was dissatisfied with Bank of America's "ridiculous fees and poor customer service" and created an event on Facebook called "Bank Transfer Day",[7] inviting her friends to close their accounts at big, for-profit banks and move their money to credit unions and local community banks by 5 November 2011.

BofA became the poster child for "ignorant and arrogant bankers" when they tried, unsuccessfully, to levy a new $5 account fee to reduce the impact of the so-called Durbin Amendment.[8] Between 29 September, when BofA introduced their new fee, and 5 November (Bank Transfer Day), the Credit Union National Association reported $4.5 billion in new

Figure 2.3: The poster for Bank Transfer Day on 5 November 2011
(Credit: BankTransferDay.org)

deposits[9] and 440,000–650,000 new customers—a 50 per cent increase in new accounts.

Customers are seeking alternatives to big banking because they believe that banks have lost touch with reality and don't care about their customers anymore … and they'd mostly be right. EPS (earnings per share) and margin have long become the drivers for large, listed financial institutions.

Avoiding risk and making profit for shareholders dominate the thinking of the modern commercial bank today. What has been lost is the balance between this and servicing customers. This imbalance has been institutionalised as banks make excuses for why things don't work the way they should for customers.

Banks argue that processes are the way they are to protect the institution (and customers) from risk—when often the processes are just bad, unwieldy and massively out of date.

Banks cut back on new innovative areas or substantially underinvest in technology such as mobile or social media, but maintain horrendously expensive branches that customers hardly ever visit anymore. Then certain bankers argue vehemently that branches need to survive. All the while customers are flocking to mobile and tablet computing faster than ever before.

So how do banks respond generally? We hear the industry say that social media, mobile and the Internet are not secure and this is the reason for using caution when introducing these new technologies. Meanwhile banks are still sending customers statements and credit cards in the mail—a channel that is so easily corrupted and so insecure that it is laughable.

The problem isn't the global financial crisis, Durbin-response fees, or even bank bonuses. The problem is there is simply too much momentum or inertia in the current system of banking and, as such, the gap between customers and how they behave, and how the institution behaves, has become almost insurmountable.

If retail banks want to stay in the game, they need to start behaving fundamentally differently—starting with re-engineering the customer experience and putting a new management layer in place that embraces continual change.

The Branch versus Online versus Mobile debate

Staggeringly, recent research released by Google shows that when it comes to financial products, up to 88 per cent of customers today in developed economies start their journeys online.[10] For deposits and credit cards, 78 per cent of time spent researching options overall is done in the digital space for an average of 3 hours and 20 minutes (that's up from 58 per cent in 2008). For mortgages and home loans, 62 per cent of their overall research is done online for a period upwards of 11 hours and 25 minutes before a product is settled on. Some 77 per cent of those surveyed said that they didn't know about the product they finally chose prior to starting the task.

This data shows a significant shift in behaviour when it comes to the selection process. Traditional marketing theory suggests that brand marketing and campaign marketing are strong influencers of behaviour when customers are selecting products, but this most recent data flies in the face of accepted theory. Fifty-one per cent of customers had a preferred brand when they started, but of those who used search to attack the task, 58 per cent *did not* search for their preferred brand! Of those who started with a preferred brand, 31 per cent ended up selecting a different brand.

> "Customers will consider an average of 4.5 banks, but will only shortlist 3.4 products for more detailed evaluation. 31 per cent of customers with a preferred brand ended up selecting a product from a different bank online..."
>
> —Karen Grinter, principal client advisor with
> Global Reviews (November 2010),
> Google Think:Banking sponsored research

So what about the role of the branch, call centre, and other channels in the actual application process? Sixty-eight per cent of those surveyed *prefer to apply online*, compared with just 29 per cent who prefer the branch experience. However, 89 per cent of the people said they are open to applying online in the future if banks and FIs get their approval processes up to scratch. That's pretty much everyone. So if that's the case, why don't more people apply online for financial products, and why isn't there an absolute abundance of evidence to show the ROI of online onboarding and fulfilment?

Research consistently shows that poor usability is the primary reason customers abandon a website, leave, and then pick a competitor's brand or product online. The same Google study previously referenced shows that the highest percentage of customers who stay with online throughout are in the $100k+ p.a income bracket. In fact, the study indicated that for 82 per cent of High Income customers, *total research* is done online today and 74 per cent of these indicate they would *prefer* to apply online for products such as deposit accounts and credit cards.

I've worked extensively with many major brands, and there are almost no global brands in the banking arena that have a dedicated usability or customer experience team designing these critical interactions and online processes to streamline or improve customer acquisition. Of the big four banks in the US today (BofA, Citi, Chase, Wells), the only banks that have put any work into the homepage experience recently are Citi and BofA. The homepage is a hotly contested property in most banks today, with every product team in the retail bank (and in some cases the whole bank) competing to get their hyperlink, product promotion, or anything else on the homepage. This is entirely counterproductive as it clutters the homepage and results in the risk of high bounce rates (we'll talk more about this in later chapters).

When we type in "Savings Account" or "Checking Account" into Google, we do get some optimised product selection experiences, but SEO (Search Engine Optimisation[11]) is still a challenge for many of these brands. Given the critical nature of online in brand selection, one would think that there would be millions of dollars a year spent on optimising the customer journey, but in most cases there have only been incremental improvements over the last five to six years. Overall, the utilisation of the web channel in retail financial services is appalling. Starbucks, Apple, PayPal, Amazon and others are two to three generations ahead of most retail banks in their level of competency online.

In 2012, there are massive changes in store on the margin and engagement front. In the US alone, it is estimated that there will be a $25-billion shortfall in fee income stemming from new regulations,[12] and a $50-billion margin shortfall as flat rates persist.[13] Meanwhile banks have not been able to right-size their operations as consumer behaviour has shifted. As customers rapidly move online, how do banks lower operation costs in branches that are suffering from dwindling support while maintaining the service commitments they've made in the past?

In today's retail financial services environment, branches, in-branch staff and agents are not the ones selling the product. The brand is. Retail financial service brands today are a collection of experiences, increasingly defined by multichannel interactions and customer discussions and debates in the social media space. If processes are biased towards the acquisition of customers or sales of products in-branch or face-to-face, then it would be very easy to argue that a contemporary retail financial institution has no idea how the customer of today engages a brand.

So how well do institutions know the flavour and depth of multichannel interactions with their brand? Generally, in my experience, most don't have a clear understanding of the mix of interactions because each channel is measured in isolation. There is no understanding that channels are related to one another because the organisation structure reinforces a one-channel-at-a-time approach to strategy.

Most banks could say which products they've sold through their branch(es) this month, and they probably track which products they sell directly online (if they have that functionality), via the phone, etc., for revenue purposes. However, if I asked the average retail banker to tell me which are the best products to sell through their internet channel, what would the technical basis of that answer be? If I were a banker looking at how to generate new revenues through my IVR or ATM channels, how would I figure out the right sales pitch and implementation? If I were trying to understand at what point a mortgage customer switches from researching a product online to ringing a call centre or visiting a branch, most banks would not even be in a position to tell me that the customer had first looked at their website, which actually led to the sale. This is the really critical stuff—the why and how of consumer behaviour.

There are two critical questions here that we will delve into in much greater detail later. The first question is, if the institution puts a product on a specific channel, will the customer engage them on that channel for that product? The second is, what is the best method to implement the solution so you get maximum take-up or utilisation? To be very specific, I'm not talking about origination, segmentation or marketing mix here. I'm talking about which product or service works on which channel, how simple it is to access for a customer, and how you measure that.

Although long-held traditions are slowly changing, bankers tend to consider the branch as the premier day-to-day banking channel, the Internet as a transactional channel with incremental revenue opportunities, the mobile as a smaller version of the web with respect to transactions, the ATM and contact centres as cost centres with limited cross-sell revenue capability. But that doesn't match how customers engage or how they use these channels.

Most developed markets research shows that customers consider the web their primary day-to-day banking channel, the mobile a rapidly emerging support channel, and the ATM where they get cash—these are daily occurrences, the staple of the banking experience. The call centre is what they call when they've got a problem, or when they can't find what they need online. The branch is where they go when they can't do their banking through the other channels due to process or bank policy, when they need a particularly sticky problem resolved, or when they need advice—and these instances are likely to occur fewer than three or four times a year.

If retail bankers viewed the world the same way as their customers, what sort of channel prioritisation would there be today? Take major brands in the space such as BofA or HSBC, each of which spends north of $1 billion on their branch networks and approximately $50 million on web and mobile banking annually. Ironically at the time of press HSBC still doesn't have a mobile app for most of its customers. In the worst case, the split of this spend should look more like $250m on web and $500m on branch today, even considering the relative cost performance of the channels. Let's not even start talking about social media. Today's spend just doesn't make sense given behavioural economics.

Go back and look at your retail channel budget today and figure out how to put at least 30 per cent of your total channel budget into the mobile, tablet, and web. Then you might just be getting closer to an organisation chart and budget mix that is closer to what your bank needs to support customers in the near future.

Which product works best on which channel?

Let us begin by making certain assumptions that relate to the complexity of the product. Obviously the more complex a product, the more handholding the customer might need to engage in that product. By law in some jurisdictions, certain investment products, for example, require a customer to be advised on the risk involved in that type of investment product. In other instances, a customer may have a plethora of choices and simply not know the right product for his particular circumstances, say, in the case of life insurance. A mortgage product is generally considered a pretty complex product (although increasingly commoditised), so it is a reasonable assumption that at some point before a customer receives approval, he's going to have to talk to a member of the mortgage product team to decide on the right option(s).

An April 2011 report by EFMA and McKinsey & Company[14] bears out this relationship between complex products and the need for advice through face-to-face channels. The report, based only on the European retail banking sector, included 3000 end-consumers, an online survey, and 150 banks. It clearly shows that for less complex products, the shift to so-called "direct" or "remote" channels occurs considerably faster.

The report identifies a number of key shifts in behaviour. Data from 2010 showed a growing percentage of consumers who stay away from the branch entirely. In 2010, 50 per cent of the Netherlands' population had not visited a branch, and in France, Germany, Italy, and the UK, those figures were upward of 20 per cent. Predictably, younger consumers (aged 20–35) were earlier adopters in the multichannel cycle than their older counterparts. When it came to product purchasing, however, there was a clear expectation that "direct channels" (Internet/ATM/Mobile) would become increasingly critical for engagement and sales.

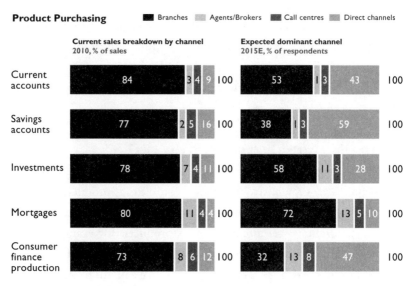

Figure 2.4: Product purchasing by channels, 2010 vs 2015E
(Source: EFMA online survey across 150+ European banks)

So investment products, life insurance and mortgages all require a face-to-face interaction right? Well, it's not as straightforward as that.

The above research almost completely contradicts Google's earlier findings. In fact, there's almost no correlation with real consumer behaviour in terms of research that leads to a product purchase. How can Google claim that 88 per cent of Internet users start their journey looking for a mortgage online, while EFMA/McKinsey say 80 per cent of consumers apply for a mortgage through a branch?

The problem is twofold. Firstly, banks don't measure the entire journey or engagement of the customer from interest and research through to selection and final application/purchase. It's simply no longer a single-point-of-contact world when it comes to sales today—it's a journey, a collection of experiences and interactions that leads to a sale, or hopefully to a relationship. Secondly, even when a product is sold online, revenue is often allocated to the "home" branch of the customer so that it skews internal metrics, and management doesn't even get an accurate picture by reviewing revenue. Thirdly, for a new customer, KYC and compliance rules in the EU still dictate that the safest option for the bank from a risk perspective is to deal with the customer face-to-face to ensure they can confirm his identity, etc. So, even if I want to apply online, I can't if I'm a new customer and the bank determines that I need to be seen face-to-face to confirm I am a real person, with a real identity. So I'm forced into the branch, and this becomes a "false positive" for branch acquisition.

Thus, I submit to you that the EFMA/McKinsey study is significantly flawed. It doesn't represent actual consumer behaviour, but represents more of a collection of metrics and compliance processes. It is based on one piece of data—where did the final step in the compliance process take place? It doesn't measure the journey.

Google's study is more representative of behaviour because it is measured in real time, as people search and engage when they need a financial product. The concept that a customer would choose the branch over the Internet doesn't really work in the case of a mortgage because the fact that the customer has applied for a mortgage in a branch has almost nothing to do with the selection process he used earlier online before walking into that branch. The key problem is this:

We need to measure accurately the total journey or engagement of the customer end to end, not just the last step in the journey.

As a customer I may very well use the Internet to research my investment options, so before I go to the advisor in the branch, or he comes to see me at my office, I may very well have decided the asset classes I want to invest in, the investment horizon, the level of risk I am prepared to take. I may have gone online and used a risk profile questionnaire to see what level of risk I will tolerate. I may have used websites or magazines on investments to look at whether it is the right time to invest in my local property market, or in blue-chip banking stocks. I may be part of an investment club online; I may even have my own online brokerage account separate from my retail bank. So while I may engage with an advisor in the final stage to execute a transaction, I may have already made the all of the critical decisions long before my meeting with the human advisor.

So while you can assume that for many customers, the *execution* of a complex product might occur through a human interaction, you cannot assume that this is the sum total of contact the customer will have regarding that product.

You have to understand which channels are used by which customers at what time, and at which stage of the purchase cycle or decision they are at. You need to cater for all of these interactions simultaneously. The good news is that for simpler products it is somewhat more predictable. So which products work best through direct channels? The answer is… it depends on which market and demographic you are looking at.

Below are some good results from a collection of 2007–09 surveys on Internet usage, where customers were asked the likelihood of their purchasing or applying for the following products online in the future. The results below (aggregated from 45 countries globally) show only those products where 40 per cent or more of those surveyed indicated that they would be *likely* or *very likely* to use the online channel to purchase or apply for that product type in the future.

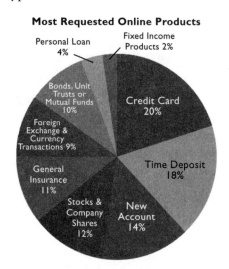

Most Requested Online Products

Personal Loan 4%
Fixed Income Products 2%
Bonds, Unit Trusts or Mutual Funds 10%
Credit Card 20%
Foreign Exchange & Currency Transactions 9%
Time Deposit 18%
General Insurance 11%
Stocks & Company Shares 12%
New Account 14%

Figure 2.5: Preference for retail banking products online, by market[15]

We do see a pattern here. With the exclusion of the investment and trading products, all of the other products are pretty simple, namely credit cards, general insurance products, personal loans, time deposits or fixed income products, and opening a new bank account. These are also things you know work through the online channel.

Breaking bad inertia

I'll discuss this more in Chapter 11, on Engagement Banking. However, the key to understanding which channel is the right channel to push a product to a customer is understanding their behaviour around these products.

Every retail banking, investment or insurance product today fills a consumer need, based not on the product itself, but on the underlying utility of the product, i.e. what it is used for. As we discussed before, people don't buy a mortgage—they buy a home. They don't get a car loan or lease—they buy a car. They don't buy a credit card—they go shopping and want the ease of use at the POS. They don't invest in stocks or ETFs[16]— they look for interest from the money you're holding.

Financial services are all about the utility surrounding a customer's money, how that money helps him live his life. Think of retail financial services products as the financial glue that allows the consumer to live in a society where money, the flow of money and commerce are essential. Understand the context of the utility of the product, and the channel delivery options become clear.

When you get that clarity, the realisation is that increasingly we don't need a physical network or distribution point to maximise the utility and fulfilment of a product. That's the scary but very liberating truth.

The problem is that in the current environment there is massive inertia around "banking". Many banks today still insist on a physical signature card although regulators have generally not required that since 2001. Banks stipulate that the customer needs to bring in bank statements to qualify for a loan, even when he has an account with the same bank he is applying for a loan with. Even the language of bankers often needs its own dictionary—with terms such as draft (not a first edition of a document), telegraphic transfers (even though a telegraph is not involved), instructions (but not like an operating manual), annuity (what?), routing number, SWIFT code…

Breaking this inertia is just as critical as building great journeys or experiences for customers. This is where I'm going to challenge the legal and compliance professionals of the typical retail banking player today because to break the inertia, the internal processes or language today, you first need to get the change approved by the compliance or legal team.

I've often joked that compliance and legal departments in banks live in the Land of No. That is, the easiest and least risky thing to say when presented with a process or policy change is, "No, we can't do that." Why? Because the processes you've long established are proven mechanisms to mitigate risk in the engagement and onboarding of customers within the legal and regulatory framework you operate under as licensed or chartered financial institutions. Right?

Again, the waters are a little muddy here too.

Take for example the humble bank statement. About 15–20 per cent of customers in developed markets have already opted in for e-statements today, but that leaves 80 per cent of customers who still receive monthly statements in the mail from their bank[17]. I signed up early for e-statements hoping it would also reduce the amount of direct mail marketing I received from my bank, but I should have realised that this wouldn't stop them! So now 50 per cent of the mail I receive in my physical mail box is still from my bank, but it's useless direct mail that I never read.

Now imagine this scenario. Let's say we lived in a world where no one had ever sent paper bank statements and it was all done electronically (perhaps like our world 10 years in the future). Imagine a scenario where you go to the compliance department and present this as your brand new plan:

Banker: "So, we're going to print out all the transaction information on a stack of paper, and we're going to stick the customer's name and address at the top of this list of transactions, and then we're going to put the whole thing in an envelope and send it out to the customer. We think this will be great for customers to get all of their monthly activity on one document at a glance, a permanent record; *and* we'll be able to stuff the envelope with other offers and deals from the bank—marketing stuff to improve cross-sell and up-sell opportunities. The ROI on this promises to be very healthy!"

Compliance Officer: "So this is totally secure, right? The envelope you send is tamper proof, and the customer has to sign for it when they receive it? Like a registered mail or courier service?"

Banker: "Ah…no, not really. That would make it far too expensive. We're just sending it through the normal mail service, in a normal envelope— that's the cheapest distribution mechanism available. We want to do this as cheaply as possible, otherwise the numbers don't stack up."

Compliance Officer: "Well, putting aside that it would still be cheaper and far more secure to send this information electronically, who or how many people would have access to the envelope through this process?"

Banker: "Um, we don't really know, but it would probably be physically handled by a handful of people, maybe a dozen or so? We have our outsourced staff stuffing the envelopes, postal workers receiving and delivering the mail, and there are machines that do some of the sorting. Of course, there is the chance that on occasion the envelope might not get delivered to the correct address, but that's a very slim chance these days and we're sure that if someone received this in error they wouldn't actually open someone else's private mail from the bank."

Compliance Officer: "You're kidding, right? You want to take pieces of paper with almost all of the secure identity information we're fighting to protect daily from identity theft, you want to put it in a format that is totally unsecured, you will allow perhaps a dozen people to handle the document with no audit trail, and there's a risk that anyone in the chain could intercept that information either in transit or at the destination in the customer's mail box!? There's no way we're ever going to approve this! Why would you even think of bringing this to us?"

The problem with inertia around current processes is that you build up a false sense of security about these processes being somehow better for the bank, more secure, less risky, and less costly than something new. You even resist new technology plays over fears that this might compromise risk or security when, in fact, over time the existing processes have become more and more risky, more and more expensive, less secure and less customer-friendly. The value proposition a bank statement provided in the 1980s in replacing the passbook was clear. But today, it's an artefact that is costly, highly exposed, inflexible, and pretty much useless from a consumer perspective.

Given those facts, why don't banks start charging customers for receiving paper bank statements and give them the option of e-statements for free? That would make a lot more sense, wouldn't it?

The inertia in the system, however, would tell you that customers LIKE receiving paper statements in the mail, something tangible and real. But is that accurate?

Forrester Research reports from 2008[18] and similar research since show that the strong majority (at least 70 per cent) of consumers are willing to go paperless. The problem is that consumers are by and large lazy beasts, and if you require them to visit a branch and sign a piece of paper to move over to paperless, then they'll probably just let things lie. However, in just the same way (understanding consumer behaviour today), banks should realise that if they told customers that they were moving all online banking customers to e-statements on 1 January 2013 and, from that point on, if they still wanted a paper statement in the mail, they'd have to opt in and pay a monthly fee of $2.50—it's probable that most people would simply allow you to switch them over to e-statements automatically.

There's no other reasonable explanation for the lack of innovation around these sorts of processes other than simple inertia. Paper statements are costly, insecure, and inefficient at translating vital information about a customer's bank relationship. There's no regulatory requirement, cost or legal benefit in maintaining them. If you were designing a bank today from the ground up, you would never willingly design paper statements into the consumer mix. So why are they still around?

I've used paper statements to illustrate an existing case that doesn't make sense from a cost, compliance or security perspective, but there are likewise a gaggle of similar scenarios that are simply outdated—holdouts from an earlier generation of banking. Inertia that is currently in the system, but that will soon disappear, includes the paper application form and signature card, cheque books, bank statements as proof of income/spending, physical identity verification, ATM receipts, channel metrics (where they compete), etc.

And here are two more:

Account opening and administration

With average account acquisition costs being in the range of $250–350,[19] you would think that someone would have connected the dots between the need for a signature card (and related physical handling) at account opening, with the cost of acquisition. The easiest way to reduce acquisition costs is to get rid of the paper. Which brings us to annual costs for current/checking accounts too. With an average current/checking account costing around $350 a year, sending paper statements, printing cheque books that are never used, charging big fees for wire transfers so that you prop up your dying legacy cheque business, all smack of a business driven by inertia.

What's my account balance?

This is the number one requested piece of information from the bank today, and while you do provide internet banking access to this piece of information, the dominant method of a customer getting this is still through an ATM or through the call centre. A far simpler mechanism would be sending the account balance via a text message when a major transaction occurs, or at set intervals (say weekly), or as defined by the customer. The cost of sending a text of his balance to a customer 10 times a month is less than the cost to you of his one call to the call centre for the same information, and less than two of his ATM balance enquiries (based on current channel cost estimates). The deployment of mobile wallets will massively reduce these ongoing costs as well.

Why is inertia such a problem?

So here's the Achilles heel of banking today:

$$Inertia = Friction$$

This friction provides a reason for a seismic shift in core distribution and engagement. Risk modelling makes way for decision engines that are better handled as predictive or real-time rules than paper-based dependencies. Friction provides the impetus to replace old, worn-out processes with better engagement and experiences. Outdated paper requirements become a competitive weakness. The requirement for physical interaction dramatically limits scale. Start-ups that have no preconceived ideas or concerns over regulation push the limit without a care in the world...

As behaviour causes business models to morph, you'll also see massive shifts in organisational structure. The head of branch gets relegated to a line manager role for the channels team, on par with the head of internet, mobile and ATM banking, and contact centres. Customer engagement becomes a competency that transcends the typical push marketing capability, and advertising becomes a supporting tool in the engagement model.

To look at opportunities for removing the inertia and the friction in the customer experience, however, it takes redesigning customer interactions and experiences from the ground up, and it takes changing the way budgets are allocated.

When you give a manager a budget, she/he will do two things:

1. Attempt to prove that the return on that investment (budget) is really high, and
2. Attempt to ensure that next year's budget goes up (or at least not down).

These might not really be mutually exclusive points as #1 is used to accomplish #2. However any new channel in this mix suffers from having to steal budget away from existing channels—or, more accurately, from stealing budget away from the managers who run those existing channels within their domain. And that's a whole lot easier said than done.

The ability to rethink how customers will engage with your business in a channel-agnostic, real-time world takes a new skill set and new incentive programme. In the future, where differentiation is connecting to the utility of the bank and maximising service opportunities, you need to look to the science of interaction design. It's more than just user experience and

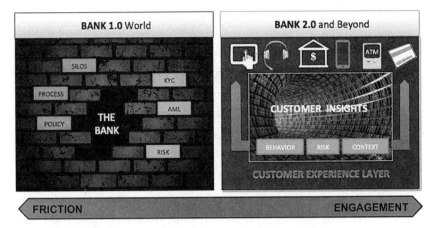

Figure 2.6: The new engagement layer attacks the friction in banking

interaction design, of course. It also requires seeding the design process with behavioural analytics, demographics, psychographics. It requires marketing and copywriting skills. It requires a messaging architecture. Most of all, however, it requires an intimate understanding of the behaviour of the customer.

The cost implications of not getting customers involved as early as possible in the design process are extremely negative, and while most institutions baulk at the upfront expenditure, the resultant losses due to poor design are much, much more expensive than getting it right in the first place.[20]

> "Since the Internet is very much a part of our lives today, consumers often conduct online research before making a purchase. Of the 500 adults surveyed in the UK, 88 per cent reported using the Internet for research while 94 per cent use it for shopping. This means that even for companies which aren't selling online, the web experience they offer visitors is key. Consumers visit a number of websites to find information and research a product or service before they make a purchase. This presents a golden opportunity for businesses to deliver a compelling and memorable interaction which will positively influence buying behaviour. By contrast, a negative online experience will elevate 'Web Stress' levels, causing customers to click away…"
>
> —CA Web Stress Index, 2009

"The rule of thumb in many usability-aware organizations is that the cost-benefit ratio for usability is $1:$10–$100. Once a system is in development, correcting a problem costs 10 times as much as fixing the same problem in design. If the system has been released, it costs 100 times as much relative to fixing in design."

—Tom Gilb, "Usability is Good Business", 1988

So if you are a bank, how do you go about getting customers involved in the process? The initial involvement may be through focus groups or one-on-one interviews with key customers about what they need, but many banks are already doing this. The better approach would be to get them actually involved in the design process. Get them trying out early "lo-fi" prototypes of the interfaces and menu structures (IVR, Web, ATM) or get them to use the existing channels and observe them using those to evaluate the design problems before you embark on the redesign.

With usability tests and observational field studies, you can normally identify 80 per cent of the critical problems with just five customers involved in the testing process. That is hardly going to break the bank, as they say...

We'll talk about social media in Chapter 8 and the emergence of crowdsourcing and new approaches to brand engagement that play a critical role in financial services moving forward.

CONCLUSIONS AND KEY LESSONS

Customer experience is no longer the sole domain of the branch, it is the domain of the **brand**. It exudes from everything you do, and customers are demanding a better experience, full stop. In fact, if I'm an average customer, I'm going to have access to your brand experience through an ATM, mobile phone or the Internet some 30–40 times more frequently than through a branch. If you're relying on the branch as the sole platform or measure for service excellence, you're totally screwed.

Inconsistencies in organisation structure and service levels between channels and silos frustrate customers who just want to deal in the most efficient way with the bank. As we will discuss in Part 3 of the book, the bank needs to do the following now to build customer experience:

- Appoint a customer champion to manage *all* channels
- Build analytics that identify failures in each channel or touch point
- Get customers involved in the design process, particularly with respect to the interface and language
- Create a team that trumps channel silos and managers when it comes to decisions around building better customer experiences
- Build a lab or crowdsourcing capability that engages the customer in an ongoing dialogue, and source ideas from this transparent platform
- Understand the total relationship the customer has with the bank across every channel

Customer experience is emerging as the new holy grail of retail financial services, but the key lessons are not so much about presence and service as they are about understanding the core needs of the customer.

To build an optimal customer experience, you must be able to measure how customer behaviour is adapting, and to measure the rate of innovation or value creation within the institution. This cannot be relegated to a channel-by-channel metric or approach. Channels and products don't compete for customer mindshare or share-of-wallet—they are now part of a complementary ecosystem, and in many cases, symbiotic.

While many institutions have the capability to measure customer experience, it is considered inferior from a data-set perspective to revenue. Where revenue tells you what you achieved, behavioural analytics, however, can tell you *why*, and, more importantly, *where you can do better*.

The future of your business is getting rid of the friction and aligning your customers' behaviour with the brand response. The better you link to consumer behaviour, the more likely I will seamlessly engage with you, as and when I need the utility of a financial institution in my life.

Keywords: Customer Experience, Behaviour, Channel Silo, Inertia, Organisation Structure, Product, Innovation

Endnotes

1 These estimates are extrapolated from customer behaviour trends in retail banking multichannel utilisation, based on data from leading retail banks, monetise and mFoundry mobile application platform providers, NCR, and from research from Aité Group, Forrester Research, Gartner, American Bankers Association and Optirate.

2 Key Performance Indicators "are commonly used by an organisation to evaluate its success or the success of a particular activity in which it is engaged"—Wikipedia

3 Customer Service Representative

4 David Bell, Australian Bankers Association, quoted in *ABC's* 7:30 Report

5 As reported in the *South China Morning Post*, 22 February 2007

6 See MoveYourMoney.info

7 See https://www.facebook.com/Nov.Fifth

8 The Durbin Amendment (Dodd-Frank Wall Street Reform and Consumer Protection Act of 2010) reduced fee income for banks of credit and debit card swipes at the point of sale in the US

9   Credit Union National Association (http://www.cuna.org/newsnow/11/system110311-5.html)

10   Research from Global Reviews and Google Finance, 2010

11   Search Engine Optimisation is a field of research and applied technology that results in websites being optimised for improved search engine ranking against specific keywords, enabling customers to find the intended websites faster and easier.

12   The Boston Consulting Group estimates that the U.S. banking industry will lose $25 billion in annual fee income as a result of regulatory changes that include the Credit Card Act of 2009, restrictions on overdraft fees in Regulation E, and the Durbin Amendment, which aims to cut interchange fees on debit cards

13   Novantas (http://www.novantas.com/retail_banking.php)

14   "Face-to-Face: A €15-20Bn Multichannel Opportunity", April 2011, EFMA/McKinsey & Co

15   UserStrategy customer-facing surveys for Standard Chartered and HSBC across 45 countries over four years

16   Exchange-traded funds

17   See ABA research on e-statement usage cost benefit statistics (http://www.aba.com/Members/Research/Documents/a1d7d123032b46eeb48cd428e8ca9b6fGreenBanking.pdf)

18   North American Technographics Financial Services Online Survey—Forrester Research Q2, 2008

19   Optirate and Andera Research—http://bankblog.optirate.com/how-much-do-you-spend-on-customer-acquisition-are-you-sure/#axzz22QFcHE7i

20   "The ROI of Usability", Usability in the Real World—Usability Professionals Association (www.upassoc.org)

Part 02

Rebuilding the Bank

3 Can the Branch Be Saved?

Ask yourself this: when did you last venture into a branch as a customer? No conjecture, anecdotes or speculation here—just cold hard facts. Do you go every week? Perhaps every month? Have you even been into a bank branch in the last 12 months? Did you really want to go into the branch, or was it necessary only because of the bank's own process or policy? How important is the branch day to day in the banking experience?

The reality is that if I go regularly to a bank branch today, I am in an increasingly tiny minority. The branch, in many ways, has become the least important channel for day-to-day banking for the broader customer base. Why? Simply because it is comparably inefficient, difficult to get to, and just not as relevant in today's hustle-and-bustle, hyperconnected world, where value is measured in speed to market and responsiveness.

When I talk to bankers about change and the opportunities new channels present, I point out that statistically support for day-to-day branch banking has been waning for the last decade, but support for mobile and internet has been skyrocketing. Instead of focusing on the opportunities that mobile and the Internet present to engaging prospects and customers, many bankers feel compelled to launch into a defence of the long-term viability of branch banking. That's entirely understandable. Branches have been at the core of banking for a very, very long time.

The root word for "bank" comes from the Italian "banco", the word for bench. This is because the money traders at the ports of Genoa, Venice and Naples literally used to sit on a bench near the port or marketplace, providing financing to traders and business people.

"The [money changers] in Lombardy had benches in the market-place for the exchange of money and bills. When a banker failed, his bench was broken up by the populace; and from this circumstance we have the word for bankrupt."

—Thomas Herbert Russell, in *Banking, Credits and Finance*

The oldest bank in the world today is Monte dei Paschi di Siena, founded in 1472 (recently bailed out I might add[1]), and its original branch still stands in Sienna today. The oldest branch in the United States is the Bank of New York, founded on 9 June 1784. Materially, these branches don't look that different from most of the modern branches we see in use today. But branches were designed back in those days as "cash distribution" points. The primary activity was depositing and withdrawing cash. Despite the fact that consumer behaviour around cash has significantly changed in the last 30 years (largely due to cards and ATMs), the branch generally still lags as a dominant "transactional" banking place. With transactional behaviour rapidly shifting, this puts existing branch networks under pressure.

In 2011 Bank of America announced it was closing up to ten per cent of its branches (up to 600 possible closures), HSBC USA sold off 195 branches to First Niagara (which then resold half of them), and, as JPMorgan Chase digested the acquisition of Washington Mutual, we saw 300 branches go the way of the dodo. JP Morgan Chase announced in June 2011 it was planning on opening some 2000 branches. It was no surprise, given the economic downturn, that Chase back-pedalled on those plans in its Q3 earnings call and then again in its Q4 earning call, bringing the number down to 1100, then 900 branches. The number of bank branches in the US peaked in 2010 and has been falling since—of course it remains to be seen whether this is the start of a trend, or simply a statistical anomaly.

In the United Kingdom, the Royal Bank of Scotland, Northern Rock, Lloyds and HSBC are all reducing branch numbers. Lloyds has been trying to sell 632 of its branches now for close to 12 months at the asking price of approximately £4 billion, but *has been unable to find serious interest*. In the UK we have seen one branch closing every day since 1990,[2] or more than

7000 in the last 20 years—that's almost half of the 16,000 odd branches in 1990.

In Australia, branch activity peaked in 2007 with 13,648 points of presence, and had decreased by seven per cent to 12,828 in 2011.[3] However, expectations are that this trend will continue and perhaps steepen.

Many traditional bankers will tell you that customers choose a bank based on branch network or the location of a branch near their home or work. That assertion simply doesn't stack up today. Seventy-five per cent of Standard Chartered's customers, surveyed online in over 40 countries, said the Internet was their first channel of choice and it drove their selection of retail banking partner; only 12 per cent chose the branch as their primary contact point. AlixPartners released a study[4] in February 2012 that estimated that 50 per cent of customers would be using mobile banking as their primary channel by 2016, but the more interesting factoid was that 32 per cent of customers in the US who switched banks in 2011 did so to get access to mobile banking. So people will move banks to get access to mobile or internet banking. Would they do the same to get access to a branch? Unlikely, especially if they're only visiting the branch two or three times a year.

The problem is this. The myopic focus on branch banking is simply a distraction. If you were building a bank from scratch today and you were attempting something the scale of HSBC, BofA or Chase and you weren't a diehard traditionalist, I can guarantee you wouldn't be thinking of deploying anywhere near the number of branches these banks have in their networks today. You'd do it very differently, just simply based on the economics.

Just so we clear the air. You shouldn't see this as a vehement attack on branches or as an attempt to advocate a total branch-less experience. As my pal Chris Skinner (Financial Services Club in the UK) so aptly puts it, we're looking at the emergence of a *less-branch experience*.

How are progressive banks dealing with this? Well, you might argue that they're not closing swathes of branches... yet. That might be the case, but I recently met with a major Canadian retail bank which has a strategic plan for the rapid deleveraging of the majority of its branch network. It is scenario-planning for a 50-per-cent-plus reduction in its physical distribution network within the next five years. That's aggressive, but it is definitely worth modelling or at least thinking about if you're thinking about the changing behaviour of customers. After all, banks are in the business of risk mitigation (I'm often told), so what is the risk of not having a branch deleveraging strategy? Perhaps you should ask Borders or Blockbuster that question.

This uncertainty around branch function, cost structure and capability serves to illustrate the key differences in goals between the institution and the customer. The institution sees the branch increasingly as a vital revenue centre whereas in the past these were more accurately classified as cost centres. Thus, this has largely been the focus of the institution over the last 20 years—improvement in branch profitability. Customers, on the other hand, expect service from a branch, and expect it because they "pay for it" with account-keeping fees, over-the-counter fees, and other such levies. In respect of sales, customers are already shifting their primary decision-making process to a digital research and engagement model. If they can complete a task online, many will. Branches that exist today because compliance forces customers into the channel to sign an application don't offer compelling value.

For an exchange of "value" to occur between the institution and the customer, both parties need to be getting something out of this real estate. What is the *value exchange* platform for the branch today?

Let's forget that branches were "always at the core" of banking historically. Let's imagine what it would be like to build a bank today, in a very different environment from the 1700s when modern, branch-based banking emerged in the developed world. Then let's think about the role of branches in the future of banking.

Always banking, never at a bank™

Yes, I thought this catchphrase was so good, I actually trademarked it, but that's another story…

As discussed in Chapter 2, with the shift to digital being apparent in many industries today (music, media, newspaper, books, retail, banking, etc.), it is clear that consumer behaviour is changing rapidly. The key to understanding this shift in the banking sector is that primarily banking is about the utility of our money.

We need banks. Why? They keep our money safe, (most of the time) they give us interest or improvement on our assets, but they also enable us to send it across the planet, pay other people in a business or retail setting, and get our cash when we need it—basically the *utility of money*. When it comes to financial services and the products banks sell to their customers, whether it is a mortgage, a credit card, a government or corporate bond, life insurance, or a merchant account, the outcome is either one of *enabling* or *protecting our life financially*.

So, at its core, banking is about utility, facilitation, or protection. Now I know there'll be some who want to spin this to talk about value-add, the advisory role, etc., but the end game is either facilitating a transaction (this includes credit offerings) or the management of assets. Banks very rarely create real value beyond the transaction platform or asset management, at least for the majority of retail customers (private banking is a little different). The value of the bank for the average retail consumer is primarily utility. Let me illustrate.

We don't buy a mortgage—we buy a home. The mortgage facilitates this purchase or life stage.

We don't purchase a credit card—we go shopping or travelling. The card facilitates our travel or store purchases in an efficient, secure way, so we don't have to carry around large bundles of cash.

We don't buy a car lease—we need a car. The lease simply facilitates the transaction, allowing us the value of the car through a supporting structure.

In the distant past, the core utility of the retail bank was simply cash distribution, and branch networks emerged as a way to allow us access to that cash. Then it included cheques—allowing us the utility of converting a piece of paper into cash. Then there were mortgages, enabling people who ordinarily couldn't buy a home outright with cash the utility of a product that brought home ownership within their grasp. Initially, we could only access that utility through a branch.

Today, the primary utility of a bank is available 24/7 digitally. In fact, it must be because of the demands of life today. We can no longer wait for the branch to open at 9am in the morning to get cash. We need to be able to pay our bills online at midnight, we need our credit card to work when we're out and about, and we need to research mortgage options when we're on the road shopping for a new condo or apartment.

The shift might appear to be subtle, but it really is a result of the impact of the Internet. We've gone from being dependent on the branch to provide the utility of "the bank", to just being dependent on the utility of "a bank". Now we can get that utility more easily through the web, mobile, ATM and a tablet rather than through a physical point of presence that may or may not be open/convenient. It's increasingly why banking has been so heavily commoditised in recent years.

As banking has evolved into pure utility, the branch is increasingly a channel that restricts, slows or complicates that utility. This is why as a customer I will tend towards circumventing the branch or switching if your bank doesn't have a mobile or tablet app.

The core function of the branch in the 21st century

To evaluate the role of the branch correctly in the modern 21st-century retail bank, we need to consider what function the branch holds today. Most bankers would typify the majority of their branch network as "one-stop shops" for retail customers. A place where they can walk in and get the answer to any banking question their heart desires, apply for any product, or execute any transaction. The reality is becoming very different.

We've already noted that branch visitation and in-branch activity are rapidly declining. The logical question then is, what is going to drive me as a customer to visit a branch?

There are really only three things that drive me to a physical branch:

1. I need a physical distribution point to deposit cash (primarily for small retail businesses).
2. I need advice or a recommendation for a product I don't fully understand.
3. I have a humdinger of a problem that I couldn't solve through other, non-branch methods.

Novantas released a study in January of 2011 that clearly showed this shift of behaviour within the US market. Every single measure of activity in respect of consumer behaviour linked to the branch is on the decline, and every indicator for direct banking shows a shift towards these channels. This is in a market with quite possibly the strongest remaining support for branch presence in the world today, so you can imagine how rapidly this is declining in locations such as the UK, Australia and Sweden, where digital adoption has been generally faster than in the US.

Table 3.1: Jan 2011 Novantas study of customer activity (Credit: Novantas LLC)

Customer Activity	In-Branch Preference	Direct Preference	5yr change In-Branch	5yr change Direct
Open an account	75%	16%	-11%	+8%
Buy products	65%	22%	-13%	+9%
Resolve an issue	36%	49%	-17%	+11%
Transfer funds	19%	60%	-26%	+29%
Check balance	6%	68%	-16%	+28%
Research products	16%	70%	-28%	+28%

An April 2011 survey from PWC[5] shows a similar trend, in that for lending products in particular, customer preference is simply not branch first. In fact, with the exception of generic "loans" at 50 per cent, preference for

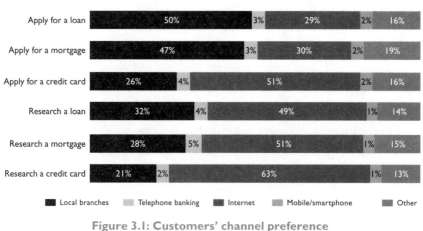

Customer preferred channel

Apply for a loan	50%	3%	29%	2%	16%
Apply for a mortgage	47%	3%	30%	2%	19%
Apply for a credit card	26%	4%	51%	2%	16%
Research a loan	32%	4%	49%	1%	14%
Research a mortgage	28%	5%	51%	1%	15%
Research a credit card	21%	2%	63%	1%	13%

■ Local branches   ■ Telephone banking   ■ Internet   ■ Mobile/smartphone   ■ Other

Figure 3.1: Customers' channel preference
for product engagement (Source: PWC survey)

end-to-end engagement on lending and credit has already clearly shifted away from the branch. For credit cards in particular, the branch is really not a significant player in the acquisition mix these days.

It's probably also important that mobile, which is a relatively new channel in the mix, already makes up 15–20 per cent generally as the channel of preference for execution of a loan/mortgage/credit card. If I asked a retail banker if he thought he could sell a mortgage through a mobile, he'd probably die laughing, but for consumers, it's all about context. I'm out and about looking for a home and my mobile is right there. Factor in the tablet and we get some really interesting plays on the engagement side.

Now before we argue whether these are the right metrics, or whether the activity will likely normalise and level out in the future, the fact is that the role of the branch in the mix is changing fast. The question that remains is what place does the branch have in the future, and how much of the branch network will survive?

However, there's some fundamental psychology at play too. Essential to understanding the role of the branch is understanding the importance that customers attach to bricks and mortar when selecting a financial services brand. While the majority of customers are increasingly abandoning the branch for their core banking activity, many of these same customers demand the convenience and availability of a physical place to go if they need it at some point in the future. The psychology is such, especially for existing legacy customers, that they can only trust a bank that has a "real" physical presence.

There's a cost-benefit question over whether banks should retain physical space to give customers a certain level of psychological comfort around the brand. There's a cost at which this makes some sense, but clearly there's also a level at which it doesn't make any economic sense at all.

There are two other core drivers that need to go into branch design and placement. For branch banking and design, different strategies need to be adopted for customers who are financially and cognitively less resourceful, and those who are wealthier, but time-poor. If you are catering for those customers who are less profitable but also less inclined to use digital channels, you have a cost burden for carrying legacy behaviour. If you are targeting mass-affluent and high-net-worth customers with $100k+ or more in ready cash to invest, the very nature of their busy lifestyles means that coming to a "space" is a luxury they can rarely afford. For many bankers this might seem counterintuitive.

The dilemma then is that the most profitable customers you want to get into a branch are increasingly likely to try a direct channel first because their time is their most valuable commodity, which prevents them from seeking out a rich, face-to-face experience. Increasingly the less profitable customers want a branch because of entrenched behaviour and lag in direct channel adoption. The balance is getting the spend right to cater for legacy behaviour and attracting the right customers, while unwinding from an expensive network that is largely inert.

Let's examine some recent innovations in branch models and the drivers behind those experiments that are likely to survive in the medium term.

Should you be building Apple Stores?

On the eve of 16 December 2010, Citi opened a glamorous, high-tech branch in New York City's Union Square. The 9700-square foot branch was designed by Eight, Inc., the same firm of architects responsible for the unique design of the iconic Apple Store. Although Citi actually launched its store concept in Singapore first, the New York store was almost positioned as the saviour of branch banking itself, and press releases even referred to the similarities with Apple's brand stores. If we read some of the reports and commentary on Citi's branch, it was clear that many bankers believed that if they just got the branch format right, made the space more attractive for customers, they'd storm the branch and all would be made right with the world.

But that's not what happened. While Citi's "store" was certainly innovative, there's no evidence that there's been any net gain in retail activity because of the evolution in branch design. In fact, Citi has generated more net activity and engagement through its iPhone, iPad and Android apps than it has through its new "Apple Stores".

Bankers sometimes argue that regulations and IDV (Identity Verification) require a face-to-face interaction. Realistically, it's more likely that existing processes are too painful or costly to change. It's simply not accurate to say that regulators force chartered banks into face-to-face interactions to onboard or identify a customer—that hasn't been the case since e-commerce laws emerged in the early 2000s. As Apple has demonstrated successfully, organisations should not seek to bias or restrict customers to buying their products or engaging their brand only through a single channel (retail). In fact, banks should be actively seeking to engage customers through digital.

Even if you assume that the first interaction for a customer is in an Apple Store or in a branch, how do customers behave once they have purchased their first device or opened an account? Does the most excellent "store" experience drive them back to the store repeatedly over time? No.

The average Apple Store makes approximately $34m in revenue annually, with $8.3m in operating income. However, if you examine the 10-K filing for Apple, revenue is split almost 50/50 between online and device-based store sales, and its retail presence split between resellers and its own stores.[6]

Since the Apple "App Store" opened on 10 July 2008, *Apple has booked close to $6 billion in revenue* just on apps.[7] Cyber Monday is used as the benchmark for US online and mobile retail sales, and figures show that iPhones and iPads account for *7–10 per cent of all online sales activity* on those days.[8]

What we know from all the data is this: Customers might start their relationship with Apple in-store, but they don't have to, and increasingly they're actually choosing not to. Even if they do, 70–75 per cent of the lifetime revenue from Apple's average customer comes from sales online—and that is increasing.

Here's a little secret that bankers should really take note of. Apple customers simply don't ever go back to the store to buy an app after they've bought an iPad or iPhone in-store. Apple's ongoing relationship with its customer base is predominantly non-store. The behaviour of banking customers is even less likely to be influenced by the physical store over time, especially as behaviour shifts. Apple has the advantage of having such highly differentiated products that many customers feel the urge to touch and play with them before making a purchase. That's not the case with bank products.

You could argue that customers need a "genius" or advisor to assist them through the perils and complexities of banking products. However, the psychology of banking consumers today is that they are going to do that research online so they are better informed. The data from Apple also shows that less than one per cent of its revenue comes from the advisory component in-store through their "Genius Bars". There's unfortunately no valid data that shows that just building a better branch leads to significant gains in revenue.

So if you're a banker and you have Apple Store envy, be sure to think about why you are attempting to build that branch of the future, or that new Apple Store knock-off. However, you can find comfort in the fact that there is a very specific psychology to branch banking which requires that incumbents simply don't drop their branches.

The psychology of branch interactions

I'm surprised that there hasn't been more work done in this arena from a research perspective. Given the firmly held belief by many bankers that customers "prefer" a branch experience, one would think there would be a broad selection of available research that backs this up and explains why there is a preference for walking into a branch to facilitate an interaction that is relatively slow, less convenient, and (in some markets) more costly than newer channels.

In the 1930s and 40s in the United States, for example, there was broad industry condemnation of "branch banking" as it pertained to the destruction of individualism and community banking practices in favour of cookie-cutter branch banking approaches built on efficiency, sales, and transaction banking. These so-called "foreign systems" of branch banking were labelled "monopolistic, undemocratic and with tinges of fascism" and as "a destroyer of individualism".[9] This also explains why the US has so very many institutions (7334 FDIC-insured institutions as of 8 March 2012) compared with other developed economies, as US regulators historically sought to institutionalise community support and make it harder for monopoly approaches.

However, since the mid-80s, branches the world over have generally been transformed into streamlined cost/profit centres, where the industry has attempted to reduce cost and improve efficiency to optimum levels. Traditionally, customers have traded off efficiency for the personalised service of their high-street, community-banker interaction. In this case, the aims of the brand for the branch, and the psychology of the customer, are in conflict.

Despite this drive for efficiency, there's still a lingering psychology of safety in the physical banking place and density which stem from long memories over the epidemic of "runs'" on the banking system during the Great Depression:

> "It is known to be a large bank and, being distant and perhaps consisting of thousands of branches, is less distinctly visualized than the local bank; and so the people are likely to think of it as great and powerful, and able to meet its liabilities. In the second place if the depositors were to initiate a run on a local branch, it would be difficult to spread their psychology and arouse depositors in distant branches."[10]

There are really then two core consumer psychologies at play in branch banking:

1. I want great, personalised service that can only come with a face-to-face interaction with a friendly, community branch manager.
2. The more branches you have, the less likely you'll go under in the case of a "run" on the bank.

There's also a correlation of AuM (Assets under Management) or size of the assets I'm investing in a brand, and the need for reassurance. The more cash that is on the line, the more I need to know you are going to lock my money away safely and that I can trust you to look after my nest egg. Thus logically, there appears to be a greater need for psychological comfort or support for wealthier customers.

Despite this psychology, customers simply aren't visiting branches as much as they were 10 years ago, and this means that you need to work out a transitional approach—an approach that bridges the new behaviour of customers, and that caters for the psychology of legacy customers who have long memories or entrenched behaviour.

Branch innovations built to engage

The concepts discussed below are not futuristic branch concepts that might or might not come to fruition; they are successful adaptations of the branch concept that are working today in different parts of the world. While you might not choose one of these specific models, the core elements that make them successful are things you should choose to incorporate in your branches today.

The flagship brand store

If there's a psychology around customer behaviour akin to "I may not intend to visit your branch, but knowing that it is there in the case that I have an issue comforts me", then flagship brand stores are the ultimate reinforcement of the security and safety of a retail bank brand—Look, mum, we've got big, glitzy retail spaces (just like Apple), we are a safe place for your money!

There's an organisational trade-off here. Lose some of the smaller spaces that are cost centres or outmoded teller stations and consolidate your big city branches as a brand like Apple or Louis Vuitton (depending on the demographic you're serving). The bank still has a "space" to showcase the brand's capabilities, but there is a recognition that the psychology of the brand is the key to relationships and acquisition, and not a transactional space.

SNS Bank in Utrecht (Netherlands) made the decision in 2009 to remove cash processing capability from their physical spaces. At that point, less than two per cent of its transactional activities were related to cash. A radical solution? The impact on the overall retail business was a dramatic lowering of costs, and a significant improvement in customer service perception and capability in-branch. While SNS is not afraid to admit it lost a few cash-focused customers, it also makes clear that the overall net gain in both service metrics and overall profitability of its spaces far outweighed any loss.

Branches are often very high cost because of the rental/rates, but the brand exposure alone from the presence makes a certain amount of sense. So how should the institution utilise these high-cost locations effectively?

The flagship stores emerging today are generally going to be a mass retail brand space, or a high-net-worth luxury service space. We hear of a myriad of "branch of the future" concepts and so forth often, but there's no use making a branch that is chock-a-block full of technology gadgetry if you don't send the right brand message—remember the psychology involved. You don't make me trust your brand by shoving digital screens and coffee machines in the space, you build trust through a great, personalised experience.

When I discuss disruption to branch banking and the channels around shifting models, I'm often told that the "advisory" capability is what differentiates the branch experience from other channels. Then when I actually visit a branch, I get offered no advice, and the service experience is lousy. Even high-net-worth customers might be lucky to be "advised" once a year at their annual review meeting with a relationship manager, and this all too often descends into a "product of the month" pitch session instead of honest, tailored advice. This must be the key focus of the flagship branch store—deliver on the brand potential.

How do you do that?

At the core is culture, not the configuration of the physical space.

To deliver outstanding service you're going to need five key components:

1. Attractive, engaging, warm and open retail spaces
2. Associates or staff on the floor who have strong people skills
3. Totally new in-branch systems designed around service and advisory, not transaction banking
4. The ability to personalise service and offers in real time around individual customers
5. A culture and metrics that reward staff for taking service initiatives, not selling products

In 1994 Umpqua Bank, an Oregon-based community bank, started a journey to shift its branch strategy and make service a true differentiator for its brand. Ray Davis, the CEO of Umpqua, and I recently met at the annual conference for *American Banker* magazine, where we debated the role of the branch in an open forum with members of the US retail financial services industry. Davis also gave some interesting historical perspective to Umpqua's strategy and how its model of "stores" emerged. He explained that when Umpqua decided to revamp its physical points of presence, it ended up being a complete transformation of the business and culture, rather than just an incremental approach to the space.

Umpqua started by bringing in the Ritz-Carlton customer service team to train its frontline staff. Ritz is famous for its frontline experience and Davis claims that Umpqua was the first organisation to engage Ritz to train its staff outside of the Ritz-Carlton organisation itself. While the *NYT* has characterised Umpqua as "Starbucks with tellers", the reality is that not all the existing teller staff had the people skills to move from transaction fulfilment to the Umpqua model it calls the "Universal Associate".

Davis said Umpqua's team started by looking at other successful retail models and asking customers what they did at banks versus what they did at retail stores. The customer feedback was universally consistent. When customers came to a **branch**, they *executed administrative tasks*, whereas when they went to a **store**, they went to *try, shop and buy*. Davis has stated that prior to its revisioning, Umpqua branches (like for most other banks) were simply not built as retail spaces to encourage shopping, but were spaces to facilitate or execute an interaction. For that reason, the key problems banks face is that although they seek to generate revenue in branches, customers don't generally picture branches as places to shop for financial services, they see them as places where tellers or application forms sit. Thus, it's much harder to defend branches in the channel mix today as behaviour is shifting to digital channels because customers find it easier to shop and browse online.

The mix of metrics that Umpqua uses to measure the success of its stores had to change. Instead of just measuring products sold or revenue per branch, the metrics shifted to emphasise frequency of visits, average service

Figure 3.2: Inside Umpqua Bank (Credit: Thread Writing Studio)

resolution times, customer satisfaction, and other so-called softer metrics. Associates in-store were encouraged to seek ways to engage customers, have them visit and engage with the brand, regardless of whether there was a sales outcome. Associates were empowered to solve problems outside of the old rule set that treated customers like a compliance procedure or financial measure. As a result, brand affinity, customer satisfaction and sales revenue all went up.

Davis cites examples of community members forming bowling teams and coming into the store to play competitive bowling on Wii gaming consoles, or groups that have held yoga sessions in the store. Now I'm generally of the school of thought that if you want to play console games or attend yoga training, a bank store is the last place that would come to mind. However, Umpqua's culture means that its stores are community places and it encourages anything that builds affinity with its brand in its respective communities.

In the case of Umpqua, it built a stronger brand and more in-store revenue not by going after revenue or by building nice places—it did it by building a different culture. There's process change as well here. Most banks deploy branches over years at the cost of millions—Umpqua has the process down to eight weeks and under $500k.

When Davis took over at Umpqua bank in 1994, it had four branches and $150m in assets; today it has over 170 stores (through acquisition and growth) and close to $12 billion in assets.[11] Is this amazing growth down to great stores? Can a bank get this growth by copying Umpqua's approach to stores?

The problem with an assumption that the "store" is the secret of success is that there are models that show the opposite—such as UBank in Australia, which has been able to grow $10 billion in assets in just under four years, and it has no stores or branches whatsoever. UBank's growth is far more impressive than Umpqua's, having done it in less than a quarter of the time, in the midst of a global recession, with a fraction of the overall investment. But what Umpqua and UBank share is a culture of great service for their loyal customer bases. The secret isn't the channel itself or the products, it's the approach to customer engagement.

That said, it's clear that a differentiation in store layout does provide a better environment if customers do decide to visit your brand for a sales discussion. Umpqua's assertion about buying behaviour in retail versus banking is spot on. You can't sell in an environment where the customer has to queue for 15 minutes just to speak to someone through a small window or bulletproof glass enclosure.

So let's examine a few best practice retail space examples in banking and look at the key features or elements used to engage customers. The most noteworthy examples in recent times are Umpqua, Deutsche Q110, Virgin Money, ING Direct, Jyske, North Shore and Coast Capital Credit Unions, and Che Banca in Italy. These are often called shops, stores, lounge branches or cafés by their creators, but at the core is a space that has been converted into a shopping and conversation space from a transactional space. A change in name from "branch" to "store" is not enough. Wells Fargo calls its branches stores, and while it has opened up the space in its branches somewhat, the fundamental problems of culture and lack of engagement remain because it only went halfway. What are the key components to reimagining the retail space?

Figure 3.3: The "check-in" desks at Deutsche's Q110 branch in Berlin
(Credit: Deutsche Bank)

Meet and Greet

Common to many of the newer designs of retail spaces is an airline- or hotel-type check-in or reception area. Some deploy an actual person to meet or greet, others simply allow the customer to self-serve. However, the meet-and-greet component is important in providing a strong initial service offering, an appearance as a brand with the wish to engage the customer.

Genius Bars and Pods

Apple has been famous for its "genius bar" concept built into its Apple Stores. As per Apple's own description, the Genius Bar gives high-touch technical support to Apple customers:

> "When you have questions or need hands-on technical support for your Mac, iPad, iPod, Apple TV, or iPhone, you can get friendly, expert advice at the Genius Bar in any Apple Retail Store. The Genius Bar is home to our resident Geniuses. Trained by Apple, they have extensive knowledge of Apple products and can answer all your technical questions. In fact, Geniuses can take care of everything from troubleshooting problems to actual repairs."[12]

Banks are trying to replicate this concept by turning to having specialist advisors roam the floor, ready to engage in a wide range of technical and product discussions. It's not unusual to see these in-store geniuses wielding iPads or other such tools to engage customers in more detailed discussions.

In the Danish market, Jyske Bank has introduced a new concept under the name, "Jyske Differences".[13] Products are presented physically as packages, and the bank's interior design works to improve customer interaction and service outcomes. Jyske calls its branches "shops" and it has a "genius bar"-type concept it calls the AskBar.

Clearly many banks see the bar, or "pod"—a modular customer engagement station—as a key component of branch design for the future. Some of these pods incorporate basic cash drawers or teller systems to give the capability of a normal branch, but in a radical new way. Bendigo and Adelaide Bank in Australia is one such bank, as is Auburn University Federal Credit Union in Alabama. However, others focus more on the sales environment and work on creating an open, inviting space away from the high-counter, bulletproof glass.

Figure 3.4: Jyske Bank employs "AskBar" points for personal engagement (Credit: Jyske)

Figure 3.5: Some pods try to incorporate basic teller capabilities into the environment (Credit: Auburn UFCU)

Digital Walls, Surface Technology and Customer Recognition

Media walls will increasingly come into the branch over the next few years to create both a dynamic advertising environment, and a place for customers to interact in-branch. Banco Santander uses a very cool media wall in its corporate headquarters (along with robot assistants), and Umpqua Bank, Citi and others are also deploying media walls too.

In addition to media walls, however, we're seeing other technologies come into play that assist in the ability to engage customers more seamlessly. YES Bank in India and HSBC Premier in Hong Kong both trialled the use of RFID technology to recognise a customer as they walked into their branch space, accelerating their slot in the "queue" system. RBS allows customers to book a spot in the queue via their smartphone banking app.

Incorporating RFID recognition or geolocation mobile triggers into the store experience allows the customer to be recognised, and the store environment to start to be personalised to the needs, behaviours and product footprint of the customer. If he or she is a particularly valuable customer, triggering a rapid personal response from a real human is also critical for service perception.

Media walls are trying to incorporate the consumer behaviour shift around touch screens and social data in-branch. These walls or screens display targeted, customised, rich-media ads, and the technology is even smart enough to analyse in real time the best way to broadcast to a passer-by, based on age, gender, etc. These digital platforms want the consumer to stop and interact, feeding them analytics about his attention span and purchase behaviour so their targeting efforts improve over time too.

Figure 3.6: Intel's Touch Wall capabilities are very soon going to be mainstream (Credit: Intel)

At this stage, much of the interaction on these digital walls is pretty simplistic—focused on messaging strategies. However the interactive nature of the environment we're in means that soon we'll see these walls combine biometric or geolocation-based recognition (probably through mobile) to tailor messages even more tightly. Messages such as "Mr Smith upgrade your Gold Visa Credit Card to Platinum today" or "Bob, your overdraft facility is approved! Just let a member of our team know if you'd like it turned on today."

High-net-worth customers are more likely to be given the opportunity to interact with their bank brand via in-store Microsoft Surface technology[14] in the near term. Surface was launched back in 2007, but these touch-screen tables are being integrated more frequently into the branch experience for flagship stores. Unfortunately, due to legal, compliance, and risk concerns, most of the banks currently deploying Surface don't actually use interaction capabilities, such as allowing the consumer to slap down his card or mobile phone to see his account balances, investments and portfolio changes (which the tables are capable of doing.) Thus, to date the platforms are more commonly expensive brochure-ware media on the bank's products, including some nice video reels and basic interactivity. This is not ideal engagement, but supplements the advisor as he's trying to sell the product of the month.

As you lead with flagship brand stores to attract your best prospects and most loyal customers, and as transaction activities move to digital, the role of other service locations becomes a little bit more niche and contextual.

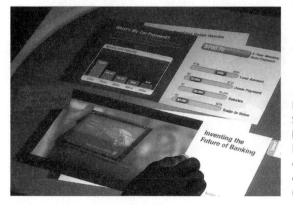

Figure 3.7: Microsoft Surface technology has been incorporated into Deutsche, Barclays and other concept branches over the last four years (Credit: Microsoft)

Bank-shops

You already realised in the 90s that people weren't getting to many of your high street branches as much as they used to because of the demands of modern working life. It was becoming increasingly difficult for people to get time off work to "pop down to the bank" during the lunch hour, and if they did, they'd suddenly find themselves presented with a queue that looked like people were lining up to buy the latest iPhone rather than cashing cheques. Branches remained largely empty during much of the working week except for spurts of high-demand activity at lunchtime and just before the branch closed at the end of the day.

The obvious answer might simply be to open branches a little later, and extend the opening times late into the evening so that people coming home from work would still have time to get to the bank. However, security concerns, issues with staff unions, the bank culture as regards branch hours, and other complications made such progression difficult. After you take into consideration the primary objective of getting people into the branch, the next logical question was where you could put a branch, knowing people were going to be there in the future to provide traffic.

When you consider the habits of people in Western societies, and increasingly in other cultures, evenings and weekends are often spent at shopping malls, cinemas and entertainment complexes, and downtown "hotspots" for restaurants, pubs and coffee shops. Thus, the bank-shop was created.

Figure 3.8: Bank-shops are designed to replace traditional branches in high-traffic, visible locations

To some extent, because bank-shops weren't a "real" branch, you could get away with selling the concept of these *nouveau* branches to management as a new initiative. Bank hours had to be more flexible because it would look a bit strange having a closed bank-shop in a major shopping mall on a Friday night when the mall saw its maximum traffic. Since then, these bank-shops have been huge successes in various locations. Location and availability (opening times) are key drivers to success here.

The other advantage that bank-shops offer, apart from accessibility, is the ability to predict the service and product requirements of the branch traffic better. While in the high street branch you have everyone from students to families to HNWIs (high-net-worth individuals) to retirees/ passbook-holders frequenting the branch, in bank-shops you can narrow down the demographics and their requirements more precisely. While customers may enquire about a mortgage at a high street branch, it is more likely in a bank-shop that customers look for information on a credit card, high-interest or fixed deposit account, or a car loan.

Pop-up branches

Taking the concept of the bank-shop to its logical conclusion, we find that there are perhaps many more opportune places where branches could be located, either permanently or temporarily, to maximise the sales or service opportunity presented by the locale and the potential audience. In reality a branch doesn't even need to be a permanent structure. As long as there is a brand presence, qualified sales staff and the ability to interact with the bank systems to support the sale or transaction, it is enough. Thus, as you move forward as bankers, you will find more ways to get access to customers in a more directed, purpose-built fashion that maximises the selling or service opportunity.

Some banks have used temporary or pop-up branch structures for rural outreach in places such as Australia, Canada, and throughout Africa. Modern plays on this could create some very attractive interaction spaces.

Mobile branches in vans or small trucks have been popular in some locations also. Here are a few other possible examples:

Table 3.2: Pop-up branch configurations in Bank 3.0

Branch-Type	Location or Event	Product or segment specialisation
Branch stall	Trade show	Mortgage (real estate trade show), car loan (motor show), etc.
Home-shop	Display village or model apartment	Mortgage (real estate)
Auto-branch	Car dealer	Car-loan and leasing options
Preferred Customer shop	Airport	HNWIs with local advisory requirement, foreign exchange desk, etc.
Ship-shop	Cruise ship	Investment advisory for retirees
Mobile branch	Popular weekend spots such as "markets"	Mobile as in a truck or car with credit card services, personal loans, etc.
University store	University campus	Student loans, etc.
Pop-up portable branch	Anywhere it's needed	Specialised segmentation or sales pitch for audience at target

The "third place"

One of the new potential forms of branches may not look much like a branch at all. If retail banks can make the case that ultimately the branch is about an advisory "space", then why not create a space for an advisor to sit in—and have that as a replacement for a branch.

Figure 3.9: Pop-up branches could be portable, mobile or semi-permanent structures

This would be a way to transition customers to a pure advisory space when you can't afford to build a flagship branch. What would it contain?

Quite simply, a place to sit and talk, the advisor or associate responsible for customer interactions, and the systems capability to facilitate those interactions. In other words, an associate with an iPad and a couple of nice, comfy chairs.

If you proclaim that your brand is differentiated by the advice you give around products, what else would you need? If transactions have shifted online, to mobile or ATM machines, you've already succeeded in getting the transactional, high-counter windows out of the branch—so you are just left with the advisory space—the "third place", as some have dubbed it.

A nice touch might be a coffee machine, but beyond that, the key would be having the ability perhaps to integrate appointment taking for the advisor's time. You can't have people queuing up to meet an advisor in the space. Firstly, it won't be large enough to accommodate a queue, and secondly, if one customer is getting advice, then he won't want others listening in.

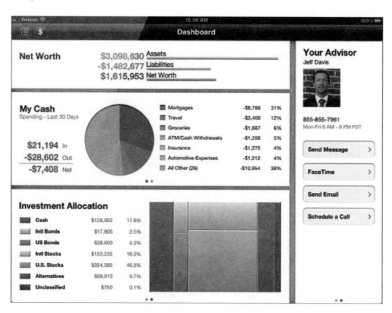

Figure 3.10: iPad tools could enable sophisticated advisory conversations, with no other branch infrastructure required except a place to sit and "advise"

If you are in an exceptionally busy location, then this becomes a mini-flagship store with two or three advisor stations, and maybe a reception space with some tools. The "third place" is really about simply keeping an advisory space in geographies where such interactions still matter, but not carrying the cost of a full-service branch in the current sense.

In Austin, Texas University Federal Credit Union has started the move to teller-less locations. Its goal was to make the space more inviting for interaction, rather than transactions. It required a minimal investment in the ATM footprint to improve serviceability, but the overall move to this type of branch saved UFCU $150,000 per location per year.[15] Customers did not notice a decline in service; in fact, as the tellers disappeared, customers commented on how they felt overall service had improved.

The "third place" is a way to transition customers away from the transactional high-street location today to a place which still provides service and advisory, at a fraction of the cost.

Automated and self-service branches

We're seeing new self-service or automated branches pop into life. If a human-staffed branch is closed to be replaced by an "automated" branch, the perception will be a decrease in service. However, if a new, hi-tech, automated branch opens in a new location, the bank is seen as innovative. Is there a basis for believing that these branches might work? It doesn't matter whether you are a traditional bank or an internet-only bank, the trend towards greater use of automated services appears to be universal. So why shouldn't this apply to branches also?

HSBC continues to have considerable success with First Direct in the UK. Starting with phone banking in the 80s, First Direct still provides all of its support without branches. So providing some automated capability for cash or cheque interactions might work to supplement the pure digital space—a "place", but not a "personed" space, at least not in the literal sense (some automated branches include remote teller support via video capability).

In Asia, it is now very common in Singapore, Hong Kong and Shanghai to see meeters and greeters tackle an incoming customer to enquire "What are you looking for today?" If the answer is cheque deposit, withdrawal or transfer, they are directed to a "bank" of automated devices that can more than adequately serve their needs for those types of transactions, freeing up the floor for more profitable transactions.

Your next generation of customers has grown up on Skype, Facebook, Twitter, YouTube, IM'ing, SMS and such technologies. This generation would think absolutely nothing of walking into ABN Amro's teleportal branches. These branches use only video-conference teller access, where one teller can simultaneously look after a number of branch locations, but all cash and cheque transactions are taken care of by devices in the foyer of the branch. Initially designed for university campuses, these so-called teleportal branches were initially very effective, but we haven't heard much about them since 2008.[16]

Increasingly the customer's banking experience will be more integrated with the technologies available. For example, instead of the customer printing off a receipt from an ATM, the ATM will automatically send his account balance and last five transactions to his mobile phone when he completes a transaction. When customers appear at the "counter", why ask them to sign their name on a piece of paper when you can get them to sign on a tablet, use facial recognition, or present their fingerprint as a suitable unique identifier.

In fact, the greatest improvement in automation is not about technology, nor about cool interfaces, but simply about anticipating the needs of customers. With better information on what your customers are doing on a day-to-day basis, which channels they use for which transactions, and what are their total product/service needs, you can use behavioural models or analytics to anticipate and service the needs of your customers better.

The first step is to improve integration of such technology into your existing branches, reducing or removing entirely the cost of zero-margin transactions such as withdrawals, deposits, transfers, etc., along with better customer "service" initiatives. The second step is to evaluate the potential for fully automated branches when you want to expand your real estate footprint of physical locations as cost-effectively as possible. The concurrent development steps are to improve the usability and interface of your customer-facing technologies so that they are not inferior options, but are choices. Then automated branches become just improved service, not only a way to reduce cost for the bank.

Third-party branches

The final type of branch evolution that you will likely see emerging is the franchise, reseller or third-party branch. You've encouraged the development of brokers for the insurance industry and other elements of the financial services arena for many years, so why not branch banking itself? As banking systems become simpler to use and more usable, and as you focus more on revenue generation over the counter, then you'll simply be able to outsource branches to franchise or third-party operators. Why will you need to do this?

As branch visits plummet further, bankers will realise that the economics of branch banking no longer work above a certain minimum population concentration. For national and regional players, rather than abandon 60–80 per cent of their community network, they need to figure out a way to transition so that the community stays connected to their brand, but through cheaper real estate and personnel models.

Ideally third-party branches will be purpose-built for specific sales activities or segments. The institution gets the benefit of having no real estate costs, and no staffing costs. The branch or "desk" needs to fund itself, so as a result becomes very revenue-focused, and streamlines all the non-essential activities that a customer finds in the traditional branch. Just like when he uses a third-party ATM when he is overseas, he'll have the choice of doing a traditional transaction over the counter for a fee to the franchisee. If he doesn't want to pay that fee, then he elects not to use the third-party branch.

Can it work? Well, the post office has been doing this sort of thing for decades, and the basic systems and service sophistication are quite similar. So why not for banking? In fact, you might need to do this to save the humble post office and bank branch together in the future as the physical place comes under fire. However, it does mean investing in systems and processes that are largely foolproof operationally.

In short, banks need to take a leaf out of the Starbucks concept of "branch" or store—a packaged, well-supported, self-sustaining business model that is primarily revenue-generating in its focus, but with fantastic service metrics. Take the low-counter handling of cash transactions out of the branch and this is entirely possible today with the right investments in systems and process re-engineering.

What happens when they don't visit anymore?

We see plenty of banks trying to reinvent their physical places to get customers back in the branch—but behavioural shift is flying counter to this effort. New customers and the most wealthy non-retired customers are increasingly branch-averse and time-poor, and they want the utility of banking to be delivered as seamlessly and as friction-free as possible. The branch just equals friction for a growing demographic of customers. Why? Because bankers have spent the last 30 years introducing more barriers to customer engagement, rather than removing them. Products have got more complex, not simpler. Compliance and paperwork have got more onerous, not faster and easier to navigate.

Turning banks into coffee shops, yoga studios, media showcases, and Apple Stores just doesn't bring customers flocking back to interact. They will only ever come back for "value". What is your core value as a bank branch? Connection to the community, the advisory capability, your ability to solve problems.

Don't think of the branch as a sales centre or a transaction centre. Essentially this was at the core of the modern branch that made it successful in the past. However, think of the branch as a place to sell complex products to customers who need advice and three fundamental mistakes emerge:

1. Leading with a "sell" when customers want help
2. There's no advice, unless it is part of a sale conversation
3. The assumption that complex products are good things

Customers want solutions to their problems and simplicity; they want a bank to facilitate their financial needs, or bridge the gap in a life-changing decision that hinges on cash or credit. The more you drive branch network towards selling or advising on complex products, the more you'll find your strategy, economics and philosophy working against the modern consumer. Inertia around transaction banking and historical concerns over a "run" on the bank simply don't wash as an underlying strategy for the bank as a place in the 21st century.

Banks often talk about products such as mortgages and investments as "complex products", but if you think back to the mortgage product of the 1970s and even 1980s, they weren't that complex. At its core, the mortgage product is still not complex—it involves a principal, a term, a rate and repayments. The only reason it has become more complex than this is that providers have sought to differentiate their product from others. So why is the mortgage product complex? Because the industry made it that way. Perhaps those providers who win in the new world will be those that reverse that trend.

By the end of the decade, the vast majority of customers won't need a teller. They won't need an advisor. They won't want complex products. They won't need a trusted financial partner.

They will want and need the utility of banking.

Work out a way to deliver that with the least friction, and you'll solve your dilemma over what to do with your branch network. Insist on sticking a new-looking space over the same old processes, complexities, culture, metrics and philosophy and you'll score a big old FAIL!

Change your culture first—then work out what the space does for you, and remember this: If you're relying on me as a customer walking into your physical brand space to reinforce my tenuous relationship with your "bank", you are royally screwed. A mobile-enabled bank/wallet will have 200–300 times more interactions annually with your customers than the physical space by 2016.

Michael Armstrong
Bank Manager

The reality of the branch,
now and in the future

As a manager who learnt his banking craft at Citibank in Australia I had an unhealthy obsession with branches—why? Well, at the time, Citi had only 24 of them up against our competitors who measured them in the thousands. We had an inferiority complex that dominated much of our decision-making.

One of my first jobs was to assist in the roll-out of the "model" branch concept in the mid-1990s. The concept, similar to what Brett talks about in this chapter, was to design branches to maximise the customer experience—their interaction with the greeter (we had an automated queuing system), their ability to receive an instant ATM card, instant cheque books, all on the first meeting. The layout was designed to ensure that customers had to walk past the "advisors", who actually sold products, on the way to the teller. Somehow this was supposed to induce the customer to buy something on the way out or in; I'm not sure it ever really worked… but I loved this job! I had to pore over floor plans, spend lots of time with vendors pondering the latest Magnetic Ink Character Recognition (MICR) encoding equipment and pontificating as a zealot on "customer experience".

The first model branch opened in Adelaide. The branch manager was so excited, as were we in head office. The result? Well, we had a state-of-the-art branch that looked great, and we still had the same customers coming in. Did it reach our expectations? Well, I don't know what we expected to happen. When our product people had to absorb the cost of the new branch, then the reality set in. Apart from a couple of other model branches, the concept quietly faded away.

This was part of a bigger continuing headache for Citibank in Australia at that time. We had no branches, so how should we compete? A vast majority of our transactions were done through non-branch channels, yet research told us our prospective customers didn't use us because we lacked a big branch network. So what did we do? We opened up a token number of branches for "branding" and then spent a whole lot more on model branches to create a unique customer experience for a special few.

I felt we compensated quite well for not having a network. We had a large mobile sales force, a well-connected introducer network made up of accountants and financial planners who sold our products, and we were part of one of the largest ATM networks in the country. Yet management always felt, "If only we had the branches that the big guys have…"

Then an earthquake hit us—the arrival of mono-line financial providers into the Australian market in the early 1990s. They came selling one product, at least initially, and they had no balance sheet, they had no branch network, yet they took a large share of the mortgage market within two years. And this was years before the Internet!

That's why when people talk about the "state-of-the-art" branch and get all excited about branch design, those groovy new seats, the big plasma TVs, calling it a shop, a spa, but definitely not a branch, well, I say, "Been there, done that—15 years ago!" For me it does not depend on the branch; it depends on what the branch can do for the customer, what services it provides, if it is the most convenient choice, and what other alternatives the customer has that are more convenient.

So, my lesson to take away from all of this is this: It's not about a branch *per se*, it's about your business proposition, how you are going to sell and how you are going to service. The branch models Brett has identified all have something in common, that is, they are about changing the way the bank can effectively engage (not sell) and service customers.

Today, we know that we can sell products remotely and we can also service remotely, i.e., without a branch. We also know that for banks most transactions are done through non-branch channels, and increasingly sales are being conducted through direct sales channels. And for the people who say only humans can build relationships with other humans, I agree, and for high-value relationships that justify a dedicated relationship manager, they can conduct that relationship anywhere, not just sitting in a branch.

So the one lesson bankers need to take away from this chapter is that your branch is not sacred. It is just a channel and your customers may choose an alternate channel to work with you. They may even prefer an alternative channel. Don't penalise them for that. Use it to your advantage.

Branch improvements today

So what is on the branch-improvement road map that we can achieve in the short term that will bring benefits to both the organisation and the customer? The following areas represent suggested opportunities for either improvement in financial operations or customer service levels at the branch over the coming three to five years:

- Reduction of friction, complexity and barriers to engagement
- Improved customer communications and language
- Better behavioural analytics, leading to better ability to anticipate and fulfil customer needs
- Retooling the branch, reskilling or rehiring key customer-facing staff
- Improved use of transactional automation and service technology
- Removing transaction capability entirely

These improvements make themselves evident through a range of projects that can be undertaken within the branch. Some of these projects cross over the above areas of opportunity, so I'd like to list the projects below as specific illustrations of how improvement and transformation are achievable.

Table 3.2: Possible projects for improvements and transformations

Project/Initiative	Desired Outcome
Cash/Cheque Deposit Machines	Remove all over-the-counter (OTC) transactions that are purely cost for the branch.
Reception Zone	Redirect transactions to self-service automated capability; improve speed to fulfilment/service for other enquiries.
Behavioural Analytics	Improved behavioural analytics on customers across all channels to understand better which "tasks" customers prefer to do in-branch, versus online, etc.
Sales and Needs Matching Intelligence	Real-time and precognitive offer management for existing customers delivered in the form of prompts, offers, or service messages delivered either to the service rep's tablet or to digital media walls, surface units or customers' mobile phones while in-branch.
Improved Staff Mobilisation	Focused service and sales training programmes, along with better KPIs that focus on more than simply the number of applications per month, or total revenue.
Reduce the Friction	Concerted effort to remove friction in the engagement layer—get rid of all paperwork entirely, reduce IDV workload for existing customers, focus on conversation over administrative and process-driven tasks. Creation of "customer dynamics" capability as owners of customers, rather than product competing for revenue from the same.
Straight-Through Processing and Credit Risk Management Systems	Enabling customers to get immediate fulfilment for an application rather than waiting the obligatory 24, 48, or 72 hours due to antiquated manual or human "processes" in the back office. Additional benefits include reduction of compliance errors through manual mishandling.
Customer-First Design	Use of ethnography, usability research, audits, customer-focused observational field studies and focus groups to improve language, communications with customers and branch utility
Deleveraging Scenario Planning	Unfortunately, it's unavoidable that you'll need to unwind a large portion of your branch presence over the next 5–10 years. So you need to start scenario planning this process and figure out a communications and customer service strategy.

KEY LESSONS

Banks are approaching a rapid decline in branch utilisation across developed economies, leading to a 30–80 per cent reduction over the next decade.[17] This will have dramatic impacts on smaller banks that rely on customer acquisition in-branch; many will fail as a result of their inability to shift. The branches that remain will not look anything like the transactional, teller spaces that most of us have grown up with.

Bank 3.0 is all about less high-counter transactional support, and far more low-counter service focus. The objective is to leave less costly channels to handle no-margin or low-margin transactions, and focus on where the value is—deep, profitable customer relationships. However, when you understand changing consumer behaviour, it also becomes clear that branches will hold far less attraction for a rapidly growing demographic due to the fact that they can get better advice online, they can do it faster digitally, and they are time-poor and can't be bothered getting to and interacting via a physical space.

The shift is that banking is no longer about the place or the space, it is all about the utility. The more you think about the brand as enabling financial utility, the more you come to terms with the fact that the branch generally no longer offers significant advantage.

Do you need branches at all? Perhaps. There is still a demographic of customers who take comfort in having a bricks-and-mortar location where they can go to meet a real person and have a problem solved. The only problem for bankers is that this demographic is dwindling fast, and by 2020 they'll be a very small minority. Given that the cycle for many banks in modifying their branch network is measured in years, you need to start planning for this deleveraging of physical network now, not in five or seven years' time, when it will already be too late.

In the end, the decision to unwind rapidly from physical networks will be an economic decision as margins continue to be squeezed, as new and better distribution models emerge, as non-bank FIs start to compete, based on friction, and as more mature metrics show that branches are by and large grossly unprofitable.

Keywords: Branch, Product, Future, Bank-shop, Pop-Up Branch, Automated Branches, High-counter, Low-counter, Sales, Service, In-Branch Systems

Endnotes

1   "Tough times at Monte dei Paschi di Siena", Euronews, http://www.euronews.com/2012/06/27/tough-times-at-monte-dei-paschi-di-siena/

2   British Bankers Association

3   Australian Prudential Regulatory Authority, Statistics, ADI Points of Presence, June 2011 (http://www.apra.gov.au/adi/Documents/2011%20PoP.pdf)

4   See http://banktech.com/channels/232601505

5   PWC Consulting, http://www.pwc.com/us/en/financial-services/publications/viewpoints/viewpoint-retail-bank-customer-centric-business-model.jhtml

6   SEC 10-K filings for Apple Inc.

7   CNET

8   IBM Research

9   *American Banker Journal*, 23 March 1939, p.2

10 *Branch Banking: Its historical and theoretical position in America and abroad,* Chapman and Vesterfield (Arno Press, 1980), p. 275

11 BusinessInsider/Upmqua Press—http://www.businessinsider.com/umpqua-bank-offers-customers-direct-access-to-its-ceo-from-its-stores-2012-2?op=1

12 Apple.com

13 Jyske Bank: Jyske Differences branch concept—http://www.jyskebank.dk/jyskebankinfo/home/home/220771.asp

14 Microsoft also calls their new tablet form "surface"—not to be confused with the table-top technology deployed in bank branches

15 YNN Austin News, 22 August 2011, http://austin.ynn.com/content/business_and_finance/business_now/280091/business-now--new-ufcu-locations-go-teller-less

16 ABN Amro Annual Reports 2006, 2008

17 Research from Jones Lang Lasalle in July 2012 estimated a 50 per cent reduction in branch numbers over the next five to ten years (http://www.us.am.joneslanglasalle.com/UnitedStates/EN-US/Pages/NewsItem.aspx?ItemID=25573)

4 Onboard and Engaged—The Ecosystem for Customer Support

The need for better support

In *Bank 2.0* I wrote about customer service and call centres as customer support mechanisms, but frankly it is clear that banks have to get out of the mindset of a channel-centred approach to customer engagement and support. In the old days a customer would walk into a branch or pick up the phone if they had a problem—those were the two channels through which banks could help a customer.

In the late 90s you started to have customers emailing you enquiries and support questions, but you didn't have the organisational capability to support the email channel. So what did you do? You told customers, "Don't reply to this email because we won't answer it," or, when they did email, you just ignored them. This still goes on today.

I'm not going to embark on a lengthy discussion around customer service, culture and how you need to build that. There is a plethora of reference works on that subject, including the work of Ron Kaufman (*Up Your Service*), Micah Solomon, Clayton Christensen, Ken Blanchard, and Gary Vaynerchuk, which are amongst my favourites. However, I will attempt to describe the problem and an organisational fix to the silos that frustrate service and sales within the retail financial services space.

> "I genuinely believe that any business can create a competitive advantage through giving outstanding customer care."
>
> —Gary Vaynerchuk (@garyvee)

This is a great quote. Even if you have a ton of complaints, you can still **lead with better customer service** as a strategy or core objective. When you give outstanding customer care, you not only create happy customers, generate new revenue and reduce costs, you also create fierce loyalty—a fan base.

Ironically, customers are just as likely to try and problem-solve themselves, using a search engine, blog, discussion board or pinging you on Twitter or Facebook, as they are to pick up a telephone, email you or SMS you. Gartner recently found that using community involvement service organisations will reduce the cost of customer support by as much as 50 per cent annually by 2015.[1] Increasingly, with better technology, banks are anticipating problems customers face and you're able to be proactive in your response, such as in the case of credit card fraud.

Yet, there are still massive gaps in your ability to support a customer, mainly because your business is simply not built to provide assistance across the board. You pigeonhole support and service through a couple of channels, and gladly hand it over to the channel team so you don't have to worry about it anymore. That means that you often have the lowest-skilled and lowest-paid staff attempting to solve a customer's issue, using a decision tree or software that applies the 80/20 (Pareto principle) rule as a framework. Often the systems can't cope with outliers (the 20 per cent of issues that require deep knowledge or expertise), and those outliers are often the issues that have the potential to create the biggest problems for customers or the brand—especially in the socially exposed era.

Ron Kaufman defines service as *taking action to create value for someone else*.[2] Too often banks fall into the trap of taking customer satisfaction surveys and then not having the mechanisms to create value. That's especially hard if the banks are not using the channels that customers are using to solve problems. So if you're a bank today and you don't provide support capability through social media, for example, it could then be easily argued that you are putting a roadblock up for customer value creation and service.

In 2009, brands started to wake up to the potential of using Twitter to support customers, but it was clunky and often ineffectual. Firstly, Twitter was a real-time, 24/7 vehicle, but most businesses don't monitor Twitter 24/7—so they have Twitter accounts signing off at 5pm saying, "I'm sorry, we'll be back in the morning/after the weekend."

Tweets

CIBC FirstCaribbean @CIBC_FCIB   26m
Signing off for today. Remember that CIBC FirstCaribbean never emails customers requesting them to verify confidential information online.

Figure 4.1: Banks have trouble adapting to a 24/7 strategy over social media

Secondly, because social media was seen as a low-priority marketing vehicle and not as a critical customer communications channel, many banks put some 20-something college graduate with almost zero training in customer relations or support in charge of the channel, often having to respond to irate or distressed customers. The "industry approach" was that if an enquiry came through Twitter, you could simply remind the customer that Twitter was not secure and they should not share any personal information, and then redirect them to the call centre.

The problem with this approach is that it assumes that a customer contacting you on Twitter either doesn't realistically expect to have his problem solved through Twitter, or that he is quite happy being redirected to the call centre (because it is more secure). However, if the customer had wanted to have his problem solved by the call centre, wouldn't he have called them in the first place? With Twitter's DM (Direct Message) feature and Facebook's messaging/inbox architecture, these mechanisms are essentially as secure as email and most customers are fully aware of that. They're making a conscious decision to trade off "security" in favour of convenience and speed. By redirecting them to another channel, you're fighting the intent of the customer, creating friction.

There are four advantages to using Twitter in customer support scenarios:

Twitter is real-time and fast

By simply monitoring comments made about your brand through your Twitter handle, you can trap issues as they occur. To take advantage of this, make it a rule to keep response times under five minutes whenever possible. This makes an immense difference. No matter what problems come up, nothing beats getting an immediate response to one's concerns. Not many channels can compete with social on this front.

It's a rule so simple that it is often easy to overlook.

Fiman Prayudi Utama
@prayudiutama

Thanks @IedFlorence for taking care of everything, again! and for your fast response, thumbs up! @IED_Official

7:26 AM - 14 Apr 12 via web - Embed this Tweet
← Reply ↻ Retweet ★ Favorite

Figure 4.2

Twitter can be as personal as face-to-face

Twitter can personalise the service experience. This means while you're speaking to your customers behind a corporate logo, there's also an opportunity to get real.

Instead of trying to corporatise and risk-reduce the Twitter channel—free it up. Empower the people supporting Twitter to solve problems, but also make every effort to replicate a **high-touch, face-to-face interaction**. You can do that by personalising your Twitter account, ending your tweets with your name or initials.

The team at ASB Bank in New Zealand has done a great job of this:

ASB Bank @ASBBank
@maknz Let us know if you need any help with the switching process? We have lots of info here experienceasb.co.nz
^SM @IanTLS
← Hide conversation

1:58 AM - 13 Apr 12 via SocialEngage · Details
← Reply ↻ Retweet ★ Favorite

Figure 4.3

Then on its Twitter page, it tells you about its team...

Figure 4.4: ASB personalises its Twitter channel—so it's more like face-to-face

For the most pressing questions from your customers, you could also switch from responding with your business Twitter account to responding with a corporate personal account. This way you can provide a personal exchange. The trick with this is managing the shift between different accounts with a personal tone versus a corporate tone—as Westpac found out a couple of years ago:

Figure 4.5: Westpac has a bad Twitter day

This takes some discipline, but the personalised approach is worth it for the kudos and connection with customers. Remember, Twitter is not a marketing channel—it's a connection channel. As such, people don't mind if your Twitter channel displays a bit of humanity, humour and personality. It doesn't have to be cold, hard, corporate communications; in fact, it will likely reduce the effectiveness of the channel if it is like that. In some ways Westpac's tweet above displayed some humanity that customers might even have found endearing, but from a corporate perspective this was simply a failure in channel management.

Use the Direct Message feature of Twitter

Social media generally has the unique ability to help the largest cross-section of customers in the shortest amount of time. But you also don't want to expose your brand to a public rant or complex customer problems if you can avoid it. As well, if you have widespread system outage or a similar problem, with a ton of incoming tweets, using DMs takes these issues out of the main Twitter stream and reduces the visual impact to the brand.

Here is the best practice approach I've seen to this type of issue:

- **Send one public tweet explaining the situation**. Anyone who finds your Twitter profile will see that tweet first.
- Then, **reply to any @mentions with a DM**. First, you won't clutter your business's Twitter stream with @replies for other customers looking for what is going on. Second, you can **go into more detail explaining how you can help each customer**. If the customer isn't following you, ask him to follow you so you can help him through direct messages more adequately.
- **Switch back to sending @replies if there is no acute problem anymore**, but only regular questions and support requests that would benefit your whole audience. Remember, customers learn from one another and the Twitter stream too.

DMs are also extremely useful when a simple @reply doesn't give all the information the customer needs. In these cases, try DMs instead of the regular "please send an email to name@company.com", which tends to prolong the time it takes to solve the problem. Twitter is all about speed.

Twitter shows great service values to prospects too

What about providing customer support via Twitter to people who aren't actually your customers yet? Helping people who have problems or questions of all sorts about banking, but not directly your brand, can be an amazing way to generate new leads and demonstrate your service capability.

There are lots of great questions floating around the Twitterverse that go unanswered in relation to banking and financial services.

Figure 4.6

Why not jump in and answer those questions without even hinting at your own bank products or services; simply be helpful and point people in the right direction. When you just help them out, many people naturally check out what you offer and can become loyal customers from the very start.

This is very different from just saying, "Ask me a question and I'll answer." Which is a fine strategy, but still reliant on the customer coming to you. That's Bank 1.0 thinking. Take the solution to the customer proactively; don't wait for them to walk into your Twitter branch before you help them out.

Figure 4.7

You either force the customer to behave your way, or you adapt and open yourself to a proactive service culture around the customer.

Facebook as a support channel?

Customers will often come to a Facebook page with support issues, complaints and compliments. Simone McCallum from ASB Bank identified the four most likely reasons for a customer to contact your brand via Facebook:

- They are frustrated and haven't been able to get support from other channels (physical, phone, online) and they are looking for an avenue to escalate.
- They have a product query and the answer isn't immediately obvious on the brand website.
- They are travelling and it is the fastest, cheapest and most convenient way for them to contact the brand.
- They want to post a comment or opinion in a public place to create an open dialogue with others in the community involved.

The trick here is that if you just have complaints on your Facebook page, you're going to look pretty ordinary as a brand. So encouraging customers who have had a positive service experience to tell others on your site would be a big win. Customers who write on your Facebook Wall and get no response from your organisation are likewise telling others something about your brand—i.e. that you don't listen and engage.

The good news is that as of today there's a positive and healthy shift towards the use of Twitter and Facebook as support and branding channels. There are companies now measuring the effectiveness of customer support channels over Twitter, such as the Engagement Index in the UK. The data from Engagement Index shows that, at least for the UK, major banks are succeeding in using Twitter to engage customers for front-line support. The problem is that the teams that manage the Twitter channel are generally totally disconnected from traditional contact centres and often still refer customers back to the call centre after an initial contact.

Siri, Lola, Skype and VoIP

We are also seeing more use of technologies such as web-chat and Skype. These are hardly universal, but a few banks have experimented with context-sensitive web-chat and integrating Skype into the web/tablet experience. In fact, when UBank launched as NAB's online direct banking brand experiment back in 2009, it deliberately integrated Skype into the customer onboarding and support mechanisms. UBank states on its website:

> "You can 'Skype™ us' from anywhere in the world for free (excluding ISP costs). UBank is the first Australian bank to enable Skype™ calls directly into our 24x7 Australian-based Direct Banking Centre."

At an FST Media event in June 2011, UBank stated that ten per cent of its customer support and sales calls were already handled via Skype.[3]

I think it is fair to say that allowing customers new ways to engage or seek out information and support actually gives them more comfort and confidence in the brand. UBank also uses Twitter and Facebook to good effect. UBank has the second-highest Facebook fan-base among the Australian banks, and ironically has more than its parent, NAB. The same can be said for First Direct in the UK, which has fantastic advocacy and is heavily engaged on Twitter, whereas its parent, HSBC, doesn't yet have a brand Twitter account.

In *Bank 2.0* I also talked about the use of advances in speech recognition, enabling customers to issue spoken commands. Obviously the next generation of this speech recognition technology can be seen in Apple's recent launch of Siri. In Siri's patent application, various possibilities are hinted at, including being a voice agent providing assistance for "automated teller machines".[4] In fact, SRI (the creator of Siri™) and BBVA recently announced a collaboration to introduce Lola[5], a Siri-like technology, to customers through the Internet and via voice. Siri's near-term capabilities include:

1. Being able to make simple online purchases, such as **"Purchase Bank 3.0 from Amazon Kindle"**
2. Serving as a recommendation engine or intelligent automated assistant—an "agent avatar", as it has sometimes been labelled

However, there are some challenges in having customers talk into their phones for customer support, or replacing an IVR system with technologies such as Lola, as a recent *New York Times* article pointed out when it called Siri "the latest public nuisance in the cell phone revolution". It outlined several scenarios of people using Siri in less than desirable situations (e.g. public transportation) for things as mundane as sending an SMS message wishing a friend a happy birthday. Here's a quote from the article that outlines some of the issues:

> "When talking to their cellphones, people sometimes start sounding like machines themselves. Jimmy Wong, 24, was at an after-hours diner with friends in Los Angeles recently when they found themselves next to a man ordering Siri to write memos and dictate e-mails. They found the man's conversation with his phone 'creepy,' without any of the natural pauses and voice inflections that occur in a discussion between two people."
>
> —*New York Times* article, "Oh, for the Good Old Days of Rude Cellphone Gabbers", 2 December 2011

The same problem presents itself with the use of IVR in the near term. Speech recognition is not yet good enough for natural speech. But clearly it's getting better, and fast.

Avatars replacing IVRs

The key advantage to integrating natural speech recognition to replace current IVR menus will be that IVRs will start to become more human again.

The logical extension of this technology married with avatars are automated customer service representatives that will look and sound like a real person and be able to answer simple "canned" questions and respond to issues such as "What is my account balance?", "I've lost my credit card", "I need a new cheque book". Why might bank customers accept such

Figure 4.8: Future IVR Video Avatar

an avatar-simulated CSR experience? Primarily because it won't feel like they're talking to a computer; it will feel more like a human experience.

"As graphics hardware in phones becomes more powerful, more realistic avatars will be possible on cellular handsets," says Mike Danielson, who's spearheading the avatar project at Motorola Labs. "On a phone with the right hardware we can expect avatar display quality that exceeds what normally appears in a 3-D game, because we will only be viewing one character at a time."

Here's what the customer's IVR experience might "look" like in the next few years, based on the combination of avatars, voice recognition technology and predictive response modelling...

Good morning, Mr Green. How can I help you?

"I'd like my account balance, please."

Which account is that for, Mr Green? Savings, US dollar savings, or Euro savings?

"Savings."

The balance of your savings account is 320,422 Hong Kong Dollars. Can I help you with anything else?

"Yes, I'd like to discuss a personal loan."

You are pre-approved for a line of credit of 150,000 Hong Kong Dollars at an interest rate of 5.25 per cent. Would you like to accept this offer?

"No, thank you."

Let me transfer you to a loans advisor so you can discuss your requirements. Thank you for calling your bank.

Are you learning from what you measure?

Banks are also not very good at being learning organisations when presented with support instances. So once a person in the business comes up with a unique solution to a set of customer problems, that intelligence is lost for all time because you haven't hard-coded it into a software interface somewhere so that it can be replicated as a process via the call centre. Or you have a channel stove-pipe that limits support only to that channel because of a hard-coded process.

For example, in 2010 I was visiting Australia, where my family had an investment property. I'd just sold the property and had to work out how to discharge the mortgage, and put the surplus cash into a new account. I thought the easiest way to do this was simply to walk into a Westpac branch (the bank that held the mortgage) and do it all in person. So what happened? I'm in the branch with the mortgage loans officer and she's explaining that she can't help me, she can't even look up the remaining balance on the mortgage, and we'll have to get on the phone to the mortgage centre "hotline". Why couldn't I have done that from home? I could have, I didn't need to come into the branch, and the branch didn't solve the problem for me. Getting me into the branch didn't make me more loyal, didn't increase brand perception, didn't solve the problem—it just cost the bank money for the relationship manager to make a call that I could have made myself. Why? Because silos were destroying the relationship potential of the interaction.

My team and I were doing a multichannel audit for a bank in the Middle East, where one branch we visited was getting 30–60 customer requests a day for credit card balances. When this occurred, tellers would have to get on the phone to the customer service hotline to find out the card balance—something a customer could have easily done themselves if that's the way they wanted the organisation to help them. It was clunky and ugly.

An even more absurd example: I recently transferred some money internally from my consulting company business account to my personal account. I had two transfers to do—one, a salary payment, and one, a credit card payment. I accidentally transferred both to the credit card.

Realising my mistake, I rang the bank and asked why I couldn't transfer the money out of my credit card to my savings account online. The answer was I could only transfer money *on to* my credit card, not out of that account. So I asked them how I could rectify the problem. I was told I had to write a letter to the bank! Seriously? A letter!

Banks appear to be building organisations that minimalise service to customers on the basis of cost.

An organisation that says, "I'll only support you if you walk in through a door, send a fax, pick up a phone, or write a letter", is not a service organisation at all these days. It's not a culture of putting customers first and delighting them, it's a culture of trying to corral costs and support processes into a one-size-fits-all approach for a "necessary evil". You call these channels cost centres and try to wring every last excess out of the overhead to minimise the impact these channels have on the bottom line. You try to reduce call waiting time, improve first-call resolution, training of call centre staff—all in an effort to make the contact centre as cost-effective as possible. If you get better customer satisfaction in the meantime, that's a bonus, but most certainly not the driver.

This cost-first, customer-second approach is coming back to bite banks collectively right now. The industry as a whole has created organisations severely constrained in their ability to serve customers, to solve problems and to connect with them. Twitter, Facebook, Skype and other new technologies are seen as outside the secure net of managed cost centres when customers just see them as ways to talk. The industry answer? "Don't talk to us unless it is on our terms, through our mandated channels." This is screwed up!

When a consumer wants to become a customer

Traditionally banks have had the expectation that a new customer will walk into a branch and say he'd like to open an account. They even see this traditional mindset characterised in movies and serial dramas. It wouldn't work for the evil criminal overlord to fire up his laptop and open a Swiss bank account online—watching someone click on a mouse or browsing a tablet doesn't have the same dramatic effect. Over decades banks have built processes, metrics and systems that assume this is the starting point in the customer relationship.

Traditionally banks have funnelled customers to the branch. In fact, they even call it the sales funnel. It's been extremely difficult from a process and compliance perspective to break out of that funnel and allow new channels such as the web, mobile, and social media to be more than just broadcast marketing channels because of the "funnel".

Today, however, banks need to be prepared to engage a customer wherever, whenever and however he's ready to talk, apply or buy. Anytime a bank prejudices a sale opportunity by forcing a customer to its channel, it creates friction, a roadblock, a reason for the customer to go somewhere else. So when as a customer I go online and I'm ready to apply for a credit card, but you tell me to print out an application form and fax it to the bank, or you tell me the only way to apply for it is to visit a branch or ring the call centre—you've failed. You've likely just lost me as a customer.

Regardless of process, policy or regulation, a bank can't force a customer to buy its way unless it has a truly differentiated product—and there is no banking product in the world that is *that* differentiated. There is a plethora of examples of how the Internet effected this shift in consumer buying behaviour, but the travel industry is probably one of the best examples of this. Let's illustrate the behaviour problem for channelling customers to the high street.

Rather than talk about buying behaviour across the entire travel sector, which has clearly been disrupted by online buying behaviour, let's take a specialised sector of travel that requires specific knowledge or advice—such as snow sports or skiing.

The snow sports industry in the UK annually supports around 1.4 million Britons. Between 2004 and 2011 there was a 79 per cent decrease in the number of people booking skiing holidays via travel agents.[6] In 2004, already suffering from the impact of online travel sites, this sector saw only 25 per cent of bookings made on the UK high street—today that figure has plummeted to just six per cent of sales. This shift is due to a combination of factors:

1. Online was faster, and more convenient.
2. Travel agents were often poor advisors on ski holidays, and were generalists who didn't have specific knowledge that was of benefit to that class of travellers.
3. There was no cost benefit in going to a high street agent; in fact, online prices were often more competitive.
4. Online resources quickly became far better at providing "advice" than high street stores.

Sounds awfully familiar, doesn't it? It should—it also describes the vast majority of sales transactions for a high street retail bank today. The behaviour of the majority of consumers when it comes to banking is pretty much identical. Except that now you also have the mobile thrown into the mix, which makes the value proposition of the high street even less attractive.

It's possible you're still not sold on the analogy here, but here's another point of evidence. In this industry, there was massive inertia around

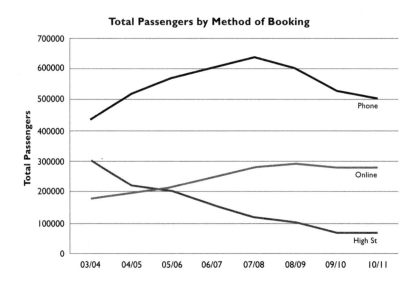

Figure 4.9: Change in travel agent activity for ski holidays between 2004–11 (Source: Ski Club of Britain)

supporting the high street that was quickly broken. Customers adapted rapidly to online ticketing and booking, and they generally didn't even bemoan the loss of the storefront. In banking, customers have already rapidly adapted to internet banking without much fuss or angst over the last decade. In fact, today most prefer internet banking. So why haven't customers done the same for buying financial services online? Mainly because banks still don't sell to them adequately online. Customers can't buy what's not available.

When customers change their buying behaviour, as they already have for banking products and services, there is no use fighting the trend, especially if you don't differentiate on product or advice. I would pit online resources in financial services these days against any generalist advisor in-branch from a knowledge base perspective. Thus, in the end, as a customer I'm left to measure the friendliness and effectiveness of a buying interaction on the basis of how simple it is or how fast I can execute it.

On that basis, if you redirect me to a branch or call centre from your website you've likely already lost me. The call centre may very well be able to serve me adequately, but I should still have the choice of applying online if that's the channel I choose to engage to buy/apply.

I'll talk more about marketing capability and engagement at the front end in much greater detail in later chapters, but for now I want to focus on the structural issues of how the organisation needs to work to reduce friction and engage more holistically with customers in the total channel environment.

Customer-centred means organisational change

Organisationally, banks will have to make some significant changes. Traditionally the key measure of success on the retail banking front has been revenue, or the number of products sold (primarily through the branch). Corporate banking has been physically separated from retail but likewise has been focused on product revenue. Therefore the business has been split into divisions such as Retail, Corporate, Treasury, etc., and, within these divisions, the business has been built to reinforce product revenue and sales through the traditional channels. So you get a product-focused, branch-focused, and revenue-focused organisational structure—traditionally key factors in a retail bank's success. Marketing continues to be focused on generating branch activity and product acquisition, and banks maintain separate departments for the call centre, internet banking (mobile and social normally sit in here), ATM, IVR, and branches.

In the Bank 2.0 to Bank 3.0 singularity that banks find themselves in now (and it's only going to get more acute), the realisation is that product and network are no longer differentiators—people and service capability are. The traditional measurement of revenue and product ratios can only make sense with reference to customers and segments today. Traditional branch metrics have become of limited use because most of the transactions take place outside the branch. Fifty per cent of high-net-worth customers (the most profitable customer group) actually use the Internet as their primary channel these days—by choice! So why do banks maintain a structure that is built to promote and build branch activity—when customers are patently moving away from this paradigm to a multicontact strategy combining branch and direct channels?

The future of the bank reveals a very different organisation structure. While product teams such as credit cards, wealth management, mortgages, etc. remain pretty much the same, the entire customer-facing organisation and supporting platform need to change radically. The hardest of these changes to swallow will be in the marketing department and the branch distribution structures. IT support becomes more about the fabric of the business, so as a result you have to split what you'd normally call "IT" into three different supporting functions with different priorities.

Here is how the organisational shift might take place within the bank:

Table 4.1: Organisational Changes

Traditional Structure	New Structure	Focus
Branch Management	Channel and Partner Management	All physical touch points, both within the branch network and through third parties, supported by Customer Dynamics, Channel Management and strong Partner Management

Marketing	Brand Marketing	Analogous to the current marketing function, but shifted to new media, with limited old media
	Advocacy Marketing	Dedicated to building a core groundswell of brand support amongst the throngs of consumers, promoting great customer experience and showcasing the voices of advocates
	Customer Dynamics	An organisational capability to generate timely and relevant offers to smaller and smaller segments, aiming at a market-of-one approach
Branch Distribution, "Alternative Channels", Call Centres, Internet Banking, ATM, etc.	Customer Channel Management	Combining service-oriented architecture, contact centre (voice, IP, email, etc.), and behavioural analytics
Information Technology	Content Deployment	Content publication supported by Customer Dynamics
	Customer Dynamics	Managing customer intelligence through Customer Data Mart and Customer Analytics
	Customer Channel Management	Managing contact centre and supporting channels
	IT	Maintaining systems backbone and core technologies
Transaction Services	Enablement	From middleware to payment systems, to settlement systems, transactional technology will be all about customer fulfilment as fast and accurately as possible.
Treasury and cash management	Enablement	Treasury will be largely automated by technology, especially as Straight-Through Processing kicks in
Strategy Groups	Innovation	A multidiscipline (Product, IT, Marketing) team that stimulates innovation and manages new programme initiatives

From branch-led to customer-led

Traditionally the branch and the direct sales force have been at the core of everything a retail bank does. It's a cultural thing. It's not so much a branch issue in reality; it is the total dedication of the institution to the traditional distribution model. Many banks today still don't classify the Internet and mobile as "core" to banking; these are typically relegated to *alternative* or *direct* channels. It's like the geeky, socially challenged cousin whom we invite over for family occasions out of respect, but everyone feels a little sorry for him and thinks he's a misfit compared with the rest of the clan. Suddenly, one morning we wake up and find out that the very same cousin is on Bloomberg TV talking about Facebook's acquisition of his new start-up and he's being hailed as the next Larry Page or Sergey Brin and we still can't figure out what it's all about, but he's just exited with $300 million in cash.

These so-called alternative or direct channels are organisationally separated from branch and "serious" distribution channels today because they've often been considered IT playthings rather than core business essentials, or because they've been hastily tacked on to the existing org chart as the business has slowly adapted and could no longer avoid a web presence (for example). Even today, when the Internet and mobile for many banks represent more than 50 per cent of their daily retail transaction load and have the potential to bring in at least 30 to 50 per cent of new product revenue, they still get fractional budget allocations compared with real estate.

While there has been a gradual acceptance of the web as an important *new* channel, this acceptance and adoption have not been even close to adequate for most institutions. I visit bank websites constantly that have very little engagement for onboarding new customers from the public website, or have zero revenue capability behind the login. This is unforgivable more than 15 years after the web became a commercial proposition.

In print, media, retail, travel, and a host of other industries, the web is a major revenue contributor today. It's not a new or alternative channel anymore. Heck, mobile isn't even a new channel anymore. They're both hygiene factors today, basic requirements. Most banks measure their internet revenue in the 1–5 per cent range and proclaim that branch is still the dominant revenue channel. Why? Largely because most banks suck at engaging customers electronically and force customers to the branch channel based on outdated KYC and compliance processes.

If you're a banker and you feel I'm being too harsh, let me ask you one simple question: In the org chart, where does your Internet channel line manager sit in relationship to your distribution head? If you don't have a head of mobile, or your internet channel manager is not at the same level as your head of branch distribution—you're doing it wrong.

In Bank 2.0 the primary shift is a move away from a physical "superior branch channel" psyche to a total customer-channel mentality. In Bank 3.0 this shift moves towards real-time engagement of customers when and where they need a solution, or building journeys that are triggered by an event, behaviour or location. These moves require a rethink on a number of levels. First of all, customer revenue and profitability drive to the top of the metrics scorecard. Revenue through the branch channel becomes a supporting metric, and when measured against real costs, comes out as a very expensive option for acquisition and onboarding. In the new mix, relationship metrics become more critical for branches, such as the net contribution to the cross-sell and up-sell targets that generate customer profitability. A monthly branch revenue figure that bears no relationship to customer measures as a core strategic driver is simply an outcome of a strategy—not *the* strategy.

Branch-Centered   **Customer-Focused**

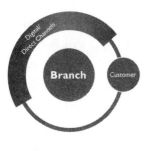

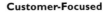

Figure 4.10: The Primary Culture Shift for Bank 2.0

Whereas in the BANK 1.0 days you would be engineering the latest product to be offered through the branch network, in the Bank 2.0 to 3.0 paradigm, the product team has to think a little more laterally about positioning product across a range of channel options rather than attempting to retrofit a product designed for over-the-counter, or direct sales force offering, to a digital dialogue.

There are sound regulatory reasons for this as well. Separating counterparty risk from operational risk is an inherent principle in the Basel II and III frameworks and, as such, a clear separation between the manufacturing and origination of a product, and the distribution of the product, is a key feature of these global risk standards.

In most of the banks I've worked with, apart from the odd "e-saver" account or similar, the creation of a new product takes place totally devoid of any thought on how the product will be distributed through non-traditional channels. Some products retrofit very easily onto digital channels—for example, time deposits. Generally, the fewer features a product has, the easier it is to multifit across different sales conduits. To be fair, many banks already customise products based on segmentation. We see credit cards and savings accounts customised based on net worth, credit cards for the female demographic (probably due to their propensity for shopping), student loans, general insurance products for families, and many more. Segmentation is a key input in the design of these products, but channel is rarely factored in during the design phase unless the product is perceived as a channel-specific solution.

Product teams need to move to a matrix approach to product generation and design, where channel is an input, or create product that is channel-agnostic. Channel-specific artefacts are created after the core product is *packaged*, and these become **wrappers** that are aimed at a specific channel or segment/channel combination. For example:

1. Physical application forms are replaced by a ***list of fields or data elements that are mandatory*** only; physical application forms or electronic entry forms are a channel-specific wrapper.
2. ***Compliance, credit risk and/or STP parameters*** are a core deliverable of the product team and supporting departments.

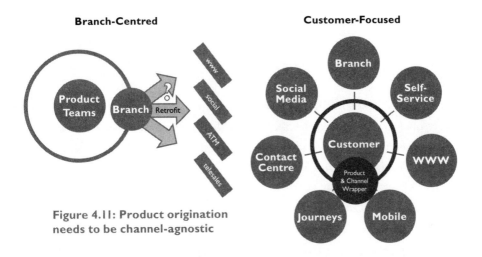

Figure 4.11: Product origination needs to be channel-agnostic

However, compliance needs to think multichannel—for example, supplying three months' worth of bank statements over a mobile phone app form is never going to happen.

3. **Benefits to the end user** are a core deliverable—not features. These are *correlated by segment*.

4. The Customer Dynamics team needs to generate a list of **cross-sell and up-sell drivers** for the specific segment, so that specific campaign instances (customer offers) can be generated at the wrapper stage.

5. *Creative design* needs to start with two core outcomes: **message** and **call-to-action;** concepts generally need to be done for at least four core media types—print, web, social and mobile (MMS, in-app or notification)—as part of each creative brief. Most current media is not actionable and so won't fit in the new customer-led dynamic.

6. In the case of a multisegment product, mapping an offer to a segment at the *wrapper* stage would produce the **media buy triggers**, rather than media buy being solely campaign based.

So the product is derived for a customer segment or segments, and it is designed to be packaged for each channel with a wrapper that amounts to either an acquisition attempt, or a cross-sell or up-sell offer. Either in the instance of a new customer or for an existing customer, the outcome should be a call-to-action that facilitates the sale, not a brand or product message.

Let's take a specific example to illustrate. A good example might be a personal loan offer at a specific time of the year, for example, a tax loan at tax time, a travel loan leading up to summer vacations, or a student loan around enrolment time. Here's how it might map out:

PERSONAL LOAN
- Loan Amount Available (e.g. 3 x monthly salary)
- Underlying Interest Rate (e.g. 6.25 per cent, or 4 per cent above LIBOR)
- Duration or Term of Loan (e.g. 3 months minimum, 24 months maximum)
- Credit Risk Rating Limit—Good to Excellent (ratings driven from internal credit risk system)
- Core data requirements
  - All Customers: Amount, Term, Preferred or Normal Rate (internal)
  - New Customer
    - » Name, Contact Details Set, Employer Detail Set
    - » Social media handles/profiles
    - » Mobile number
    - » Annual salary, current credit card balance
    - » Bank contact if not your bank

TARGET SEGMENTS
- Customers with salary account and 12 months' history
- Customers with good to excellent credit risk rating
- Customers with maturing personal loan (redraw offer)
- New target, working professionals aged 25–45
- New target, expat professionals as possible preferred segment up-sell
- Inactive customers with deposit in excess of US$25,000
- Etc.

BENEFITS

- Existing customers: Pre-approved or Approval in 60 seconds
- Funds the same day
- Choose the term that suits your budget
- Competitive rate
- Offer 0.5 per cent privilege rate for preferred customers for 30 days
- No penalties for early pay-out
- Automatic redraw facility for existing HSBC customers
- Themes: Renovate Your Home, Upgrade Your Car, Take a Dream Holiday, etc.

Wrappers by channel (Customer Dynamics team to define)

Table 4.2: Customer Engagement Product "Wrappers" (by channel)

Public Website (New and Existing Customers)
Landing page, possible dedicated URL (i.e. getaloan.com, newcarnow.com…) for link with print campaign
Third-party "Apply Now" rich-media banners
Link to Internet Banking process for existing customers
Internet Banking (Existing Customers)
"You've been pre-approved" banner and secure message
"Pre-Approved Credit Options" contextual hyperlink on account summary page
"Transfer Credit" hyperlink on credit card summary
Add new listing under Account "Personal Loan" with maximum pre-approved amount, e.g. $50,000 pre-approved
Add Pre-approved Credit Options to left-hand navigation
ATM
Rich-media ad playing during idle time
"You have been pre-approved" message for existing customers on close of transaction—call-back request option
Promotion on coupon for selected segments: "It takes less time to get a loan approved than it took to get your cash…"
SMS/MMS
Personalised message or notification with web/app link; "Mr King, HSBC has pre-approved you for a personal loan—interested?"

Social Media
Facebook integration of a student loan application that uses Facebook profile data to kick-start KYC
Advertising travel loans or travel insurance on Pinterest, Instagram or Facebook when an individual posts something about a travel destination they'd like to visit

Mobile App
New button/in-app banner—"Pre-approved Credit Line"
For existing customers, just two fields—term, amount (preset drop-down list for options)
Call back with approval and compliance procedure notice

Branch
Banner stands as per themes, TV and poster board promos?
Pop-up cross-sell on branch dashboard
Focus on preferred customers for month of January, offer discount interest rate
Digital application—green, i.e. no paper?? Can they sign on digipad? (Check with IT and branch services)

Other?
See if they can integrate personal loan as a payment option on cathaypacific.com and BA.com instead of credit card for existing customers (does cookie technology allow this level of granularity?)

This presents a fairly vanilla product offering with some interesting execution options for either customer acquisition or cross-sell. Obviously the wrappers could be further segmented into different groups of customers, or different themes. We haven't touched on traditional print media as a promotion element here, but you could use this for *drive to web* or *drive to branch* also. Clearly, however, the approach of using a core product offering and "wrapping" the product for use within an appropriate channel gives a lot more flexibility than trying to retrofit a branch product after the fact.

I know many banks have already been looking at options for deploying product over new channels, but generally the banks start with the standard branch or physical distribution options first. In the new world, retail banks need to be agnostic as to which channel is used first or most prominently for the product promotion and roll-out.

The wrapper approach allows much more specific channel metrics for each product and customer segment as well, garnering much more constructive data than is currently captured. Basically you'll know who, when and via what channel the customer committed to a product—rather than assuming the branch is always the first place he'll look.

From selling to service-selling

Firstly, the objective has to be about the right product at the right time to the right customer. This takes some intelligence, but increasingly you'll have great pools of information available about your customers. Banks just have to tap into this wealth of information and apply it. Secondly, you'll need to be able to have a conversation with the customer that appears more like a service exchange than a sales exchange. How is this possible? Well, if the offer is presented as a solution to a potential problem for the client, they then equate this with better *service* from the institution, rather than a pure sales pitch. This is really the only way to tackle the psychological hurdle of the "sale". Move from selling to ***service-selling.***

Anytime a bank presents a badly positioned or poorly selected product to a valuable customer, the more likely it is to fail, not just once, but cumulatively over time. Time and time again today customers see front-line staff saddled with the "**offer of the month**" to position to them in the branch or contact centre. As effectiveness has reduced, you increase the offer of the month to perhaps three or five different products that the staff member can choose from on the fly, depending on what he knows about the customer, but it is still hit and miss. You need to have intelligence built into the system in respect of the next best offer or the next best action for the customer. This requires the implementation of customer analytics, business intelligence and offering management solutions to take a range of offers each month, and match the right offer with the right client. It also requires each of the product teams to come up with a range of offers each month that can be triggered by key data points for specific customers.

Most product teams are used to running just one acquisition-type campaign on a new product three or four times a year—and it takes a great deal of work with creative agencies and so forth to pull it off. Thus, approaching these teams and asking them to come up with core benefits or sales messages for 10–15 different offers each month requires a fundamental change of philosophy internally.

There are three elements that make an "offer" viable for use across multiple channels. Firstly, an offer is not a campaign—it is a simple sales message tailored to a market segment or individual client profile. Secondly, it is designed to be actionable—with a simple, understandable proposition that has specific benefits for the client it is offered to. Lastly, it does not require a great deal of preparation or a steep product learning curve in order for a staff member to be able to pitch an offer.

There are four classes of offer types that need to be developed for the sales conversation regularly, and these need to be reinforced with training or with messaging architecture for support across digital channels.

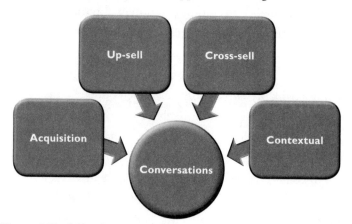

Figure 4.13: Offer development for effective sales conversations

Acquisition is for targeting new customers and is the most difficult to be driven from an analytics perspective, but there is a way. For example, you may have customers who have taken a credit card with you, but have no savings or current/checking account. By looking at their card history, purchases, payment history, etc., you can get a picture of potential needs. Maybe at certain times of the year they make certain big purchases that might be better funded by a lower-interest-rate credit facility, etc.

For **cross-sell** and **up-sell**, you already have all the information you need in the bank's various systems, but you rarely use this information effectively. The analytics should be looking for opportunities around the following categories of offer:

1. **Products that the customer has purchased before,** but currently does not utilise, such as general insurance, a term deposit, etc.

2. **Products that a customer could use** due to his transaction history or linked product activity, but doesn't—for instance, a customer who has a car loan with the bank, but not motor vehicle insurance.

3. **Products that improve a customer's life,** or aspirational products, such as upgrading a customer from Gold to Platinum status on their Visa card, or pushing them into the "preferred" bracket even though they don't meet the minimum balance requirement.

4. **Alternative products that give the customer a better deal** than the current solution. For example, for "revolvers" who maintain a high credit card balance, an offer to shift some of the balance to a line of credit facility at a lower interest rate.

5. **Bundled offerings** or products that go well combined with other products, such as mortgage insurance or contents insurance with a new mortgage, car insurance with a car loan, or Platinum credit card with a mutual fund investment.

6. **Future point-of-impact offerings** that are time sensitive or might be linked to a future action, purchase or trigger. For example, a tax loan at tax time, or a great travel loan deal when the customer takes his annual family holiday.

Customers are increasingly expressing and sharing needs/desires through social networks, which banks could mine for leading product and service opportunities.

Customers rarely (if ever) receive such well-thought-out offers. High-value customers often have a spread of products with various financial institutions that could easily be consolidated with one or two institutions, but the fact is that they often make a choice of a product because of expediency and because their primary institution does not anticipate their needs more effectively and in a timely way.

Offers also need to be delivered **contextually**. We'll talk more about engagement banking in Chapter 11, and journeys in Chapter 13, but the key to contextual up-sell or cross-sell offers is understanding when and where a customer needs a product or service from the bank and then delivering that offer at the right time, through the right channel.

The offer management or generation process needs to be a dedicated function within the bank. The marriage of the product team and the channel needs to occur through a function such as a customer propositions or customer dynamics team, but one with real clout. For example, if the product teams aren't supporting the process, then the contact centre or web channel is not obliged to promote their product of the month. The customer dynamics team, however, can assist the product team with the right data and analytics so the crafting of relevant offers is made easier. The product team can even second members of their group to the customer dynamics team to ensure the offer messages and positioning are correct.

Responsive architecture

Channel management is probably the most significant change both operationally and technically for creating a competent service organisation across the institution. Currently banks are sticklers for maintaining multiple technology and operational silos around customer channels. This situation is untenable as you move into the networked economies of the 21st century. Why?

Firstly, customer channels will continue to evolve and emerge, presenting opportunities but also risks around increasing complexity. For example, the introduction of the iPad as a device now requires you to think about a new channel, potentially new integration requirements, potentially a support hook into the app too. Are you going to create a new silo for the app, or does your organisation have the ability to add this into the current channel architecture without significant investment or development of your core platform?

Secondly, bank management is increasingly facing the question of who should own all these new channels. In reality a customer-focused channel team could deal with all these new opportunities agnostically, without having to offset investment in one channel against some pre-existing budget thinking or bias within the marketing and IT teams (for example).

Forget the empire-building—no one owns the customer

Let's take one example in respect of sales channels and advertising as an illustration. We're seeing a significant shift in the consumption of TV-related content today due to the concept of the "screen" along with new distribution platforms such as Apple TV, Google TV, Hulu and so forth. Content consumption is shifting rapidly from fixed-point-in-time/fixed-channel broadcast over cable and free-to-air, to people downloading the content when they'd like to watch it—preferably commercial-free. So, as this shift occurs, the advertising will change as well. Advertising in this medium currently takes two basic forms: sponsorship of a programme so it is "free", but the consumer is subjected to advertising; and in-programme advertising, increasingly with content tailored to suit the consumer's interests and likes/dislikes (Hulu and others try to match offers to ads you've previously "liked", for example).

There are going to be opportunities here to create ads that are responsive and able to be leveraged in real time, instead of the passive TV commercials we all tend to tune out on (except at Superbowl time). If I'm a retail banking customer watching my favourite TV show on my iPad (as many increasingly do now), I could click through to an ad regarding a mortgage or car insurance, directly through to the application process, or a special offer based on my unique relationship with my financial services provider. So who manages this new opportunity? Is it marketing, the product team, the iPad app development team? One team can't own this—it would screw up the result.

Again, to illustrate, as NFC[7] point-of-sale (POS) technology evolves and daily offers and coupons can be streamed direct to the customer's mobile or to the POS unit itself, you're likely to compartmentalise this as a payment solutions issue and relegate it to either the cards division or even MasterCard, Visa, Discover, and Amex to solve. However, the reality is that the bank actually needs to find a way to optimise the point-of-sale experience for each individual customer—who would own that?

Creating the right precognitive service selling offers requires more than a cards team—it requires a deeper understanding of customer behaviour through analytics. It also requires partnerships with retailers, mobile operators, secure payments providers, perhaps a wallet provider, and others. Without a customer-focused, overarching channel team, you're screwed.

All these challenges cannot simply be met by the current technology platform and organisation structures that most banks employ. How will the platform be optimised to serve a true multichannel services concept?

The figure below illustrates the complexity most banks find themselves saddled with today: multiple channels, largely married with current systems on a case-by-case basis, with independent technology bridges and interfaces. In addition, content that is created or published currently is purpose-built for one channel only each time it is required. In the future, ATMs, phones, the Internet, mobile internet and app phone devices, in-branch systems and the call centre will all leverage sales offers generated by a Customer Dynamics team—just imagine publishing that content across these channels with eight or nine different content and channel platforms.

Consider the development effort required every time you find a channel is not adequately configured to handle the latest capability of the end-user's device. Optimised channel management goes hand in hand with better content, service and experience. This is a goal that cannot be achieved in the current IT environment without considerable expense that is largely avoidable if an overarching team is created for customer sales

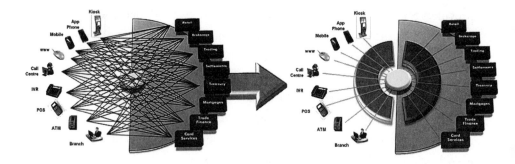

Figure 4.14: Moving away from Bank 1.0 architecture

offers. This streamlined environment will also enable the bank to respond to product opportunities in real time across every channel, rather than face production lags due to silo-ing.

As an organisation, your institution is rapidly going to have to re-engineer itself around the customer more effectively. The current departmental structure effectively creates competition for resources that could otherwise be optimised in servicing the customer. For example, removing duplication of silos such as the call centre, internet banking, and email handling for different business units (i.e. retail versus commercial banking, personal internet banking versus commercial internet banking, etc.).

It means creating a consistent service across all channels because branch performance is no longer the key measure for customer experience. Customers now evaluate the bank on its performance across *every* channel—a great branch experience will not save you if your internet thingy sucks...

Conclusions: Tactical channel improvement

So what is on the contact centre improvement road map that you can achieve in the short term that will bring benefits to both the organisation and the customer? Over the next few years think about the following initiatives:

Table 4.3

Project/Initiative	Desired Outcome
Staff Retention Programmes	Consider homesourcing as an option for retaining your best service staff. Assign new cadets to the call centre for at least three months within their first year of service so they learn customer pain points.
Full Integration of Email, VoIP/IM, Twitter and Facebook directly into the contact centre	Integrate the technologies customers use into the contact centre—picking up the phone is not a superior choice for customers. Don't forget to develop a communication policy for all employees that covers use of the above, plus blogs, social networking sites and virtual communities.

Project/Initiative	Desired Outcome
IVR Menu Redesign	Think about prioritising menu options based on traditional traffic analytics, thus reducing IVR navigation for those calls that are most frequently made. Incorporate voice-recognition "emotive" IVR technologies to redirect upset customers to a specialist "customer advocate" and defuse difficult situations.
Single-Screen Customer Dashboard	Improve customer knowledge, process and workflow with a single-screen interface for CSRs, akin to the internet banking centre for customers. Reduce the current workarounds with multiple disparate systems, separate logins, screens, etc.
Improved Service Culture	Work to create a total service culture within the bank that gives contact centre staff pride in their role within the customer equation rather than letting them feel like they have been relegated to the call centre dungeon. Empower staff to solve problems rather than creating a process that frustrates resolution through convoluted organisation structures.
Customer Analytics	Use customer analytics to understand better the reasons for the call, and work to anticipate customers' needs both collectively and individually. If a customer calls regularly with the same request, utilise analytics to serve up an IVR menu that prioritises those requests by CLID (Caller Line ID) function.
Dynamic Offer Management	Create a customer dynamics team (incorporating product specialists, marketing staff, customer advocates, etc.) to craft offers for segments that emerge from the customer analytics. Create tons of sales scripts and offers for unique, tailored cross-sell and up-sell opportunities that feel like better service for customers, rather than just a sales pitch.
Reform Legal and Compliance departments	Give the legal and compliance department KPIs for enabling customer solutions and improvements so they are working for the customer and not just mitigating risk for the brand. Turn these teams into internal consultants who help manage customer-facing teams through the channel/journey design process, with a focus on risk as a value-add.

KEY LESSONS

Call centres, or contact centres, have been hailed by industry as a significant improvement in the ability to provide rolling support for customers in an increasingly mobile and time-poor environment.

IVR systems and channel migration have provided a significant cost savings imprimatur for corporates. This revolution, however, has not resulted in greater customer satisfaction. Increasingly, contact centres are experiencing problems with very high staff turnover, those in management are demanding improved sales results and corporations are grappling with the question of outsourcing versus onshoring.

The vision of the ultimate contact centre currently appears to be a convoluted mix of unified messaging platform, IP-based architecture, automated voice response systems and first-call-resolution KPIs. But do core building blocks still have to be put in place for this channel to be truly effective?

This chapter tackled the issues of staff retention and effective measurement of the performance of the call centre. But it also looked at the deeper issues of the contact centre becoming the platform for all multichannel contacts with the customer—processing and recording contact history and optimising responses, whether through a sales opportunity, or through a better IVR design.

The construction of a simplified contact centre dashboard or interface would reduce workload for CSRs, improve first-call resolution opportunities, and result in better-quality sales positioning.

Keywords: Customer Advocate, Up Your Service, IVR, Voice Recognition, Siri, Lola, Skype, VoIP, Multicontact Strategy, Communication Policy

Endnotes

1   Gartner Research, Customer Relationship Management Report 2011

2   Service Measures and Metrics; "UPLIFTING SERVICE: The Proven Path to Delighting Your Customers, Colleagues and Everyone Else You Meet"

3   Reported via Twitter

4   Patently Apple

5   SRI International (http://www.sri.com/blog/meet-lola-virtual-personal-assistant-banking)

6   Ski Club of Great Britain

7   NFC: Near-Field Communication

5 Web—Why Revenue Is Still So Hard To Find...

Why aren't we buying more online?

In the United States, United Kingdom, Australia, Germany, France, Hong Kong, Singapore and many other developed economies, the Internet has been the primary, preferred day-to-day channel for banking for more than five years. That is, it is more popular—or preferred as a channel—than the bank branch. That's not news to most bankers. However, given that it is the primary channel for most customers, you need to take a good hard look at why branches still dominate the revenue intake for most retail banks. There are three possible explanations for this disparity:

1. Customers transact online, but prefer to buy offline
2. Banks don't record revenue accurately via channel, and/or
3. Banks don't sell online effectively

Of these three possible explanations, 2 and 3 are pretty obvious, but I would say that 1 does not line up with consumer behaviour in other industries. So either we assert that customers buy everything else online, but still prefer bricks and mortar for banking—or we come back to the fact that banks generally don't facilitate customers' behaviour online well. Regardless of where we think banks are today (some might actually believe customers still prefer the branch), by 2015 all indications are that even in banking the buying behaviour will swing massively to digital. Part of this is the generational shift around Y-Gen, but part of it is just consumer adoption of technology in the buying cycle.

I've been working with retail banks for over 15 years in the deployment of bank websites and internet banking capability, and I can say that the only reason I've ever found for banks not to be making money hand over fist from the online channel is that they simply don't enable online acquisition and fulfilment effectively. It's never been about adoption rates or customer acceptance of the channel. I've never seen a well-designed, highly usable product application process online fail to bring in new revenue from day one.

Internet banking utilisation has never been higher than it is today, and this is reflected in economies such as Australia, where three of the top 20 websites used daily are banking websites.[1] Facebook, YouTube and Google frequently appear in the top websites regardless of country, as do Apple and Amazon; eBay and PayPal make regular appearances too.

However, the question remains as to what people do online when it comes to banking.

If we look at behaviours online, we see that online purchases are well-established behavioural norms now. Since 2006 the US economy has been recording record increases in online purchasing annually. Cyber Monday is singled out as the biggest day for online deals each year—it is the Monday following Black Friday (the Friday after the Thanksgiving holiday) in the United States. Between 2006 and 2011, online purchases

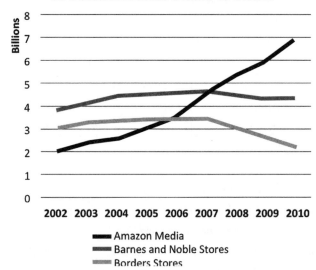

Figure 5.1: US books sales by distributor (Credit: Fonerbooks.com)

on Cyber Monday have more than doubled from $610m to $1.25 billion.[2] Sales of books, online media through iTunes, NetFlix, Hulu, etc., and the success of sites such as Zappos, Amazon and others are testament to the shift in consumer buying behaviour—to the point where consumers now are walking into stores, scanning barcodes and product details to check prices online before purchasing real-world goods.

Clearly, the issue of whether people will buy online has been settled many years ago. Today e-commerce in the US accounts for around ten per cent of total retail sales, depending on how the spend is classified (e.g. including automobiles, fuel and groceries). But in the books industry, it's a very different story, with Amazon alone catering for over 50 per cent of all North American sales revenue. In media and TV content sales, iTunes data tells a similar story.

Clearly, the more suited a product or product range is to digital distribution, the more significant the impact online sales on revenue has been. This is where the problem arises in the retail financial services space.

The false comfort of compliance and process

A mortgage, a car loan, a credit card, or a deposit product are all much more like a book, an app or an album, from a distribution mechanism, than a pair of shoes, a TV or an automobile. From a pure sales and engagement philosophy, the product doesn't require a complex distribution process because it's not physical—it's already essentially a virtual product.

Even for products such as TVs, tablets, mobile phones and shoes, people are increasingly turning to online purchasing, but financial services have generally lagged. If we take away regulatory and compliance requirements and embedded process around the way banks sell products such as mortgages, it's clear to most that it's actually pretty easy to sell financial services products online.

Banks talk about "complex" financial service products, but the complexity is not with the product itself generally—it's in the application process or the features banks have attached to it. Investment products are certainly complex, but a current/checking account, a CD or fixed deposit, a credit card, a personal loan, even a mortgage product, are at their core pretty simple. The complexity of financial services is often in the process—either the approvals required for a personal loan, a credit card or a mortgage, or the application process itself, which requires identity verification, background details, proof of income, etc.

In this way, banks have come to believe as an industry that people don't buy financial service products online because of their complexity. But from a buying behaviour perspective, if the purchase process were simpler, the products in fact lend themselves considerably to digital buying behaviour. If banks as a whole could just crack the process and application issues, then the online revenue upside potential would be almost unlimited.

Banks generally, however, are not incentivised to remove the complexity. It is perceived as increasing risk from a compliance perspective, and if the institution is branch-led, then the incentive to move a customer from an online "lead" to a branch "sale" is very strong—because banks have to continue to pay for the branch real estate and feed the physical channel metrics.

The challenge here is that if someone makes it easier to purchase those same products online, and your buying process is biased towards physical compliance processes, you're quickly displaced. A great example of this in recent times is Square®. Square took a fairly simple product (a credit card point-of-sale terminal) that had heaps of complexity in the buying process—typically known as "merchant onboarding"—and re-engineered the application. By removing the complexity, they had dramatic results—taking one-fourth of the industry's market share in the space of two years.

Amazon did the same with books. Apple did the same with iTunes. It has always been a very tough lesson for incumbents.

Incumbents who relied on complex, restricted distribution mechanisms or processes that were complex were ripe for disruption. In the recording industry—where incumbents spent literally hundreds of millions trying to stop illegal downloads but failed to fill the void with good, legal options—buying behaviour still leaned towards digital downloads even if they were illegal. The buying behaviour was such that the incentives for a simpler purchase (i.e. a download versus an in-store experience) were so strong that people would engage in illegal behaviour as a preference.

iTunes succeeded where an entire industry failed—why? Because Apple attacked the friction of the existing pricing and distribution model, and the incumbents inevitably ended up creating more friction to protect their traditional businesses.

In the same way, banks and regulators can't force consumers to engage only in-branch. If they attempt to do so, behaviour will simply circumvent this over time.

This is a key issue facing banks today. Banks don't sell well online because of compliance and KYC processes, although in almost all cases, the actual regulations around those processes don't absolutely require physical distribution. Otherwise Square and PayPal would simply not have been allowed to do what they did. In terms of basic banking, the next disruption here will be the mobile wallet connected to a simple value store—nothing in the current regulations would stop a non-bank value store from powering a mobile wallet. If the mobile wallet value store serves as a proxy for a debit card, then increasingly a bank "account" becomes optional for day-to-day payments. If, as a consumer, I'm visiting a bank that requires a signature card for account opening, then this should be ringing all the warning bells, because none of the non-bank competitors will need that for account opening, and surprise, surprise, the regulator doesn't either.

What sells online?

In a recent report by the Australian Communications and Media Authority (ACMA), it was found that 62 per cent of adult internet users bought a good or service online during the six months to April 2011.

"The adoption of online shopping among the general population is fairly widespread, it is not something that is on the margins," ACMA's manager of communication analysis Joseph di Gregorio told reporters.[3]

Convenience is the primary driver in online adoption, with 75–96 per cent of users consistently giving their main reason for going online to apply as either time-saving or convenience.[4] Convenience simply means it must be quicker and easier for a customer to get this online, compared with picking up the phone or going down to the branch/high street. **Price** or competitive rates and fees are also drivers, but more so in the consumer market, and less so in the financial services space. But remember, people online are cheap. They love a deal and a deal will often get them over the line…

The counter to convenience is **complexity**. If a customer has to spend 45 minutes online filling in forms, only to have the application process potentially fail at the last moment because he/she doesn't live in the right location, or doesn't have the right details on hand, it is extremely frustrating. Thus, by their nature, less-complex products or application processes will work better in the online and mobile space.

Table 5.1: Preference for retail banking products online, by market[5]

India	Singapore	Hong Kong	United Arab Emirates
Credit card	Time deposit and monthly installment plan	Time deposit and monthly installment plan	Credit card
General insurance (travel, life, home, medical)	New bank account	Stocks and company shares	Personal loans
Bonds, unit trusts or mutual funds	Credit card	Credit card	New bank account
New bank account	Foreign exchange and currency transactions	Foreign exchange and currency transactions	Car loans
Personal loan	Bonds, unit trusts or mutual funds	General insurance (travel, life, home, medical)	Stocks and company shares
Stocks and company shares	Stocks and company shares	New bank account	Time deposit
Time deposit and monthly installment plan	Fixed income products	Fixed income products	Monthly installment plans

This is where it is key to understand how the web supports the sale of a product. Take a real-world example such as buying an automobile. Researching a new car online is a major boon to the automobile industry—

there are online reviews, comparison tools, configurators, video test drives, and many resources that help me as a consumer select a car to buy. However, how do I "buy" a car online? Unless I've got a pretty hefty credit card limit, how would I pay for it? How would it be delivered?

Understanding the difference between the needs of a customer that lead to a sale, and the sale itself, is critical in understanding how to support the sale online. As products increase in complexity it is less likely that the entire process of purchase or application can be done through online fulfilment, and indeed due to compliance rules and regulations, it is often simply impossible. Thus, the online purchase or actual *sale* may not necessarily be the ultimate goal for a financial product.

In simplistic terms, there are three main phases in respect of the customer-product relationship that we can encapsulate through the online channel in varying levels of sophistication. They are:

- **Pre-Purchase or Product Selection**
  What marketers might typically call the "research" or selection phase. This is where customers seek to be informed on options available, choose their budget or quality options, etc. Increasingly the Internet is a primary element in pre-purchase selection.

- **Purchase or Execution**
  What bankers call "acquisition"—the moment the customer selects the product and agrees to the purchase or fills in and submits the application form.

- **Post-Purchase or Maintenance**
  In finance parlance this is where customers monitor their investment products, or where they make a claim on their insurance product, or where they check their statements— everything that happens after they sign up for the relationship with the bank via a specific product.

Figure 5.2: Typical phases of customer engagement online

Not all products are created equal in respect of their suitability to the online channel. Primarily this is due to the sophistication or complexity of the product as explained above. So let us talk about the following broad grouping or classification for retail banking products:

Table 5.2: Grouping or classification of products as they pertain to multichannel interactions

Simple Products	No advice required	Credit Card, Current/Savings Account, Personal Loan, General Insurance, etc.
Informed Purchase	Advice sometimes required	Mortgage, Life Insurance, Overdraft, etc.
Complex Products	Specialist advice required	Securities, Investment Funds, Mutual Funds, Derivatives, Structured Products, etc.

Putting this together, you can determine through analytics, customer behavioural analysis and customer research a typical pattern of utilisation or suitability of the online channel in supporting each respective phase of engagement for each class of product. So let's analyse this in greater detail and look at some examples.

To illustrate the issue of online engagement, let us take the example of a mortgage product. Now, subprime aside, there has been a significant increase in the mortgage business over the last few years globally, and a borrower is definitely finding it easier nowadays to get access to mortgages than he did, say, 20 years ago. As noted in the earlier Google Finance

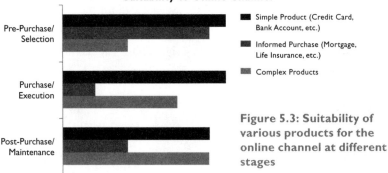

Figure 5.3: Suitability of various products for the online channel at different stages

research, 88 per cent of internet users start their selection process of a mortgage provider or product online. So the fact is, even if a customer does walk into a branch to do the mortgage application, the reality is that in the vast majority of cases the customer was "sold" on the product online or heavily influenced by his online research.

Right now banks are not very good at separating lead generation capability and the whole online application process. Banks also undervalue products that are researched online and, as a result, don't do a good job with content support. Too much of the content the customer sees online is still effectively brochureware, and doesn't actually help him through the purchase journey.

In the near term, customers will be using their smartphone and tablets to access information about a product on the move. Banks need to start to think about informational requirements contextually also.

That means finding the customer when and where he needs a bank or a bank solution…

Findability and Context

Google revolutionised search engine behaviour in the late 90s when it launched its portal of the same name on the unsuspecting public. Prior to that, we had lived quite happily with the equivalent of the Yellow Pages or Sears mail order catalogue system online. With the launch of google.com we learned that finding stuff on the web could be really, really easy.

The other component that is really critical today for bank websites is the ability to search quickly and easily within a site for information around a product. The thing that Google has done is create an expectation that if we type in a keyword we'll be able to find information about that "directive" quickly and simply—much faster than by navigating. But most bank websites don't really cater for search well, and the results are hit and miss. Consider integrating Google search onto your website—though you'll still need to optimise content on your site to cater for keyword search, etc.

Prior to the revolution in search engine technologies and interface, businesses relied on URL marketing through traditional media, banner ad click-through and third-party link population to get people (or eyeballs as they are called in dot-com speak) to come to a website. But as early as 1998, Georgia Tech reported in its annual www survey that 84.8 per cent[6] of users found websites by the use of search engines. This was even B.G.— Before Google. So imagine what those stats look like today!

In some of the most persuasive and conclusive statistics found to date, AT&T Interactive and Nielsen have released statistics from a March 2011 study that illustrate the unique behaviour that mobile searchers exhibit when it comes to their real-life shopping patterns. The statistics help underscore the importance of local and mobile marketing online.

Fifteen hundred US consumers who owned feature phones, smartphones and tablets were queried about local mobile search behaviour. The study found 43 per cent of local searchers on mobile devices physically showed up at the business location they found in search results or through online ads targeted to mobile users. Perhaps even more impressively, 22 per cent of those users actually made a purchase. So that means almost half of smartphone owners ended up in a store they had found through search, and more than one in five made a purchase. But that was in 2011, and already the data shows that mobile search is increasing. There's even a running joke around mobile search, online buying behaviour and in-store purchasing that suggests Best Buy should be renamed Amazon's showroom. This increasing tendency for consumers to seek out a retailer to touch and feel the product before purchasing online is now known as "showrooming".

Smart mobile devices will account for 25 per cent of all paid search ad

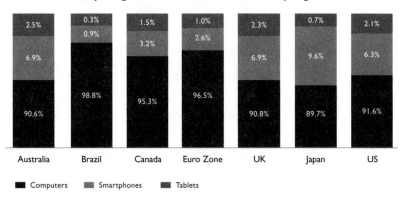

Figure 5.4: Search is not just about PC screens anymore

clicks in Google's network by December 2012, up significantly from five per cent in January 2011. Click-through rates (CTRs) on mobile phones are a staggering 72 per cent higher than on desktops, according to Marin Software's "State of Mobile Search Advertising in the US"[7] report.

But as search moves on to mobile, organisations also need to understand that search is dependent on context, what people are doing that requires them to search. For example, if they're out and about and they use their mobile phone to do a search on mortgages, they're likely looking at a house or apartment to buy and are trying to figure out how much they can afford to borrow. What an amazing opportunity to target that consumer.

> "...this kind of next-generation search in which Google understands real-world entities—things, not strings—will help improve our results in exciting new ways. It's about building genuine knowledge into our search engine,"
>
> —Larry Page, Google CEO, 6 April 2012

Google initially focused on trying to embed search in the most popular websites, such as Facebook and so forth, to facilitate context. Google calls this type of search technology AdSense, while Yahoo calls it ContentMatch—search that appears on content websites and not in a search engine page itself.

In August 2011 Google launched **Google Related**, a feature that shows users additional content relative to the content on the page they're already viewing, as they're viewing it. So, say they're reading an article about the launch of a new product or service they're researching or considering. With Google Related, they'll also have the option of viewing other content relative to that topic—such as videos, product reviews, or other mentions of the product across the web.

Now imagine doing the same with geolocation data—tying in where the consumers physically are or what they're looking at or for through their mobile devices. Ultimately, Google is trying to find ways of augmenting their view of the world through this data with projects such as Google Glasses, or Project Glass as it is known internally.

The development of Siri for the iOS platform is really another example of interfacing with the world of data and giving the consumer more contextual access. Search is going to become less like a search, and more like just helping them with the data they need to make decisions in everyday life. In that way, you need to start thinking very seriously about when and where a customer needs a financial services product, not just what they need and search for.

The other thing that affects revenue online, of course, is how easy (or hard) your website is to use.

Usability

Usability is a term used to describe how easy a system, product or interface is for individuals (users) to use. The term has come to include a broad range of references in recent times, including the art of user-centred design (UCD), interaction design (IxD), usability testing (UT) and other such fields of endeavour. The primary notion of usability is that an object designed with the user's psychology and physiology in mind is:

- More efficient to use—it takes less time to accomplish a particular task
- Easier to learn or is an intuitive design—operation can be learned by observing the object
- More satisfying to use

By applying this to the engagement process for a customer seeking a banking product through a digital interface (web, ATM, mobile phone, tablet, kiosk, etc.) you can improve the closure rate of new product applications, and improve the return on investment spent in the underlying technologies.

In some instances, customers are still being asked to print off application forms and take them into a branch, or fax them into a call centre. This is a usability problem—because instead of simplifying the process for applying for a product, you've just increased the complexity by introducing both the step of printing the form and the requirement to visit the branch physically. You've completely missed the intent of the Internet from a user perspective—**convenience**! It would be better not to have the application form online at all in this respect. If he'd wanted to take a form into a branch, why did he come online?

Improper language and poor design of the interface are the most common issues facing banks in respect of usability. Poor usability occurs for a variety of reasons, including:

1. IT guys have designed the site with no customer consultation
2. Compliance or legal overload process and data requirements
3. No one asked customers what they want or need
4. The design process didn't involve end users until the testing phase
5. Pages are designed based on physical processes or forms from the branch world
6. Processes or language are too bank-centric rather than customer-oriented

Improvements in interface design have come rapidly in the last few years. Organisations such as Apple, Google, and others have put huge emphasis on making systems simple to use and have been rewarded with record sales and cult-like followings. Again, such processes need not be expensive. Indeed, employing interactive design methods will probably save you development costs for a system.

Unlike traditional interface design, which takes place entirely behind the scenes and without any reference to customer usage, the objective in interactive design is to use low-fidelity (or lo-fi) methods of prototyping and multiple iterations to get to an optimal interface design. These methods are designated lo-fi because they don't require any special technology, software or skills. In fact, the most common methods of design in a lo-fi environment simply involve pen and paper. You can test these lo-fi prototypes also, getting input from customers before you've even started coding.

Let's take an interface for a credit card landing page within an internet banking portal. The first thing to do is to think about who the audience is, and what the objectives, metrics or success measures of the page might be:

Table 5.4: Credit Card Landing Page (Internet Banking)

Intended Audience/Need	Metrics
New Customers (Application)	# of new card applications (acquisitions)
Existing Customers (Payment)	# of new direct debit authorisations
Existing Customers (Usage)	# of redemptions (bonus), offer take-ups

Then you need to work out a sketch of what the page might look like, refining the design through exposing it to both customers and key product/business stakeholders.

Stage 1: Informal whiteboard sketch

Brainstorming the key content elements that meet the needs of the intended audience and meet the required metrics of the bank can be done on a whiteboard, tablet or a sketch pad. You can include credit card product specialists, customer advocates from the call centre or branch, and even staff who are customers in these exercises. IT guys are not required…

Stage 2: Formal Sketch (Lo-Fi) ready for usability test

The beauty of the lo-fi approach is that it can be done with very basic tools. A pen and paper, whiteboard, tablet, butcher's paper, anything on which you can quickly sketch the ideas that flow from an interactive design session. It can be formalised by transferring this onto PowerPoint, Visio, or Photoshop, but the objective here is speed and testing concepts.

How can you test a paper prototype with real customers? Easy, give them a pen or pencil and ask them to mimic a mouse and show you where they

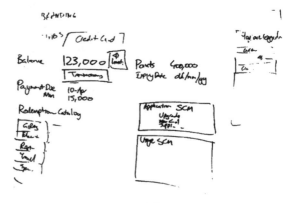

Figure 5.5: Lo-Fi Wireframe Sketch

would click for a specific task. Customers can easily make the conceptual leap to visualise how this would work in a live/real setting.

Stage 3: Creative concept and implementation

Figure 5.6: Formal Website Sketch

A key issue is that marketers generally don't understand the interactivity or the dialogue-like elements of the "interface" and IT guys just don't get access to customers on a regular basis. So in the typical design process, you have two groups fighting for the "right" to determine which way the screen

Figure 5.7: Creative Concept

design should go when neither is adequately qualified to be the voice of the customer. Even creative agencies have a tendency to get carried away with gimmicks or "design" that ends up attractive but pretty much useless.

In the example of the Grow Financial Federal Credit Union, it redesigned its website to cater for Y-Gens with a flash website (Grow4students.org) that tried to mimic a college dorm room. To open an account they had to click on the neon Open sign, etc. The site failed and was replaced by a more traditional website within months, largely because a creative design like this doesn't mean a usable website for customers.

Figure 5.8: An example of design killing usability on a Y-Gen-targeted site
(Credit: Grow Financial Federal Credit Union)

Some simple usability principles include:
- Clear engagement messages/images on the home page linked to journeys
- Pages that are not cluttered
- Intuitive design—I shouldn't have to work too hard to find where I need to go
- No Flash, animations, or pop-ups!
- Good use of keyword and content so sites can be indexed via search engines

- Clean code that is easy for browsers to load. The more complex the code, the more likely you will have issues on mobile and tablet platforms.

If you want to get your web stuff right, you must have customer advocates as part of the design process as a minimum, and ideally, real customers. Remember, staff are real customers too, so they make an excellent (read: inexpensive) source of usability test subjects. But in the end, nothing beats putting real customers into the design and testing process.

Make sure that, at a minimum, you employ interaction designers and usability testing for any major site deployment or product release on your website. If it has a form customers interact with, or it is a redesign, make sure it is tested by real customers—not employees.

This is a cheap way to make lots of revenue off your web channel.

Screen (web/tablet/mobile) first

Unless you've been living in Outer Mongolia (and even *there,* the iPhone is hot), the mobile has become huge over the last few years. Despite the massive success of the app phone and devices such as the iPad, banks have been traditionally slow to adopt these new technologies when it comes to website deployment and customer experience. All that is changing pretty rapidly right now.

Increasingly organisations are grappling with the multiscreen environment in more sophisticated ways: planning not just for the basic land grab of a iPhone app, but exploring Android, Windows Mobile, BlackBerry (while they are still around), iPad apps, and perhaps early HTML5 website deployment. You realise that while your customers might download an app, new customers or prospects could increasingly be using their mobile or iPad to access your websites.

Try using a finicky website, with tiny little buttons and hyperlinks designed for mouse clicks or embedded flash marketing promos on a tablet or an iPhone and you'll be sorely disappointed. The site is pretty much useless.

Citibank did a great job of redesigning its US retail banking website to work with tablets in its recent revamp. We're going to see a whole lot more of this in the coming years—websites that detect our browser type and serve up a site for our mobile mini-browser or tablet seamlessly, even websites that detect who we are and where we are and serve up content based on location and our individual needs. Citi even sends us to a mobile-optimised online banking sign-on by default on a mobile mini-browser.

Figure 5.9: Citibank and BofA's websites are designed tablet-ready
(Credit: Citibank.com and BankofAmerica.com respectively)

Bank of America's site has also been tablet optimised in the last 12 months. By contrast, Chase and Wells Fargo[8] still have links that are almost impossible to click with a finger on a tablet.

By 2015 mobile device access to the Internet will dwarf PC access, so that means you have just three years to learn everything you can about people accessing your organisation via a screen instead of a browser from a PC. Today tablet penetration is still relatively small, but by 2015, tablet sales should surpass PCs alone.

Designing sites that work on all types of screens is generally called "responsive design". The term **responsive web design** is related to the concept of developing a website design in a manner that helps the layout get changed according to the device or **screen resolution**. More precisely, the concept allows for an advanced four-column layout, 1292 pixels wide, to auto-simplify into two columns on a 1025-pixel-width screen. Also it suitably formats on a **smartphone and tablet** screen.

Images in responsive web designs are called **context-aware. Responsive web design** images are primarily fluid images that can be replaced by

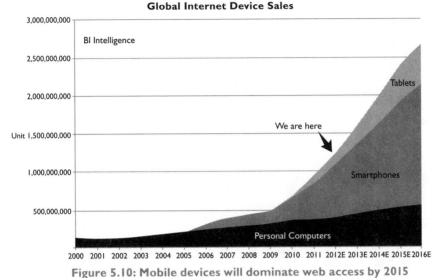

Figure 5.10: Mobile devices will dominate web access by 2015
(Credit: Business Insider)

context-aware images, an updated version for better designing. This particular technique serves the purpose of responsive designing in the true sense as the images serve at different resolutions, ranging from larger screens to smaller ones. The scaled images appear to change fluidly with the help of updated developer tools and coding languages, allowing designs to look sharp in every context.

This is quite a specialised arena of web design and there are as yet very few developers and designers really capable in this arena. However, this will be a hot emerging area over the next three to four years.

If you still think that mobile web design and application development are a niche industry, you need to change your way of thinking. Mobile isn't a trend, nor is it even the future, it's the present. Don't believe me? Here are some thought-provoking statistics to consider from Mobithinking from February 2012.

- There are over **1.2 billion mobile web users worldwide**
- In the US, **25 per cent of mobile web users are mobile-only** (they rarely use a desktop to access the web)
- Mobile apps have been downloaded 20 billion times
- Mobile device sales are increasing across the board with over 85 per cent of new handsets able to access the mobile web

One of the most interesting facts here is the second item, which indicates that many users will likely only ever see the mobile version of your site. That's an astounding revelation.

More than ever before, the web is something we carry in our pockets, not something that merely hangs out near our desks or in our homes. This is a global trend that will only continue to see growth in the coming years.

Remember, customers might download your app, but a prospect won't.

Cross-sell to existing customers

There is a very simple but extremely valuable tip that I'm going to divulge here that has the potential to generate millions of dollars in revenue for you over the next three to five years. It is so simple that you will kick yourself for not recognising this already, and it is so fundamental to the use of your website that it should drive your total budget decision and marketing approach from this day onward. There may still be some resistance from those who prefer the status quo, but when you check out the analytics of your own site, the evidence will be overwhelming, I assure you.

Here it is. Look at the following website and tell me where more than **90 per cent of daily visitors** click on this site…

Figure 5.11: Typical retail bank homepage (Credit: HSBC)

Is it the "Red Hot Dining" billboard-style marketing advertisement?

Is one of the other hot offers on display?

Is it the "$6000 Scheme" or similar offers on the right hand side, or perhaps the search box in the top right hand corner?

Give up?

More than 90 per cent[9] of customers visiting this website click on one section of the site. It is, of course…

Personal Internet Banking

LOG IN

Now most banks consider the "Internet Banking" portal, or "secure-site" as it is sometimes called, a *functional platform for transaction capability*. Mainly the focus is on account balance, fund transfer, bill payment, term deposits, etc. It is normally run by the IT team, who are the "functional" guys.

The fact is, today your marketing team is probably spending 95 per cent of its budget related to web marketing on either building public websites that pitch product, OR launching new campaigns on third-party sites, social media, PPC, etc.

That's clearly not right. Based on these simple analytics, you need to be spending *at least* **80 per cent** of your web marketing budget on building offers and campaigns for *existing customers* through the *internet banking portal*! But that ain't happening at any bank I know of today.

The other advantage of pitching product behind the login is that the compliance and acquisition process is dead simple. You already have all the customer information, so compliance is simply a click-based, existing customer acquisition or sale conversion rather than copious forms to provide proof of who they are, their credit risk assessment, etc. These are simply the easiest customers to acquire and process online because you already have their profiles.

A strong word of warning, however! Don't opt for a simple banner ad approach here as all you'll do is upset your most valuable audience. You have to think about this and provide *relevant offers*.

So don't pitch a Gold credit card to someone who already has a Platinum card. Don't pitch term deposits to a customer who is already a Premier account holder with a managed fund. Don't pitch retirement plans to a student, etc.

For this you need business intelligence and segmentation that create compelling, targeted offers that appeal.

There are some other issues with selling behind the login, though—issues that have come as a result of marketers picking up some bad habits along the way.

Combating banner blindness

In a fairly brilliant piece of early usability testing, Jan Benway and David Lane of Rice University discovered in 1998 that users were starting to filter out "advertising banners".

The ad agencies that were still thinking of the web as just another channel to push traditional media campaigns had shot themselves in the foot a little by producing little magazine ads and billboards everywhere. They just retrofitted these and called them banner ads. Let me explain.

In October 1994, *HotWired* (*Wired Magazine*'s former online brand) made history by placing on its website the very first banner ad. It looked like this…

Figure 5.12: The very first banner ad appeared on HotWired in 1994

The ad was produced for AT&T by Modem Media and TANGENT (which went on to become part of Razorfish). Initially banner ads were hugely popular and all through the dot-com age we were talking about banner ad conversion rates, click-through rates, eyeballs and other such metrics, which were very exciting ways to measure this huge new phenomenon. In '96 and '97, when banners became the next big thing, all the big brand guys were getting online, experimenting with this cheap but very effective medium. Response rates on banners in these early days were better than any responses on existing media offerings. Perhaps it was because of the novelty value.

But as advertising agencies rushed to put more and more ads on this new medium, they lost the advantage the new platform gave them. You see, the internet and banner ads could have been something fundamentally different. Why?

The web, compared with print media, TVCs, billboards, etc., is a very different medium. It provides the ability to interact, to engage, to have a dialogue. Traditional media did not allow this unique capability. However, ad agencies that flocked to the web lacked the fundamental creativity to adapt to this space because they were caught up in the concept of the **message** being the all-important element. The web is about **experience**, not simply a message. Therefore, by flooding the web with banners that were static and simply duplicating what they were already doing with other media, they missed the opportunity to capitalise fully on this new medium.

In late 1997 some agencies started to experiment with rich media in banners, but their objective was really akin to trying to create something like a mini TV commercial in a banner ad, again not an experience, but the concept of a "rich message".

Ad agencies were myopically focused on the concept of trying to create brand recall, and not thinking about how to engage in a dialogue with the user—which the web enabled. This was the fundamental shortfall in the early attempts to utilise banner advertisements. The same happened with Flash introduction pages, which were originally argued by traditionalist marketers as a great way to introduce the web equivalent of TVCs. The idea was that you could force a consumer to view a 15-second TVC before *allowing* him to get access to the content on the website—a serious mistake.

As a result of advertisers simply presenting more and more of the same to customers who were increasingly being bombarded with much more "noise" across the media spectrum, it became clear that banner ads were simply being dismissed by customers as just more "noise".

If you are going to serve up banner ads, you now have to retrain your customers into thinking that these are relevant, timely and appropriate. So start figuring out how to identify your customers and serve them content that is tailor-made for them. Here are two simple strategies utilising ad-serving and simple cookie technology:

1. When existing customers come back, you know who they are. So in the same way that you would serve a tailored offer up within internet banking, serve up cross-sell or up-sell offers that are super relevant within the public site or through third parties. Don't get lazy and offer them the same offers the general public is seeing.

2. If a visitor comes to the site and is trawling through the credit card section, personal loans or mortgages landing pages, next time he visits, offer to continue the journey. Place a banner on the home page panel that says something like "**Still looking for a great mortgage?**" This is technically very simple to do—you just need a marketing team that is not thinking *campaign,* and is instead thinking *offer to target audience.*

Internet channel improvement today

So what is on the Internet improvement road map that you can achieve in the short term that will bring benefits to both the organisation and the customer? The following areas represent suggested opportunities for either improvement in financial operations or customer service levels at the branch over the coming three to five years:

- Improved customer content, communications and language
- Better cross-sell/up-sell capability
- Better findability and search engine optimisation
- Improved analytics on customer behaviour
- Better offer management and generation capability
- Improved use of application processing automation and service architecture

These improvements make themselves evident through a range of projects that can be undertaken within the branch. Some of these projects cross over the above areas of opportunity, so I'd like to list the projects below as specific illustrations of how improvement and transformation are achievable.

Table 5.3

Project/Initiative	Desired Outcome
Usability tests of all sites	Assess any issues with current website language, layout, design and process.
Customer Information System	Improved behavioural analytics on customers across all channels to understand better which "tasks" customers prefer to do in-branch versus online, etc.
Content Management Systems	The old dot-com favourite is back, but this time enabled across the organisation so you can "publish" new content continuously. The best analogy is to imagine that your bank is publishing a product catalogue and investor information magazine, based on your product, to customers daily.
Sales Intelligence and Automated offer capability	Real-time and precognitive offer serving for existing customers delivered in the form of prompts, offers, or service messages, especially within the internet banking portal.
BPR (Business Process Re-engineering) on select processes	Reduction of layering between sales and service departments, including the removal of duplicate "skills" within "competing" product units. Creation of "customer dynamics" capability as owners of customers, rather than product competing for revenue from same.
Straight-Through Processing and Credit Risk Management Systems	Enabling customers to get immediate fulfilment for an application rather than waiting the obligatory 24, 48, or 72 hours afterwards due to antiquated manual or human "processes" in the back office. Results in improved service perception and reduction of abandonment due to ongoing process demands (i.e. proof of income, faxing of three months' bank statements, salary certificates, etc.). Additional benefits include reduction of compliance errors due to manual mishandling.
Customer-Friendly Language Initiative	Use of ethnography, usability research, audits, customer-focused observational field studies and focus groups to improve language and simplicity of application forms and communications with customers within the branch (and beyond)...
Search Engine Optimisation	Organic search engine optimisation should be the strategy of every institution, but it requires rethinking what content you actually put on the site because it needs to be driven by what customers are actually looking for.

These initiatives are designed to optimise your capability to generate revenue and keep customers coming back time and again to interact via the web.

KEY LESSONS

After 10 years the Internet is still perceived as a "threat" by some traditional bankers or, at best, just not understood by most bankers. Far from being simply a "functional" transaction platform to save costs, the web is the greatest source of new revenue that exists today. Understanding what to sell and how to use the channel in the sales process is the key.

Bankers need to start treating the web as the equivalent of the branch in strategic importance to the brand. Anything less than equal footing simply means loss of new revenue opportunities and loss of customers to alternative providers.

Let's just put it in very simple terms. Ten years down the track, most retail banking revenue will be either web, mobile or tablet-based. If you haven't already started down that path, then you've got to start moving very fast.

Keywords: Findability, Usability, Cross-Sell, Up-Sell, Public Website, Internet Banking, Wireframes, Interaction Design

---

Endnotes

1 Alexa.com

2 comScore.com

3 "Convenience and Price driving online sales", News.com.au, 16 November 2011

4 User Strategy Survey Data, ACMA report, November 2011

5 Various (UserStrategy online survey for StandardChartered.com, Alexa.com, GoogleLabs Trends, etc.)

6 GVU's WWW User Survey—http://gvu.cc.gatech.edu/what/websurveys.php

7 "State of Mobile Search Advertising in the US"

8 At the time of printing

9 Webtrends data for www.hsbc.com.hk. 93.7 per cent of Chinese-language users and 95.2 per cent of English-language users click on the log-in button for personal internet banking. Results are paralleled in the US/UK/Australia and most developed economies.

6 Mobile Banking—Already Huge and It's Just Getting Started

The greatest device ever sold

With contributions from Scott Bales, Chief Mobile Officer, Movenbank

In July 2007 Apple launched the iPhone (what we call the iPhone 2G generally today). The most impressive thing about the iPhone is not necessarily multitouch, Siri, retina display, ease of use, or core functionality, but unquestionably the iTunes platform that brought us apps. Prior to the launch of the iPhone, we'd never even heard of apps, and yet today, just four and a half years later, here are the stats on apps:

- 600,000 apps for Apple and close to 400,000 for Android[1]
- More than 30 billion downloads for Apple, and already 15 billion for Google Play (previously known as the Android Marketplace)
- $15.1 billion in apps revenue for 2011, expected to exceed $70 billion within just another four years.
- Daily downloads of 48.6 million per day—Apple
- New app submissions per day: 455 (88 games/367 non-games)
- No. of active publishers/developers: 147,000 on the US store
- 400m iTunes account holders (with active credit cards on file)

So, from its humble start, iTunes was always more than just a place to go to download music or TV episodes. It became the core delivery platform for a whole new category of software and user experiences. On 5 March 2012, Chunli Fu of Qingdao in eastern China downloaded a free version of Disney's physics-based puzzle game, "Where's My Water?" It was the 25-billionth app downloaded since the iTunes store started offering apps for Apple's iOS devices.[2]

Now, before iTunes, the iPhone and apps, there had still been software—both for PC screens and for phones. Prior to the so-called "Jesus Phone", there were Java apps, games and so forth we could buy and download for our phones, but these certainly didn't become ubiquitous, primarily because the usability wasn't good enough, and there wasn't a marketplace that distributed these apps.

So here we are, just a few years later and there's probably not a single person in the US, UK, Australia, Germany or France who doesn't know what an app is. Some estimates put worldwide mobile application store revenue as high as $15.1 billion in 2011,[3] with estimates in the range of $46–52 billion by 2016.[4] That revenue was exactly $0 in 2007.

And yet, there are bankers out there who still persist in the belief that mobile payments via our iPhone will take **years** to "take off". In a debate on this via Twitter one weekend recently, an illustrative comment was "I can see it, just not for some time…"

The ongoing proliferation of mobile phones globally is connecting the world's population at rates never seen before in history. Together with the drive for financial inclusion in the financial services markets, there have been new opportunities for non-traditional financial services to establish themselves and, in many cases, thrive.

Suddenly companies with a large base of customers and broad distribution networks, be they mobile operators, retailers or online brands, have an opportunity to participate in financial services previously only available to banks and associated financial services providers. To put it simply, by leveraging the power of vast connectivity, the mobile phone is enabling new and existing consumers to be reached by an entirely new ecosystem in which an entire generation of anytime, anywhere consumers can be reached in engaging mobile services.

With 6.2 billion mobile connections globally, mobile phones have far greater reach than any other distribution network in the world. TV sets reach about 1.4 billion people, print newspapers reach 1.7 billion,[5] the Internet reaches 2.2 billion.[6] Already 1.2 billion people are accessing the Internet via a mobile device—25 per cent of US mobile phone users are already mobile-only Internet users. Mobile's reach goes beyond geographic and demographic barriers. Whether a taxi driver in Mumbai, a supermodel in Milan, a fishmonger in a local Kenyan market, or a banker in New York—we are all part of a global network that connects the world's population.

Mobile phones have been a large driving force behind the modality shift of consumer behaviour in banking around the globe. Consumers now expect access to banking through their mobile phones, as a shift away from the Internet and other traditional banking channels. comScore actually goes as far as to say that mobile banking is seeing 74 per cent growth per annum, and could see more than 50 per cent of US bank customers using mobile by 2015. Today that number is already one in five, and is expected to increase to one-third of consumers in 2012.

Many of us would be familiar with the rapid rise of M-Pesa as the world's leading mobile-centric financial system. M-Pesa started as a project funded by the UK Government Department for International Development (DFID) to provide a means for more efficient collection of microfinance loan repayments (see the case study later in this chapter). While the initial goal for M-Pesa was quite humble, no one was prepared for its incredible growth. The system addressed a long-time systemic deficiency in the Kenyan financial system that excluded a majority of the population. In 2012, the World Bank estimated that 25 per cent of Kenya's Gross Domestic Product runs through M-Pesa each year—not surprising, considering that around 50 per cent of the Kenyan population is on M-Pesa, which also has a positive effect on the users' financial lives.

Only one per cent of Kenyans have a telephone land line. Around ten per cent of Kenyans have a bank account. So how do you enable financial inclusion for the poorest populations in Africa? You turn their phone into a bank account. Registration for M-Pesa also increases the likelihood of users having some savings by more than 20 per cent, according to World Bank findings released in 2012. The survey found that 65 per cent of M-Pesa users reported having some savings compared with 31 per cent of those who were not M-Pesa users.[7]

Since M-Pesa's creation, the GSM Association (GSMA) has identified 130 similar deployments across the globe, with another 93 in the pipeline.[8] But here's the thing. In Kenya I can SMS you money, and I can use my feature phone to withdraw cash from an ATM. Ironic then that in the US, I still need a cheque book and a plastic card at an ATM machine. Why is it that we think the US is an advanced banking economy when it is already five years behind Kenya in the mobile payments game?

There is some light at the end of the tunnel, though. In parallel, Near-Field Communication (NFC) technology is gaining rapid momentum in the mobile banking and payments space in the developed world, where much of the conversation has shifted from the technical ability of banks, merchants or carriers to provide the platform, to the economics of NFC as a replacement for traditional plastic cards. Some, however, remain sceptical, labelling NFC "Not For Consumers". This is particularly the case in the United States, where point-of-sale technology is entrenched, and typically funded by the retail sector—which is loath to replace it unless absolutely essential or incentivised by card issuers and banks.

The industry is now showing signs that it is at a stage where ecosystems players will cooperate after Google Wallet and others have brought several key players or payment vehicles together. With the recent creation of the ISIS consortium, we are just starting to see signs that the big brands have shifted from a turf war built on a "who is going to win"' mentality to cross-industry collaboration aimed at building an ecosystem that benefits everyone.

The core problem around payments in retail is an assumption that someone will win. By waiting for a clear winner in the mobile wallet stakes, many banks are simply going to miss out. There is one player that could turn all this on its head though—we'll talk about them in a moment.

The debates about NFC and mobile payments rage on. There are questions over which handset platform to support, which devices are certified, the lack of real NFC standards, how to enable the secure component on the various cellular networks, and so forth. To a novice this all sounds very complex. Shouldn't we worry about adoption rates? When will mobile hit critical mass? ISIS versus Google Wallet versus Visa's play versus PayPal, etc., etc.?

There are those who will argue that it will be many years before mobile payments become mainstream. We'll hear figures such as 2014, 2016 or even 2020 bandied around as to when mobile payments will hit mass adoption. However, the primary measure to focus on when looking at these sorts of predictions is, first and foremost, exhibited customer behaviour— the predilection to a shift in the way customers pay, bank, purchase or shop.

If we look at consumer behaviour, the story is very simple. The great mass is not only ready for mobile disruption and mobile payments, they are racing towards it as fast as they can whenever the opportunity presents itself.

Mobile's ability to shift banking

The real power of mobile lies in behaviour and the way it empowers users. Mobile is, by its very nature, "personal". It is your device—a tool for an individual carried in a pocket, bag or hand. Today, people take their mobile smartphone everywhere with them.

The average US smartphone user now uses apps upwards of 94 minutes a day, compared with just 72 minutes a day surfing the web. That's more than radio, newspapers, and magazines, and it's fast catching up with the time allocated daily to television. According to a survey conducted by marketing agency 11mark,[9] a whopping 75 per cent of Americans use their mobile phones in the bathroom regularly. For people aged 28 to 35,

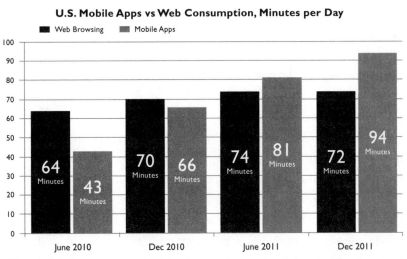

Figure 6.1: App usage continues to climb on smartphones (Credit: Flurry)

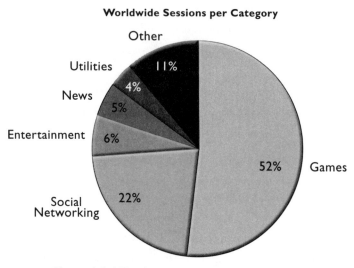

Figure 6.2: We play games more than anything else on our app phones (Credit: Flurry)

that number shoots up to 91 per cent! Sixty-three per cent of people have answered a phone call in the bathroom, and 41 per cent have made one. Seriously, folks… that's kinda gross. But that's not all…

Two-thirds of mobile phone owners in the United States sleep with their mobile phone.[10] When you factor in 16–29-year-olds that number is in excess of 90 per cent, where the phone is often kept on their bedside table, where it is the last thing used at night and the first thing used in the morning. There are entire websites dedicated to breaking the addiction of taking your mobile phone to bed with you. Smartphones have had a significant effect on the way we communicate, the way we socialise, behave, curate, share, and connect.

What makes mobile phones dramatically more personal is the nature of communications on the device. The mobile phone is seen as an individual's personal space, so SMS, emails and messages on the device remain an individual's most sacred communications.

Not only is the mobile phone a personal device in our personal space, it is a key service enabler. Our lives have shifted onto the small screen of the mobile phone. Facebook has already seen roughly half its daily traffic shift to the mobile phone,[11] while on Twitter 55 per cent of traffic now comes from mobile devices.[12] Why? What's behind this shift in behaviour?

The answer is quite simple. The mobile phone is a transportable medium, one that is equally powerful on the bus or subway travelling to the office, waiting in the queue at the bank branch, or sitting in a park. It doesn't matter if we want to listen to music, read the news, or catch the latest episode of *American Idol*. All of these activities can be catered to on a mobile screen. It has become a behavioural norm in recent times for emails to be sent from BlackBerrys or iPhones; mobile apps allow customers to buy coffee, shop for birthday gifts, or book a restaurant while on the move.

But mobile has one more key trick up its sleeve that drives it as a channel of choice—**contextualisation**. Through the years of dot-com and social media, the idea of smarter user experiences has resulted in concepts such as the "segment of one", personalisation, targeted content and relevance.

These concepts result in optimised experiences for the end user, but mobile takes that optimisation to a whole new level. Suddenly time and location relevance can be applied, creating such unique experiences that they may only exist for a short amount of time at a specific location. Take, for example, the mobile user who opens Foursquare after finishing work for the day. Instantly they see a location-specific perspective of where their friends are now, and where they can get a Happy Hour special with the information at hand—showing that the mobile device is not just a part of a virtual world, but increasingly a guide for the physical world.

Increasingly financial services will be about where the consumer is and why he needs a bank product or service—hence, the smartphone and tablet are both uniquely positioned to tap into this opportunity.

The landscape

The mobile landscape is rapidly changing. In *Bank 2.0* I talked about the threat to Motorola's mobile business, which essentially is today just worth the patents that Google has bought although they may resurrect some latent production capability for a Google Phone sometime. Today it's RIM and Nokia that are on the ropes because of the dominance of Apple and Android. However, before we talk about the mobile phone market generally, let's put some definitions around the various terms that get thrown around in relation to banking and mobile:

- **Mobile Payments** refer to the enablement of payments services from a mobile device. Instead of paying with traditional instruments such as cash, cheque or credit cards, a consumer can use his mobile phone. Strong examples of this include the role PayPal and Dwolla play in the person-to-person payments space (see Chapter 12).

- **Mobile Commerce** refers to the enablement of commerce transactions using a mobile device, such as the purchasing of content, services, etc. Groupon, Amazon and eBay all have offerings that fit into the mobile commerce world.

- **Mobile Money** is a term that was driven by the success of financial-inclusion initiatives in many African nations, where entire financial ecosystems were built that enabled bank-like services to be delivered over a mobile device. In these ecosystems, the primary role of the service is to create a market-optimised banking network that replaces cash while enabling nations with poor infrastructure to leap forward in adoption cycles. The main difference between mobile money and other vehicles is that in this case mobile is both the transactional and customer acquisition channel, and often the mobile is the only way to interact with the business. M-Pesa, G-Cash, WING and MTN Mobile Money are prominent examples.

- **Mobile Banking** refers to the adding of mobile as a channel for existing bank customers. In the majority of cases the features and functions of mobile banking are not dissimilar to those of Internet banking, only optimised for a smaller screen. In some cases, banks have elected to add services such as a location-based directory of branches and ATMs, and loyalty discounts.

With the recent news that Barclays' PingIt had 120,000 downloads in its first five days, that Square already has more than two million merchants on its payments platform (around a quarter of all US card merchants/retailers), that Starbucks is doing 25 per cent of its North American payments via a cardless app[13]—it seems like mobile payments are taking off phenomenally.

> "We are the number one company not in the U.S. but in the world in terms of mobile payment, transactions and dollars."
> —Howard Schultz, president and CEO of Starbucks

The interesting thing is that many bankers are looking at all of this activity as if it has little meaning or impact on their business at this point in time. I think part of that may be that there is a fundamental misunderstanding of how the mobile can be utilised in the banking and payments space.

Mobile banking delivery versus payments

One of the key problems for bankers is that banks divide the cards business and "banking" through separate divisions or business units that handle these two functions. The only time they ever seem to meet is in the form of a debit card or within internet banking. The cards business, while being a strong revenue earner generally for banks because of credit card fees and interest margin, is philosophically not considered banking *per se* by most diehard bankers. For customers, they simply see the card as a part of their bank relationship, they certainly don't get any division of labour along product lines.

For a long time these two worlds have remained largely separate operationally. The popularisation of the smartphone is destined to destroy that view of the world.

Banking historically has been about two primary things—storing or protecting assets, and helping in the conduct of trade and commerce. Rudimentary cheques (or bills of exchange) were around almost 800 years before physical currency and, prior to bank branches, "assets" such as grain and gold were often stored in temples and palaces. At the core of banking were assets that you either kept safe, or mobilised to effect trade. In many ways, that's still at the core of the bank value proposition.

Now with internet banking being the primary day-to-day channel for banking in most of the world today, and branch frequency/visitation down

90 per cent from the peak in the mid-90s, it turns out the branch is pretty much "alternative" banking today. The pendulum has shifted.

If we attempt to characterise day-to-day banking today, we really end up with two core classes of activity. Payments and day-to-day banking based on our assets, including applying for new products, wealth management engagement, etc. If we look at customer engagement, transactional activity or the role of an advisor with respect to our assets, we'd be hard pressed to identify activities that aren't done through either **Payments Channels** or **Delivery Channels.**[14]

Given the way retail banking is structured today, this means that many banks look at a mobile wallet as an instantiation of payments—the ultimate, downloadable payment channel "function" or utility. However, they look at mobile banking separately, as a mobile-enabled version of the Internet banking platform, ultimately just a channel migration of transaction activity from branch to digital—hence, a delivery utility.

Some progressive banks are even looking at onboarding customers entirely electronically through the web, mobile, ATM or call centre— without a signature. More delivery channels. The branch is the premier delivery channel still, and more so as transactions shift out of the branch, and it becomes about high-touch sales and service (delivery of revenue and service).

The problem philosophically for retail banks is that the mobile device is collapsing this view of the world. Payments and traditional day-to-day banking utility will be packaged into one portable, handheld "channel".

It doesn't make sense to have one app for "banking" and one app for "payments" or a wallet. Customers need the utility of both the bank and payments capability in one device. That presents an organisational shift because it merges the two disparate parts of retail banking. While philosophically being a challenge, it does present massive opportunities.

What is possible is that, for me as a customer, my day-to-day connection with my money can be far tighter than it is in a traditional banking relationship. Whether it is simply the fact that I can see my balance before and after I make a payment (not possible with plastic, cheques or cash), or whether my bank can start to advise me day-to-day on how to utilise my money better, the opportunity for mobile is not the wallet, and not mobile banking. It is re-imagining the utility of banking from a mobile perspective.

We'll talk more about the emerging business of mobile payments in Chapter 12, but the key concern for banks is that right now the major banks in the US are essentially relying on either ISIS, Visa/MasterCard, iPhone or Google Wallet to provide a piece of software that emulates the card in the phone. It means they are designing the future bank as they have the cards and payments business today—as two separate worlds.

That is a guarantee that at some point in the future you're going to lose the opportunity to link day-to-day payments activity to the bank account more tightly. It means that someone else will own the opportunities for contextualising payments and it won't be the bank.

That means that banks will have to pay someone else who "owns the wallet" if they want to contextualise offers to customers at the time of payments or based on a possible banking event—i.e. when the utility of a bank product or service is required.

Mobile in Commerce

Given the power of mobile, it's not a surprise that financial services would shift to mobile phones. Our daily lives constantly require us to interact with our money, whether it be paying bills, buying a coffee, or paying for the daily commute to the office. Money is at the centre of multiple events in our daily life. The key word here is utility. While money is a frequent influencer in our lives, it's an ability to act that usually determines whether we use our money.

Take for example a middle manager who walks past an Apple Store and falls in love with the new iPad. What influences his decision to buy in that moment is usually determined by his ability to access the utility of his money, rather than whether or not he has the money. One of the primary reasons the credit card was invented was to give people with money the ability to increase the utility of that money by giving them a card that could be used to make a purchase, rather than their having to go to their bank to withdraw the necessary amount of cash. In the modern world, credit cards also enable them to act on impulse. Let's look at another scenario.

Tesco in South Korea created a virtual store in the subway where commuters can buy their groceries out of a virtual wall. Consumers only need to scan QR codes with their smartphones and products are added to their virtual cart and then delivered to their homes as soon as they are back.

Therefore the mobile's real strength lies in the device's ability to plug the individual into the utility of money in a way that

Figure 6.3: Tesco subway customer in South Korea ordering groceries on his phone

is contextual to the purchase use case. There is far less risk in our daily Starbucks purchase than the purchase of a new 60-inch LED TV, therefore the user experience should reflect the complexity and context of each individual situation.

So the smartphone has the power to change the way we view banking. It has the power to introduce context, meaning banking becomes a utility that we can use, when and where we need facilitation of a purchase, a loan, or a payment. Context means that banking can solve problems as they happen, rather than waiting for us to go to the "bank".

Not everyone on the planet owns a smartphone, however—so the question is, when will smartphones be ubiquitous?

Bringing banking to the unbanked

The Mobile Marketing Association of Asia has stated that out of the six billion people on the planet, 4.8 billion have a mobile phone while only 4.2 billion own a toothbrush.[15]

According to *Business Week*, more than 20 countries have mobile phone penetration rates of over 100 per cent, with the UAE's penetration reaching as high as 233 per cent.[16] According to Chartsbin, the number of countries with over 100 per cent penetration is nearly 60, and this is reflected in the roughly 4.6 billion mobile subscribers, although some estimates put this figure at 5.9 billion mobile subscribers by the end of 2011.[17] The Mobile Marketing Association probably counted anyone who has a subscription in its estimates versus the number of toothbrushes accounted for. If the penetration rate in these countries is lowered to 100, the number of people who have cellphones drops to around 4.2 billion. That's still the majority of the planet.

Only about 15 per cent of the world's population has a smartphone today. However that is quickly ramping up.[18] Smartphone sales accelerated from 26 per cent of the world market in Q1 2011 to 34 per cent in Q4 2011, according to data from Gartner, IDC, Canalys and Strategy Analytics. The data shows there were approximately 1.6 billion mobile handsets shipped in 2011, of which some 483 million were smartphones.

Smartphones also continued their pattern of outselling PCs, which first happened in the fourth quarter of 2010; the gap between smartphone and PC sales is now widening steadily.

Android today powers around 50 per cent of handsets shipped—compared with 25.3 per cent in 2010—just three years after its launch. This indicates that the open platform, which allows handset makers to install it without paying a licensing fee, has been a massive success for adoption. In total, close to 1.5 billion smartphones have been sold since the first quarter of 2007.[19]

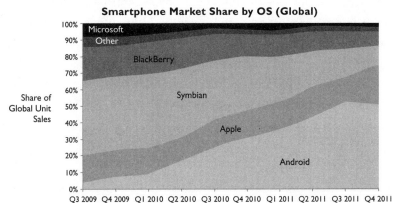

Figure 6.3: Normalised smartphone market by OS (Source: Gartner)

With all the noise around the iPhone we'd expect it to be continuing to dominate smartphone sales, and we'd be right. Sales of the iPhone rose from 13.4 million to 17.3 million by Q3 in 2011, but the iPhone 4S turned that on its head. On 24 January 2012, Apple revealed that it had sold 37.04m iPhones in fiscal Q1 of 2012 alone. That means it sold more iPhones in Q1 of 2012, than in the whole of the previous year.

The 37.04-million figure divided out over the period of 98 days in the quarter gives us 377,900 iPhones sold each day. That's higher than the world's average birth rate, which clocks in at 371,000 per day. So it's not hard to figure out it won't be long before just about everyone we know owns a smartphone.

Nokia's Symbian, which the company has said will be phased out, nevertheless sold 19.5 million handsets in 2011, but Nokia's total market share halved in 2011. Interesting that Nokia was selling more feature phones than Apple up until the iPhone 4S was launched—and that trend has now been reversed.

The problem for the mobile proposition is that if we look at even the most sophisticated economies such as the US, feature phones are still used by about half the population. This is naturally because people take some time to swap out their old phone, and upgrade to a smartphone. The question is when will the smartphone be accessible to the majority of the world's population?

At the Mobile World Congress in Barcelona in February 2012, Eric Schmidt tried to tackle this question. Going by Moore's Law, Schmidt says that smartphones that cost $400 today will be $100 on contract in 2013. He also claims smartphones will reach the $70 price point in 2012, and that's not on contract, but as an actual price point. He said that those $70 smartphones will re-enter the market one year after that at a price point of just $20. So, by 2015, 70–80 per cent of the world's population will be able to afford a smartphone.

The mobile as a bank account

With somewhere around 4.5 billion people owning a mobile phone, there's a very strong case for pushing financial inclusion through the mobile phone and mobile payments, especially in developing economies where mobile penetration is 5–10 times the penetration of the basic bank account. In fact, by 2020, what we consider a bank account will most likely be defined by the mobile phone. The mobile phone is likely to be the basic bank account of the world by the next decade.

Although mobile payments are quickly gaining traction in more developed markets, peer-to-peer m-payments, such as mobile money transfers, are an established and fast-growing fact of life in many developing economies. A large proportion of households in developing countries lack access to basic financial services, which impedes economic growth and development. A large body of evidence shows that access to financial services and, indeed, overall financial development, are crucial to economic growth and poverty reduction.

A lack of formal financial services infrastructure and activity limits market exchanges, increases risk, and limits opportunities to save. Without formal financial services, households rely on informal services that are associated with high transaction costs. Thus increasing access to formal financial services for the majority of households in developing countries remains an important policy goal for institutions such as the United Nations, the World Bank and IMF. It has also been recognised that even for those with bank accounts, physical distances to branches or points of financial service add significantly to transactions costs.

Mainstream financial institutions generally shy away from developing economies because of the premise that low-income populations do not save and are bad borrowers. However, the microfinance revolution effectively shattered these myths by demonstrating that when poor households have access to financial services, not only do they save, they also have high repayment rates and low default rates when they borrow. Muhammad Yunus, the founder of Grameen Bank in Bangladesh, was awarded the Nobel Peace Prize in 2006 for his efforts to revolutionise microcredit on the subcontinent.

Beyond microfinance, however, one of the largest sources of income for developing economies these days is the large population of expatriates living and working overseas who remit funds back to their families in their home countries. Peer-to-peer money remittances enable an expatriated worker to send money across international borders to family or friends.

According to the World Bank, 175 million migrant workers each year send billions of dollars' worth of international remittances to family and friends, many of whom do not have bank accounts. Mobile is a huge part of this. Mobile remittance companies will see some $55 billion in international remittances made through mobile devices by 2016, according to a December 2011 report from Juniper Research. Already $12 billlion in mobile remittances was processed in 2011, up from $330 million in 2008. This is in addition to the sum of $4 billion PayPal processed as P2P payments via mobile—this $12 billion is specifically mobile remittances to developing economies.

India, Mexico, China, the Philippines and Poland were the top five recipients of remittances in 2008. In 2010 Poland's growth and high wages moved it out of the developing economy category as measured by the World Bank, and Bangladesh took its place in the Top 5.

Nearly five billion people worldwide have little or no access to traditional financial services due to the lack of ATMs and bank branches,

Table 6.1: Top recipients of migrant remittances among developing countries in 2010 (Source: World Bank)

	Remittance inflows in 2010, est. ($ billion)	Growth of remittances in 2009-10 in US$ terms (%)	Growth of remittances in local currency terms (%)	Growth of remittances in local currency terms adjusted for inflation (%)
All developing countries	324.7	5.6%	3.9%	-2.7%
East Asia and Pacific	92.5	7.4%	4.9%	0.8%
Europe and Central Asia	34.9	1.3%	5.8%	-0.5%
Latin America and Caribbean	57.6	1.7%	-2.9%	-6.9%
Middle-East and North Africa	35.6	6.2%	8.1%	2.2%
South Asia	81.2	8.2%	4.6%	-6.3%
Sub-Saharan Africa	21.9	5.5%	5.1%	-4.0%
Largest recipients				
India	53.1	7.4%	1.5%	-10.4%
China	51.3	5.3%	4.3%	1.0%
Mexico	22.0	0.2%	-6.3%	-10.0%
Philippines	21.4	8.1%	2.3%	-1.4%
Bangladesh	10.8	2.7%	3.6%	-4.3%
Nigeria	10.0	4.8%	5.0%	-7.7%
Pakistan	9.7	11.1%	15.8%	3.7%
Lebanon	8.4	11.3%	11.3%	6.5%
Vietnam	8.0	17.0%	27.1%	16.4%
Egypt	7.7	8.1%	9.3%	-2.2%

poor regulation, low levels of financial literacy or other weaknesses in a country's infrastructure. Clearly, with the wide reach of mobile phones, which now outnumber ATMs by two thousand to one, mobile operators have a potential solution to the access problem and can extend these remittance services to millions of people in remote, rural areas, thus offering a relatively inexpensive alternative to exorbitant private money-transfer services.

With the help of the mobile phone, the GSM Association[20] (GSM refers to Global Systems for Mobile Communications, the primary standard for digital mobile phones in use by 80 per cent of the global mobile market) estimates that the international remittance market will grow to $1 trillion by 2012. ABI Research meanwhile predicts that the global mobile fund transfer market will generate $8 billion in revenue for mobile operators by 2012—from just over $10 million in 2006. Edgar Dunn[21] (Mobile Banking and Payments Consultancy) research estimates that by 2015, more than 1.4 billion people will be utilising mobile payments services.

A case in point are the mobile telephone money transfer services that allow mobile phone users to make financial transactions or transfers across the country conveniently and at low cost. The two most successful of these are M-Pesa in Kenya and G-Cash in the Philippines (see the M-Pesa case study later in the chapter).

The Edgar Dunn research also found that the number one barrier to successful deployment of mobile payments and wallets was government regulation. Mobile operators and collectives such as the GSM Association are lobbying governments to ensure that regulation governing the deployment and usage of mobile financial services is proportionate to the risks involved.

As reported in the *Nairobi Star* in December 2008,[22] M-Pesa with all its success represented a clear threat to the Big Four banks in Kenya. The Big Four have a combined market coverage of around three million account holders and 750 banking outlets. M-Pesa, in comparison, has more than 15 million customers and 37,000 sales agents and outlets across the country. The massive threat that M-Pesa holds for the Big-Four banks is patently obvious. A similar story can be told in other markets where new payment mechanisms have been successful. The problem for mobile payments in this environment is to what extent do such mechanisms impinge on banks, and should they be regulated as banks are?

Regulators and governments probably do need to provide an infrastructure for mobile payments to be truly successful. This framework might include:

- **Regulation of low-risk money transfer services,** which involve small amounts of money compared with traditional banking services, outside traditional banking regulation.
- **Enabling non-bank organisations to facilitate the transaction**; to become an agent of a bank or a remittance provider to facilitate the cash-in and cash-out activities on both sides of the mobile money transfer.
- Whenever possible, **implementing regulation on the systems level** without interfering with the customer interface.

What is the outcome for banks? Well, as G-Cash from Globe in the Philippines, and M-Pesa from Safaricom in Kenya show, the biggest threat to banks is from telecom operators. So banks need to team quickly with network operators so as not to find themselves competing against these. Given the limited number of network operators in each market, banks should move quickly in case they get locked out by exclusivity agreements or other considerations. To illustrate, the Bank of the Philippine Islands (BPI) and Globe Telecom have recently announced the launch of a mobile microfinance institution, PSBI (Pilipinas Savings Bank).[23] PSBI is a traditional bank that has been converted for use in the mobile and microcredit arena.

Secondly, rather than treat mobile payments as a threat, banks need to see it as an opportunity to open otherwise unprofitable markets for low-income segments. Banks will need strong partners and a strong platform to succeed.

If you want to bank the world, the mobile phone is the easiest and cheapest way to do it, as Kenya and the Philippines have shown.

What does the future hold?

With most of the world's population still on feature phone hardware, though, the question is, who will really dominate the mobile platform in the coming years as feature phones are swapped out for smartphones?

Scenario 1: Android dominates

To succeed in this strategy, Android would need better standardisation of its OS on platform, and better developer support. The problem today is that there's no consistent upgrade path for Android devices because each device is different and it requires the hardware manufacturer to support the upgrade process.

Scenario 2: Microsoft-Nokia partnership dominates feature phone replacement cycle

Don't count Nokia and Microsoft out just yet. In just five years Apple turned this industry on its head. Windows Mobile 7 (Mango) and Windows Mobile 8 are significant improvements on the mobile OS play and might just save both Nokia's and Microsoft's mobile divisions. The question here is, will the large percentage of Nokia customers still using a feature phone upgrade to a Nokia/Microsoft smartphone when they can afford to do so? If they do, then Nokia and Microsoft will emerge as a major player over the next two to three years.

Scenario 3: HTML 5 disrupts the App Store

iOS (Apple), Android (Google) and Windows Mobile (Microsoft) all rely on the concept of a marketplace or store for distributing their content. HTML 5 is the emerging browser technology that could render apps obsolete. HTML 5 would turn any browser or OS user experience into an app-like interface. The shortcoming with HTML 5 in the near term is that we can't use it to access native functions on the phone—like a mobile wallet or NFC capability, for example.

Until HTML 5 can give us access to the more interesting hardware features on the phone, then HTML 5 can't deliver what apps deliver today. Undoubtedly this is where many are trying to take HTML 5. More on that in a moment when I discuss Beyond the App Store.

M-Pesa Success Story
Mobile remittances taking the
developing world by storm

Kenya's mobile payment service, known as M-Pesa, provided by the main mobile phone company in Kenya, Safaricom, in conjunction with Vodafone, represents a good example of how low-cost approaches that use modern technology can effectively expand the financial services frontier. M-Pesa (M for mobile, "Pesa" for money in Swahili) is the product name of a mobile-phone-based money transfer service that was developed by Sagentia (now owned by IBM) for Vodafone. The concept of M-Pesa was initially to create a service that allowed microfinance borrowers to receive and repay loans conveniently using the network of mobile provider, Safaricom, and utilising their air-time resellers. This would enable microfinance institutions (MFIs) to offer more competitive loan rates to their users as the cost of dealing in cash is reduced. The users of the service would gain through being able to track their finances more easily. In 2006, when M-Pesa was launched, over 70 per cent of Kenyan households did not have bank accounts, or relied on informal sources of finance.

When the service was trialled, customers adopted the service for a variety of alternative uses, and complications arose with Faulu, the partnering microfinance institution (MFI). M-Pesa was refocused and launched with a different value proposition: sending remittances home across the country and making payments.

Today, millions of Kenyans use M-Pesa to make payments, send remittances and store funds for short periods. Many of those without bank accounts are able to use this service, at low risk and cost. As noted in a recent article in the *Economist*,[24] Kenya's M-Pesa is the most celebrated success story of mobile banking and payments in a developing country. What started as a mobile money transfer service has become a success story of financial services development with a technological platform that makes it cost-effective and safe.

And it has contributed to the financial health of the nation significantly.

By the end of its first month, the service had just over 19,000 subscribers. Within three months, there were 268,499 registered M-Pesa customers and within the first year, one million. By 2012, that number had climbed to 15 million customers. Almost half of the Kenyan population of 35 million have embraced M-Pesa in its short five-year history. Also impressive has been the increase in the number of monthly transactions, which increased by 4627 per cent over the period from July 2007 to July 2009. M-Pesa averages 11 to 14.6 person-to-person transfers each month, with over 56 billion Kenyan shillings a month (US$675m/month) moved through the M-Pesa network. Mobile money transfers in total crossed the 1-trillion shilling mark in 2011.

With over 37,000 outlets and reseller agencies around Kenya, M-Pesa outstrips the top four banks' reach by more than 50 to 1. This is why M-Pesa has become ubiquitous so quickly. M-Pesa also facilitates bill payments for more than 700 companies across Africa.

M-Pesa has now expanded its field abroad. In October 2009, Safaricom launched its M-Pesa services in the UK through Western Union, Provident Capital Transfers, KenTV and others. While there are some AML

With 37,000 outlets, 15 million users and close to $700m per month, the M-Pesa mobile payments network is a huge success.

restrictions on the usage of M-Pesa for transfers by a single individual, the system still allows a Kenyan working in the UK to deposit pounds or euros in the UK with a remittance agent, and have his family or associates collect that money in Kenyan shillings back in the home country with the use of their mobile phone.

M-Pesa has extended its reach further across Africa with its relaunch of M-Pesa in Tanzania. While the take-up in Tanzania has been slightly slower than in Kenya, there are still more than nine million users in that country. Vodafone has also partnered Roshan to provide M-Paisa, a local variant of M-Pesa, in Afghanistan. Early in 2010, Nedbank and mobile operator Vodacom teamed up to launch M-Pesa in South Africa.

Scenario 4: Apple Rules!

If Apple continues on its current growth path, with the launch of the iPhone 5 and its mobile wallet capability, it's likely to blow their current estimates out of the water. Then the iPhone will likely end up being the single most popular mobile phone on the planet. For this to work in markets such as Africa, for example, Apple will need cheaper mid-range units that make it into the hands of the more average consumers in markets such as China, India, pan-Africa and Indonesia. It will then take years for a competitor to displace them broadly.

Beyond the App Store

With the knowledge that Apple has had more than 30 billion apps downloaded, and more than 600,000 apps in its store, we'd expect the future of apps to look very bright indeed. However, the iOS marketplace is suffering from a lack of surface area. Simply put, "app discovery" in the App Store is a nightmare with so many choices, and so much content.

In February 2012, Apple acquired Chomp, a leading app-comparison tool for $50m. According to Chomp, its "proprietary algorithm learns the functions and topics of apps, so we can search based on what apps do, not just what they're called". Currently the fastest way to find something in the App Store is to know the name of what we're looking for, so finding apps by utility or function could be an invaluable capability.

The incredible growth in the App Store presents a problem in itself for Apple. The closed ecosystem may be a windfall of revenue for Apple (and for some developers), but specific content easily gets lost in the crowd unless we know exactly what we're looking for. Apps represent a particularly tricky taxonomy problem. Not only do all of the normal categorical complexities of subject matter apply, just like in books, movies or music, but apps also have functions, they do things. So the hierarchy of what they *are* has to be overlaid with the hierarchy of what they *do*.

Another problem is cross-platform compatibility. Developers tend to prefer the iOS platform because of the traffic afforded it by the dominant iPhone and iPad platforms, but Android also gets solid demand, requiring development across at least two platforms. With Microsoft and Nokia emerging as a potential competitor, yet another platform for app development emerges.

The ecosystem might be prepared to put up with native apps' drawbacks if there were no viable alternative. However, an alternative is fast emerging. HTML5 promises developers a platform that enables apps to run directly from smartphone browsers. HTML5 can support many features, such as video, graphics and multimedia content, without having to resort to proprietary plug-ins and application programming interfaces (APIs).

HTML5 enables developers and content providers to deliver a consistent experience across different devices while emulating native apps' ability to download and cache data for use when not connected to the web, which reduces the user's need to be constantly online.

From the developers' perspective, using HTML5 could dramatically reduce the time spent coding as one app will run across different platforms. HTML5 works with any online payment technology, enabling developers or content companies to provide customers with a choice of payment methods. Finally, HTML5 allows developers to embed links to specific web pages into specific parts of an app, a technique that can be particularly useful for promotions and advertising. To date, this "deep linking" has not been easy to do in native apps.

Of course, HTML5 won't be a silver bullet that eliminates all the downsides to native apps in a single stroke. Although HTML5 will reduce developers' dependence on app stores, which typically take a commission of between 10 and 30 per cent, they will still incur some marketing, distribution and transaction costs.

The benefits of cross-platform speed to market, along with lower distribution costs, mean that the likes of Facebook will be championing HTML5 as an alternative app experience. The restrictions will be around native mobile function and feature access. That will likely be solved by mobile browsers that have the native plug-ins.

So how long does the App Store have? Maybe another two to three years of dominance. Beyond that, more journeys that are app-like via HTML5 will increasingly be the norm.

Unfortunately for banks, this means supporting at least iOS and Android app platforms for the foreseeable future.

KEY LESSONS

If we had asked most bankers five years ago when they thought mobile banking would become mainstream, they would likely have told us "not in my lifetime". Yet in the last five years that is exactly what has happened and now banks everywhere are talking about NFC, wallets, mobile banking, etc.

Over the past ten years, mobile has matured and established its place in the financial services world, in both developing and developed nations.

Mobile as a distribution network not only reaches a far broader audience, but also engages them at a very personal level.

The strength of mobile is its ability to enable the utility of an individual's money in a convenient, anywhere, anytime, always plugged-in service.

Mobile's role in financial services has already matured and grown to mainstream scale. With the large payment networks now heavily investing in mobile, it will bring about a revolution.

Already with developing economies moving towards 50 per cent smartphone adoption rates, no bank can avoid a mobile presence if it wants to be relevant to most of its customers.

By 2016 mobile banking will be the primary channel for most customers. Four years is not a lot of time to develop this channel competently to support the vast majority of your day-to-day retail business, especially when banks currently have very little experience on cross-sell and up-sell via digital channels such as the mobile.

Social media, offer and geolocation integration promise to make the mobile experience much more relevant to consumers, and hence place further demands on financial institutions.

Keywords: Mobile Payments, Mobile Wallets, iPhone, M-Pesa, Mobile Banking, Unbanked, Remittances, Marketing, Promotion

Endnotes

1   Sources: http://148apps.biz/app-store-metrics/, http://www.androidtapp.com/android-apps-statistics-summary-for-2010/, http://techcrunch.com/2012/05/07/google-play-about-to-pass-15-billion-downloads-pssht-it-did-that-weeks-ago/, http://venturebeat.com/2011/01/26/mobile-app-revenue-2011/ and http://bits.blogs.nytimes.com/2012/06/11/apples-stash-of-credit-card-numbers-is-its-secret-weapon/

2   Apple.com Press Releases: http://www.apple.com/pr/library/2012/03/05Apples-App-Store-Downloads-Top-25-Billion.html

3   Gartner: http://www.gartner.com/it/page.jsp?id=1529214 (revenue estimates include app sales, in-app revenue, subscriptions and app-based ad revenue)

4   ABI Research ($46 billion), Juniper Research ($51.7 billion)

5   http://www.wan-press.org/article18612.html

6   Internet World Stats

7   World Bank Report on Financial Inclusion 2012

8   UNCTAD report on Mobile Money Trends (http://unctad.org/en/pages/newsdetails.aspx?OriginalVersionID=134)

9   http://www.11mark.com/IT-in-the-Toilet

10 Pew Internet & American Life Project: http://www.dailyfinance.com/2010/09/03/do-you-sleep-with-your-cell-phone-most-americans-do-study-find/

11 ReadWriteWeb

12 The Realtime Report

13 Starbucks processed 42 million mobile payments in just 15 months. In the 11 months between Jan and Nov 2011, more than 26 million payments were made, with reloads on the 'card' totalling more than $110 million (Source: VentureBeat/Starbucks).

14 Credit to Terence Roche @Gonzobanker for this insight

15 See analysis of assertion here—http://60secondmarketer.com/blog/2011/10/18/more-mobile-phones-than-toothbrushes/

16 http://images.businessweek.com/slideshows/20110213/the-20-countries-with-the-highest-per-capita-cell-phone-use#slide1

17 http://mobithinking.com/mobile-marketing-tools/latest-mobile-stats#subscribers

18 See Google's recent research on global smartphone growth: http://googleblog.blogspot.com/2012/05/new-research-shows-smartphone-growth-is.html

19 Gartner (http://www.gartner.com/it/page.jsp?id=1924314)

20 GSMA: gsmworld.com

21 Edgar, Dunn and Company: edgardunn.com

22 *Nairobi Star*, "Big Banks in Plot to Kill M-Pesa", 23 December 2008

23 *Finextra*, "Philippines mobile phone-based microfinance bank set for launch", 13 October 2009

24 *The Economist*, 26 September 2009

7 The Evolution of Self-Service

Self-service banking—where it all started

Self-service devices in the banking world have traditionally been focused primarily on the ATM (Automated Teller Machine), with its mass launch in the 1970s in the US, and gradually over the 80s across the rest of the world. The ATM solved one of the biggest problems for a retail/commercial bank, that is, distribution of cash for customer withdrawals. Cash machines are an essential part of most consumers' daily lifestyle; the ATM celebrated its 40th birthday in 2007, and today 75 per cent of all cash in the UK is dispensed to consumers via ATMs.

The invention of the ATM meant that one of the biggest fixed costs in any retail banking operation—the branch—could be reduced through branch rationalisation (closures). In addition, the variable cost component, staff, could also be reduced through downsizing. So, ATMs provided one of the biggest one-off saving hits for branch banking. The automation of one of the basic functions of a bank not only reduced costs, but also increased customer convenience, allowing access to cash 24/7.

That is where the story seems to have ended for ATMs. While there was the initial big roll-out and the promise of further automation of services through self-service, the promise has never really been delivered. Sure, ATMs have evolved in terms of their look, efficiency, speed, but their function, on the whole, is still concentrated on cash delivery.

The first mechanical cash dispenser was developed and built by Luther George Simjian and installed in 1939 in New York City by the City Bank of New York, but it was removed after six months due to the lack of customer acceptance. The first self-service device of any note that was a commercial success was the Automated Teller Machine launched by Barclays Bank in

1967. That device relied on a prepaid token to retrieve envelopes with a fixed amount of cash within. From this relatively primitive beginning, the ATM has gone on to revolutionise the banking habits of most retail customers.

The drive for efficiency

The initial drive for banks to launch ATMs was to promote an innovative image in what was still a branch-dominated world in the 1960s and 70s. There was little effort at migration of customers from branches to ATMs in an era of tight banking regulation in most of the world.

Regulation meant that banks were limited in what they could offer in terms of competitive interest rates and, with credit rationing, especially in housing loans, there were set quotas on what could be lent and at what level of interest. In this environment there was little incentive to be competitive. In effect, banks were cross-subsidising their services, including branches, with the income earned on their lending and deposit services.

So, while self-service devices were around by the 1970s, there was little incentive to encourage active migration to the new devices when branches were still the main platform of service and were being well funded by cross-subsidisation from heavily regulated lending services.

With deregulation of the financial industry in the UK, US, and Australia in the 70s and 80s, financial institutions could no longer hide inefficiencies behind margins. With competition allowed in the deposit and lending markets, margins were quickly squeezed and services had to be justifiable on their own account. This was especially the case in countries with large branch networks, such as the UK and across the rest of Europe. The largest fixed cost for retail banks were branches and the highest variable cost was staff. When looking at the activities of the branch, the accountants found that a huge majority of the work performed related to the teller function, which consisted of cash deposits and cash withdrawals. If you take out these two elements, you take out up to 70 per cent of the branch staff costs.

Forrester states that 69 per cent of bank customers in Europe use ATMs on a regular basis. UK cash machine withdrawals hit a record high in 2011, new figures reveal. In 2011, UK consumers used ATMs 2.87 billion times, taking out £191 billion, according to data from the Payments Council.

Over time this has meant that cash withdrawals have continued to trickle along in-branch, but increasingly many banks are simply opting to discontinue cash withdrawals over the counter, such as SNS Bank in Utrecht. Others, such as some UK banks, are mandating minimum withdrawals of £100 at a teller. Others no longer allow cash deposits over the counter. One bank I heard of recently in the US now requires customers to wrap cash notes in bundles by denomination, and coins packaged by denomination, with the account number written on the bundles, before they will allow a customer to make a deposit. The ATM has a vital role to play in this ongoing battle around branch transaction handling costs.

But the ATM, as we know it, is not going to last long. Why?

Are ATMs more than just cash dispensers?

The ATM was initially all about moving cash-withdrawal teller transactions out of the branch and reforming cost structures. However, as ATMs became embedded in the behaviour of the vast majority of retail customers, banks inevitably wanted these automated tellers to do more than just dispense cash. Like branches before them, ATM machines started to get costly. First of all, the real estate required to house the ATM units could run into hundreds of thousands of dollars a year on their own. Secondly, the cost of servicing and replenishing ATMs got more expensive over time. Lastly, there was the call for making these devices "pay for themselves" either through a fee or product revenue.

Thus over time we've seen quite a few experiments in form factor and interface to encourage better utilisation of the ATM as a platform for engagement. I want to talk about where I think this will end up.

Most recently we've seen banks incorporating cheque deposits, bill payments and other functionality. Bank of America has recently been pushing its ATM cheque deposit capability by advertising strongly. Chase, Barclays and RBS have been advertising the ability of their ATMs to dispense cash via our mobile phones. HSBC in Hong Kong launched touch-screen ATMs with barcode-scanning capability in December 2010 so that bill payment was expedited. What's the industry view of the near term for ATMs?

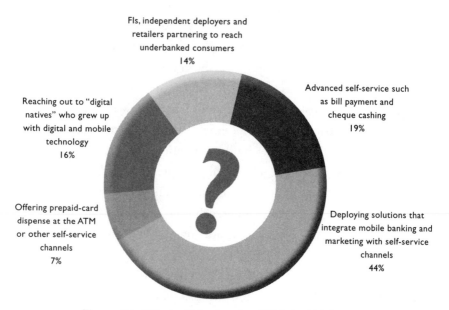

Fls, independent deployers and retailers partnering to reach underbanked consumers
14%

Reaching out to "digital natives" who grew up with digital and mobile technology
16%

Advanced self-service such as bill payment and cheque cashing
19%

Offering prepaid-card dispense at the ATM or other self-service channels
7%

Deploying solutions that integrate mobile banking and marketing with self-service channels
44%

Figure 7.1: What will be hot for ATMs in 2016?
(Source: ATMMarketplace.com)

The ATM Future Trends report from early in 2012 identified the above "trends" as the hot prospects for serving "cash-preferred" consumers in the next five years. The survey suggested ATM installations would grow six per cent between 2009 and 2015, and cash withdrawals would increase eight per cent each year through to 2016. It predicted a branch decline of 2.5 per cent between 2010 and 2013, which would stimulate increased ATM usage (I think that's extremely conservative).

In reality, branch decline will start to accelerate more rapidly between 2013 and 2016 as digital behaviours around screens and mobiles really start to bite into visitation and sales, so it's pretty obvious that ATM usage will get a bump as banks try to replace their "place" with more capable self-service platforms. As can be seen from the previous data, at the core of this will be self-service mobile integration from both a marketing/messaging and transactional/cash-withdrawal basis. However, the trend for ATMs to be used more for bill payment and cheque deposits will be totally undermined by the utility of smartphones. Thus, the likelihood that ATMs will split form along the lines of full-featured versus simple cash-dispensing is more likely, in my opinion.

Recently the team at Abu Dhabi Commercial Bank (ADCB) in the United Arab Emirates was looking at ways to improve the suitability of offers for card usage delivered to customers. There were suggestions around using location-based messaging technology through telecommunication providers to target the consumer when he was at various shopping malls around the Emirates, but the Telco network operators proved unable to deliver this reliably and consistently. So ADCB looked at behaviours—how did customers behave when they went shopping?

Behavioural analysis suggested that a customer who went to a shopping mall was almost always certain to do one of two things: go to an ATM machine on arrival and pull out cash, or, alternatively, use his debit/credit card to make a purchase at a store. So ADCB worked out that it didn't need the mobile operators to work out *where* customers were; it only needed to look at live transaction data through the POS/ATM networks for location triggers.

Thus, today ADCB can provide the customer with a time-sensitive, location-sensitive offer based on his behaviour and can then simply send him an offer via SMS or an app notification when he uses his card. This is far more constructive than flooding him with inane broadcast messages that are more miss than hit.

For most of the credit card customer base, ADCB did not have the customer's mobile number on his profile. How could it send him offers if it didn't know his mobile number? How would it incentivise the customer to give his mobile number to ADCB when it didn't have it in his profile? ADCB simply introduced a message on the ATM screen as customers were waiting for their cash to be dispensed asking if they wanted to receive a discount coupon for the shopping mall they were already at. All they had to do was enter their mobile number. The request was taken up by more than 30 per cent of the customer base over the space of just a few months.

Of course, the next step will be attempting to integrate customers' phones directly into the ATM experience so they don't need a card at all.

A number of banks are now incorporating contactless capability into their ATMs so that the customer is able to use an NFC-enabled phone or a contactless card to withdraw cash. China has a very well-saturated local e-purse scheme and has been upgrading ATMs in the thousands over the past year or so with contactless in order to be able to support top-up/balance-checks, etc. of this e-purse card at the ATM. Bank of Communications in China introduced cardless withdrawal via app and contactless in January 2010, and it already has a couple of million customers using its ATM devices *sans* cards. Japan and South Korea have had similar capabilities for many years.

In my research with NCR, they suggested that 2012 has seen a steady increase in demand for contactless ATMs and its so-called "contactless kits" (already being shipped today). As a result NCR believes that 2013/14 is when the tipping point for contactless ATMs will occur. Within Brazil and Australia, for example, there are customers investing now in contactless ATM hardware although work is still being done on the software/transactions these ATMs will feature. NCR is running pilots and proofs-of-concept trials for contactless ATMs in countries as varied as the US, Brazil, Canada, France, Poland, Slovakia, Spain, Turkey, South Africa, New Zealand and Australia.

According to NCR, between September 2009 and May 2011 they shipped around 3000 contactless modules, but by end of 2011, that had more than tripled, to over 10,000 units, and they expect more than double that number in 2012.

Contactless capability is cool, but more than mobile and NFC integration, what will influence the evolution of the ATM in the next five to ten years?

The influence of multitouch and usability

Spain's Banco Bilbao Vizcaya Argentaria (BBVA) has arguably the best ATM design out there today, thanks to the design team at IDEO, and the collaboration of the teams at NCR and Fujitsu. This is a fundamental rethink of customer experience on the channel and it works fantastically. It is generations ahead of most ATM machines in the market today. This project commenced in 2007, and by May 2010, BBVA had installed five pilot ATM units in Madrid.

The most impressive thing about this is that someone actually stopped to ask the question about what customers really want and need from an ATM, and how the bank could humanise the experience. It wasn't just an iteration or a user interface redesign. BBVA aimed to revolutionise the experience of using an ATM by making it highly usable, secure and massively efficient all at the same time.

At first glance, the BBVA ATM looks to carry a reduced footprint, and is more space and security-friendly.

Figure 7.2: The BBVA Ideo ATM

However, the thing that captures your attention is the large, well-placed touch screen—a screen at 19 inches that looks remarkably like a large iPad (although designed prior to the iPad's release).

The interface design is the real innovation in my opinion. In designing the new ATM, BBVA and its team worked hard to change the entire interaction. They started with paper prototypes, cardboard cut-outs and mock-ups for customers to play with and give feedback on. Thus the entire interface was redeveloped from the ground up around the interaction. They didn't start with a hardware platform and say "What can we deploy on this device?" BBVA's cross-discipline team, led by the innovative design team at IDEO, started with the question, "How do we make the ATM interaction more human, natural, intuitive and, in doing so, also more efficient, secure and cost-effective?"

Figure 7.3: The iPad-like interface to the BBVA ATM

The end result is a best-in-breed interface (and form factor) that is two to three generations ahead of most bank ATM platforms in the market today. Some of the features of just the interface alone are things such as:

- Personalisation of the interface around the consumer's relationship with the bank
- The ATM learns what withdrawal types he makes over time, and offers that as his default
- To select different denominations, he can swipe through the currency/denomination options visually on screen (as shown in the figure above)
- There are big, clear, on-screen buttons for interaction, no annoying hardware buttons on the side that sometimes don't even line up with the screen itself
- Animation and embedded video to guide the first-time user although the simplicity of the interface makes that largely unnecessary, and
- A single slot that can be used for dispensing cash, or for deposits.

There were other more subtle improvements also…

> "'We observed plenty of ergonomic awkwardness when using the machines while carrying handbags, or even more so, with shopping bags,' says [IDEO's Pascal] Soboll. A flat surface was added to the design that could accommodate a purse or coffee, and a bigger kiosk footprint made space for groceries."[1]

BBVA is already rolling out more than 3000 of these new ATM devices around the world currently, and thus far the reception and feedback have been unanimously positive.[2]

I've watched my three-year-old son, who has grown up with an iPad, and my older kids interact with screens generally in recent times. My kids understand laptops and TV screens, but my three-year-old's primary interactions with screens has been through an iPad. Thus, when he sits with me when I'm surfing the web on my laptop, showing him YouTube videos, he's always touching the screen to navigate to the next video he wants to watch—that's how he's learned behaviour around screen interaction. We're now learning that screens are much easier to use if they are touch-screen; we're also seeing laptops now that incorporate both multitouch and traditional interaction devices (i.e. keyboard and mouse).

So what happens today when we visit an ATM? How often do we find ourselves touching the screen of an ATM that isn't a touch screen? I know I've done it without thinking on more than one occasion.

Interface designers and usability experts such as Jared Spool, Don Norman, Jacob Nielsen and others often talk about design patterns. The fact is that over time we learn to use these new design paradigms and they influence our expectations of new devices that emerge. Thus, if someone brought out a tablet today that only worked with a stylus or one finger at a time, instead of multitouch, he could be pretty much assured of it bombing commercially. The problem is accentuated over time, of course, but people see older devices as somehow deficient in their capability, and this leads people to trade up.

Has anyone recently picked up an old BlackBerry or Nokia phone (non-touch) that has an icon menu system? We immediately expect it to react as a multitouch app phone of today would. When it doesn't, we realise we have to switch back, but we've already decided that this is outdated, outmoded technology.

That's happening right now in the ATM business, and our expectations for ATM interactions are not set by the dominant standards in the industry, nor by Diebold or NCR. Our expectations are set by Apple, iOS, Android, Microsoft Windows 8, and the Xbox.

I've used ATMs recently that haven't had their interface updated in 10 years or more, and they are looking very old and shabby indeed. While the interface or form factor of an ATM is unlikely to be the dominant factor in our choice of a bank, it's a basic hygiene factor that consumers will expect to get sorted. According to surveys from consumer research firm Buzzback, 88 per cent of consumers globally are more likely to choose to transact regularly with a business based on their experience with its self-service devices.[3] Remember, your brand capability is being assessed based on utility, and not on product, rate or place anymore. A total channel experience involves one that optimises any customer-channel experience to make it a positive engagement.

You might be able to survive for a time with a hardware platform that still uses eight buttons to help you navigate, but every time a user touches the screen and then has to devolve his interaction back to an old hardware platform, your brand credibility is taking a hit. Just go and watch how many customers touch the screen of a non-touch-screen ATM and you'll know I'm right on this one.

How the mobile changes ATM interactions

The next big thing in ATMs will undoubtedly be incorporating the utilisation of the smartphone and apps. Initially this is as simple as incorporating an ATM locator in mobile banking apps so customers can locate the nearest ATM machine. The next logical step would be the use of the mobile phone itself as the ATM interface, rather than an ATM screen. After all, you can do everything you can do on an ATM on your phone, except get cash out—so if the ATM only dispenses cash, then that's fine. The phone can display our balance, allow us to select an account, choose how to receive the cash, transfer funds, pay our bills, etc. It just can't give us hard currency.

Now admittedly the mobile wallet will reduce the reliance on cash over time, but cash is not quite ready to disappear completely, so we'll need the humble ATM for quite a while yet—at least well into the next decade.

NCR has been working on this technology and Fast Company profiled some of their imaginings recently.

In a couple of scenarios, NCR has imagined an ATM device that is powered by our mobile phone entirely. For high-traffic areas or areas with limited space (such as a convenience store), this could be ideal. The device is essentially a cash dispenser and it can do away with the touch-screen interface in the ATM device because that is provided by the functionality in our phone. I had the opportunity to visit NCR's prototype showroom at their World Trade Center offices in New York recently, and the design of the cash-dispensing device working with the smartphone was not a leap in the slightest—it was totally logical and intuitive.

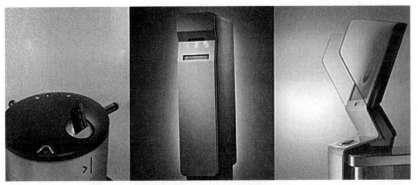

Figure 7.4: NCR has been experimenting with ATM form factor (Credit: Fast Company)

The other thing that is interesting is that as these devices evolve into highly interactive interface devices, the ATM can also be much more than just an ATM. It can be a discount coupon dispenser, ticketing machine, mobile phone top-up kiosk, etc. In Qatar, the largest telecommunications provider, Qtel, has deployed more than 100 ATMs that do not dispense cash at all. Instead, the ATMs let customers drive up and deposit cash to pay their phone bill or purchase calling cards.[4] The success of the NCR-built self-service terminals has been such that Qtel has stopped accepting any bill payments or selling prepaid vouchers via their traditional customer centres, freeing Qtel's staff to focus on new sales and attend to more customers.

It appears then that the self-service device is likely to evolve down two separate paths: a rapid cash-dispenser in a very simple form, and a fully functional kiosk platform that may dispense cash but will also be highly interactive and could also dispense new prepaid cards, discount coupons, and have heaps of marketing integration, including with mobile devices.

The more complex question is how to make revenue out of self-service devices today. Is it as easy as installing an ATM—"Build it and they will come"? The problem with selling a product is that there has to be a need that requires a solution. For the ATM, the need is very obviously cash, and cash is easy to sell!

Cash is used as a medium to buy almost anything. Its need is universal and is so obvious that marketing does not even have to sell it. So long as the ATM is visible, it will have customers. But generating real revenue from the ATM is a lot tougher.

HSBC

Contribution from Michael
Armstrong, former Senior
Manager, Asia Pacific

When self-service fails to deliver

In Hong Kong, HSBC had established a highly successful Internet-based offering built on commodity insurance products. The key to success of the online proposition was:

- Easy-to-understand products with readily identifiable need
- As few questions as possible
- Instant payment solution—credit card
- Instant approval—customer can print out confirmation of coverage immediately.

HSBC had great success with travel insurance because it fit the criteria listed above. The need was apparent: if we go on holiday, we need insurance; the required information was essentially dates of travel, name, and credit card number. About one year after launch, the website was handling over 50 per cent of all applications for that policy type, thus all indications were that HSBC had done a great job.

Then one morning, as I settled in over my morning cappuccino and blueberry muffin, I saw an article in the paper from a rival insurance company proclaiming its success at selling travel insurance through self-service kiosks. These kiosks were actually "smartphones" that were plugged into a touch screen to turn them into self-service kiosks. The large touch-screen LCD display allowed everything from buying tickets, finding the nearest 7-Eleven, as well as making a phone call (a little 80s-ish, that last one). The kiosk used web-based architecture and had a built-in printer and so it could provide receipts/tickets, etc.

The company that owned the kiosks placed them in high-traffic areas close to train stations, high-volume bus stations and where people were likely to gather—most importantly at the Shenzhen border between Hong Kong and China. It was apparent that the company did not see itself as a phone operator, but rather as a multifunction kiosk operator. It made its money from renting out applications on its kiosk/phone. The model is similar to what Apple now does with the iPhone and iTunes. It built the hardware and then allowed third parties to sell applications or products and services via their platform for revenue.

A competitive insurance company approached the owner of the kiosks with a proposition to sell simplified travel insurance for travellers going to China. It obviously did its thinking as it only requested the use of the kiosks that were in the train station where the trains left for the Hong Kong/China border. In addition it requested its app to be on the kiosk just as passengers approach the Hong Kong Immigration after getting off the train. The number of people who travel that route can be in the hundreds of thousands on a busy weekend, such as during Chinese New Year.

Next it ensured that the application was very, very simple and very focused. It only offered one type of travel insurance for people travelling to China from Hong Kong. The customer was only required to enter his Hong Kong Identity Card Number and the number of days of travel. No name, no contact details, no address. Payment was made by the contactless smartcard used for transport in Hong Kong known as the Octopus card. The machine then printed a receipt confirming the details. The entire transaction could be completed within 15 seconds.

The keys to the success of their proposition were:

- **Simple and focused product** with a readily identifiable need: travel insurance—I travel, I need insurance.
- **Context and location**. It had the very high-volume pedestrian traffic points covered, for an audience likely to need its product. The customer could see the sign, remember he wasn't covered and then head to the kiosk and buy.
- **Keep the questions short.** It only asked two questions, ID number and the duration of travel.

- **Instant payment** through a contactless-card payment system
  that 98 per cent of the Hong Kong population carries.
- **Instant confirmation** through the printout facility—a
  confirmation was printed in five seconds.

Well, if this company could do it, why couldn't HSBC? So HSBC
approached the same vendor. We knew that the application form we
currently used on the web needed further simplification so we tried to
replicate what our competition had done, but could not get away with
entering just an ID number due to compliance restrictions within the bank
(that is, compliance wouldn't agree to a simpler form). Nor could we do
a contactless one-second payment swipe using the Octopus card. We still
needed the customer to enter the 16-digit credit card number.

For the location we decided to hire kiosks at the Hong Kong
International Airport. We figured an airport would contain the key
ingredients: lots of traffic, and people who had forgotten to get insurance!
We tried hard to think where to place the 10 kiosks we had hired. With an
airport so large it was very difficult to find locations where a majority of
people would have to walk past. We placed some in the pre-Customs area
where passengers check in, as well as post-Immigration, where they might
mill about. To highlight the offering, we created colourful banners around
the kiosks. We thought we had the elements for success: a simple product,
a simple application process, and a great location.

The results were disappointing. Our sales measured in the single digits
for most days. As a percentage of overall sales, the channel was statistically
insignificant. What happened? Through surveys with our target customers,
we found we had violated the rules we set out earlier:

- **Product**—*good*
- **Location**—*not great*. Too dispersed to gain a critical mass of
  customers.
- **Application**—*still way too complicated*. Customers did not
  feel comfortable completing the application, even though it
  had been shortened significantly, while standing at a public

kiosk. We found there were too many buttons for them to press and therefore too much chance of their making an error, or abandoning the process before it was completed. There was also the added possible pressure of people standing behind them.

- **Payment**—*took too long* compared with a stored-value smartcard.

In the end our attempt was too clumsy and took too long to complete. The application had been perfect for a web-based application. We knew that because of the tremendous success of that channel. There is a big difference, however, between sitting in the office or at home completing an application on our PC, as opposed to standing in a busy airport trying to get our credit card out of our wallet while keeping an eye on our bags and using an unfamiliar interface.

The other factor in this story that contributed to the ultimate defeat of the kiosk project was that travel insurance could also easily be bought via mobile phone. Instead of completing the application on the kiosk, customers could just phone the insurance hotline and get instant coverage there and then. In terms of total application time, the phone would have been by far the quickest way to get covered when out at the airport.

Where customers had the choice they still preferred buying travel insurance over the web. We believe this was because the customer felt they had the control when applying for the product themselves: comparing quotes with other providers and, when they did commit, print off the details immediately rather than wait for confirmation through the post.

I believe the key lesson from this experience is never to take the customer for granted; never assume that because something has worked elsewhere on a different channel or a different location, it will work for us. We must always consider the different factors that, when combined, can result in success or failure. We always need to think of the products, location, sales process, payment and fulfilment, and we need to be continually testing new ideas to see what sticks.

The next 10 years

The key lessons from user research on self-service transactions are:

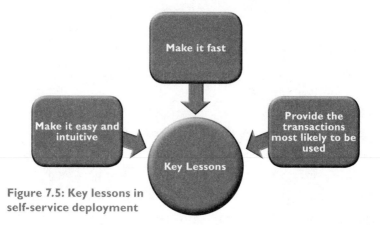

Figure 7.5: Key lessons in self-service deployment

The problem for banks today is that the ATM machine of yesteryear looks pretty shabby compared with the multitouch iPad app-enabled, revolutionary devices of today. The key values are clearly simple, compelling and easy interactions that enable the key transactions. However, there are other longer-term challenges and opportunities that are likely to morph the ATM environment further.

Form factor, extended utilisation and revenue

One reason banks have the opportunity to exploit the uniqueness of the ATM proposition is the sheer number of ATMs/self-service devices and spaces out there. There must be some other use that banks can put to the machine with a touch-screen display, dispensing capability and network connectivity. The obvious item that springs to mind is something such as concert or movie tickets. And perhaps gift vouchers that could be issued following an order made through the Internet channel. There is an opportunity for ATMs to be the physical fulfilment component of marketing campaigns to be conducted where distribution is important, e.g. redeeming vouchers for prizes or offers that need to be redeemed.

The fly in the ointment for this proposition is the Internet. Tell me what non-cash functionality cannot be conducted over the Internet that could only be done via an ATM?

Increasingly concert tickets, boarding passes complete with barcode information, etc., can be printed out by the user at home using his PC and a printer. This way the consumer cuts out the intermediary completely and the fulfilment role that the ATM could potentially fill is now redundant.

Again, the ATM is a location-specific distribution point and relies on offering something that is timely and relevant for where it sits. There is little point offering the printing of an airline boarding pass at an ATM—this is something I can easily do at home, or do at the airport on a dedicated kiosk. On the other hand, if I receive an SMS on my mobile phone saying that I need to redeem a voucher and claim it from a nearby shop within the next hour, then the ATM does become relevant as it can fulfil a specific purpose in a location close to me. Here are a few functions that will be used to leverage the ATM platform in the short term.

Mobile wallet and value store refills

The promise of the mobile wallet connected with the value store that we discussed earlier is best seen in the use of general purpose reloadable cards such as Visa Prepaid, or the Octopus card in Hong Kong, and the Oyster in the UK. The intention of the cards was that commercial transactions could be facilitated using the stored-value card with no cash involved. Increasingly we are seeing the emergence of NFC mobile phones that integrate generic value stores or prepaid components into a mobile wallet.

Depending on how the cards are topped up, the ATM could have a role in being a "hub" where money can be transferred across from the bank account onto the card. However, it seems clear that a well-designed mobile or online experience would be just as capable of topping up a value store as an ATM/self-service kiosk.

Bharti Airtel's Indian subscribers will be able to withdraw cash in 2012 by using their mobile phones at participating Airtel stores (acting as corresponding banks), without going to a branch or ATM. The company, which recently launched Airtel Money (AM)[5] to allow users to transfer money, as well as pay bills, is in discussion with various banks to launch the cash-withdrawal service through its ATM networks also. The service allows users to spend up to 50,000 rupees or around US$1000 per day, but each transaction is limited to 5000 rupees. Currently they can pay bills, buy movie tickets, pay at participating restaurants, spas and shops, and send money to other Airtel subscribers.

In Singapore the NETS cash card, which is used in motor vehicles for payment in car parks and highway tolls, can be topped up using bank ATMs. But the majority of the add-value transactions are still undertaken at specific terminals placed in logical locations, such as car parks and shopping centres where the traffic and the need are, thereby limiting the usefulness of the traditional ATM in performing this transaction. It probably makes sense that these platforms will converge increasingly over time.

The competing infrastructure is the use of direct bank account debiting and improved person-to-person or peer-to-peer capability. In this method, the customer's card is automatically refilled by debiting the customer's bank account when it reaches a set balance, or initiated through a notification, SMS or email. This is a popular means of top-up due to its "set and forget" nature, and not having to go to a physical place.

Cash conversion

While it may be difficult for the ATM to find a relevant role in converting cash to a value store balance, it does have some potential of going the "other way", i.e. converting a remittance from an electronic message into cash. In the realm of mobile wallets, the role of the ATM could be leveraged as the "cash converter". Imagine receiving a PayPal payment from a friend, being able to go to any ATM, put your phone number in and take the payment as cash without having to use a card! This would be compelling enough to promote as a unique play.

An example of this need for cash conversion is Globe GCASH, a Philippine service that relies on SMS to transfer funds between two parties. Apart from people to people over the mobile phone network, many overseas remittances are conducted the same way. The cash is given to the agent who then "wires" the funds to the beneficiary's account.

The problem there is how to convert the funds into cash. GCASH has a number of ways, including through its network of physical agents, but also through a bank's ATM network. The ATM is the obvious option as the funds can be immediately converted into cash. Services such as GCASH are particularly popular with foreign workers, especially in Asia and the Middle East, for remitting funds to their families back home.

A similar scheme operates in Kenya called M-Pesa. It also provides for person-to-person fund transfers using mobile phones. Interestingly, with the M-Pesa scheme, it is the cash conversion which is one of its biggest issues. The shopkeeper who signs up as an agent for M-Pesa is required to keep a cash float which can cause problems in isolated areas, and results in the merchant having to travel to the nearest town to replenish the cash. M-Pesa has attempted to solve this problem through ATM cash withdrawal through PesaPoint, Equity Bank Code and Diamond Trust. More on the M-Pesa case study can be found in Chapter 6 on Mobile Banking.

Personalisation, data and analytics

ATMs could truly become automated "tellers" in the next few years—you might integrate Avatar access to customer service and voice recognition, as well as integrate with payment cards, NFC[6] and a number of other key technologies that enhance the customer experience. The problem with many of these plans is the assumption that people will be standing at an ATM or self-service device interacting for lengthy periods of time. At this stage the reason ATMs work well is that they are a quick way to get cash. The more you complicate that, the more likely the value proposition of the ATM is actually decreased.

However, with data integration and personalisation, the ATM experience could become more about meeting our needs than just "How much cash do you want?"

When we visit the ATM it could inform us of any outstanding bills we need to pay, whether we want to redraw that personal loan we have, whether we want to upgrade that credit limit or transfer the outstanding balance of our credit card to a cheaper line of credit facility at a better interest rate. The ATM will offer to deliver messages to our mobile phone relevant to our transactions or our relationship with the bank. The ATM will give us service messages relating to questions we left with the customer service team last time we called, such as "Your recent request for a credit line extension has been approved!" These are simple, value-add mechanisms.

With IP-based and multimedia-capable ATM devices, you can do so much more than you are currently doing with your ATMs. The concept of a standard ATM interface needs to change immediately, to be replaced with something that can be populated in real time over the secure IP connection with the bank CRM system.

Advertising

There are estimated to be more than 2.2 million automated teller machines globally.[7] In the UK alone, over 130 million different "cardholders" will access ATMs annually, and over 21 million access ATMs each week. This translates to 75 per cent of the UK's available cash being distributed through an ATM.[8]

ATM users are a sought-after target demographic for media buyers. The vast majority will have bank accounts and good credit ratings. ATMs may also be the only cost-effective way to engage with some customer segments especially difficult for other types of media to reach, e.g. men aged between 18 and 35. People feel comfortable using ATMs. They are a trusted customer interface, in most cases used by cardholders at least once a week. In fact, in the US, the average usage of ATMs is 10.6 times per month.[9]

For some banks, ATM advertising is replacing direct mail altogether. Diebold estimates that response rates of up to 20 per cent can be generated on self-service terminals—20 times higher than the average for direct mail campaigns.

The results of any ATM-based advertising campaign can be measured in great detail, usually in real time. According to NCR, ATM advertising is 65 per cent cheaper and 200 per cent more effective than direct mail.

There are three opportunities for presenting an ad or message to consumers at the ATM:

1. **Approaching the ATM**
   a. Vinyls or "skins" that advertise a product or concept
   b. Dynamic video advertisement in free play while ATM is inactive
   c. Personalisation of the interface based on mobile device detection or facial recognition

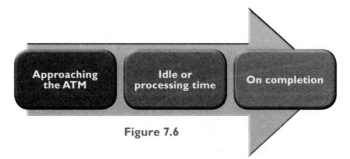

Figure 7.6

4. **During the transaction**—i.e. idle machine or processing time

   a. Instead of giving the boring "please wait while your cash is delivered" message, or just letting the screen sit while customers await the next step, present a quick video offer or message for users of the ATM

   b. The transaction time is not lengthened by branded content and consumer feedback demonstrates that it is preferable for waiting time to be filled with something engaging rather than a revolving egg timer.

3. **On completion**

   a. A final message after the card is withdrawn

   b. *Printed coupon on the receipt.* The receipt is transformed into a branded, take-home element of an ATM advertising campaign. It can act as bar-coded discount voucher, sampling offer, or a proximity prompt for a high street retailer

   c. *A support message to your mobile device.* Whether it is your account balance post withdrawal to reduce fraud and reduce coupon printing, or whether it is continuing the story where you left off at the ATM, your mobile will be a useful integration point for personalised messaging, post transaction.

Use of biometrics on self-service

On the technology front, the biggest potential improvement for the ATM is the enhancement of security through the use of biometrics. The most obvious use would be using a fingerprint or facial recognition to verify the user prior to undertaking the transaction.

Biometrics have two advantages: first, they eliminate fraud. If biometrics are used, it will then be more difficult for criminals to observe

PIN input and then replicate through theft of the cards or through cloning. The second advantage is simply a faster, better user experience. With so many personal numbers and passwords required, the ability to access accounts through a unique biometric feature has an appeal. Biometrics can be added to an ATM very cheaply. NCR estimates it would only add about $120–200 to the average price of an ATM unit. Given the broad acceptance of fingerprint technology in laptops, mobile phones, etc., customer acceptance would not likely be an issue.

While the biometric hardware is cheap, the effort to modify the software and authentication processes involved requires significant investment at the bank's end. For this reason, currently only two countries have incorporated biometrics in their ATMs: Colombia and Japan. Colombia is obvious because there are obvious security concerns due to the prevailing law and order situation there. Japan is more interesting because security is not as much of a concern; here, consumer perception essentially drives the need for incorporating biometrics in the ATM. In fact, Japan uses a form of contactless biometrics, as Japanese consumers are very hygiene-conscious and do not want to touch surfaces touched by other people.

Biometrics have more appeal in emerging markets, especially in poorer, less sophisticated markets where ATMs are a relative novelty. The potential for growth is limited by the need to distribute PINs and retain integrity over the process, i.e. keeping PINs and cards separate, especially in poorer areas where people may not find it easy to remember PINs, and the distribution of PINs presents a security risk.

The more interesting biometric integration with ATMs involves that of facial recognition as you approach or walk past the ATM (think Minority Report, the movie). ATMs could recognise me as I approach and show tailored messaging based around my current product portfolio, or my recent financial activity. Already digital signage is incorporating facial recognition and can tell if a customer is male or female, young or old, sad or happy. It won't be long before this capability is built into the self-service platform to provide a more personalised experience.

Using commercially available facial recognition software, a team of researchers at Carnegie Mellon University was able to identify around 30 per cent of the college students who had volunteered to be photographed for a research study on use of augmented reality and facial recognition.[10] They simply compared photos of the participating, anonymous students to images publicly available on Facebook. By using other public information from their social media profiles, the researchers also could identify the interests and predict partial Social Security numbers of some students.

> "It's a future where anonymity can no longer be taken for granted —even when we are in a public space surrounded by strangers."
> —Alessandro Acquisti, associate professor at
> Carnegie Mellon University (Source: *New York Times*)

In future, advertising billboards and digital signage that use facial detection might detect a teenage female and show her an ad for, say, a Lady Gaga branded perfume. But what if the next generation of digital signs could analyse skin quality and then publicly display an ad for acne cream, or detect sadness and serve up an ad for anti-depressants?

Think this is all a bit far-fetched? If I'm a Facebook user today, chances are if I'm tagged in a photo somewhere, my biometric data is already being stored and utilised by Facebook. Facebook currently uses this to suggest "tags" for other photos where my face is recognised, but Facebook also uses this technology ingeniously to verify my identity if I log in from a new location or forget my password. To recall my password, it doesn't ask me those classic password reset questions such as "What is your mother's maiden name" or "What is the name of your first pet?" It asks me to identify photos of my friends. This is a simple use of the biometric capability already built into Facebook.

Figuring out the right mix between personalisation, responsiveness to individual needs, privacy rules and security will be an important distinction in creating a positive self-service experience.

Initially, providing customisation around age- and gender-related services will be enough of a differentiation from a user-experience perspective. This is all part of a push to make our digital experience more personalised and human.

The long tail of ATM networks

In Australia, cash usage for retail payments has fallen more than 25 per cent in the last five years. In both the UK and US markets, cash usage as a payment method will decline between 17–20 per cent over the next five years. Now this is not the death of cash. In fact, it is likely that cash will be with us into the next decade. However it is quite possible that there will be a number of developed economies that will see a 50 per cent decline in use of cash at the retail space between 2005 and 2025. Putting the figures this way is certainly a compelling argument for the "death of cash" in the medium term. What impact will that sort of behavioural shift have on the ATM business?

In the early stages of a cash decline, the ATM networks of today become untenable, and banks realise that, just like branches, the ATM networks are mostly just a cost. Initially ATMs and other self-service devices were devised to take cost out of the branch. With mobile banking and mobile payments rapidly emerging, ATMs will start to look like outdated, costly infrastructure too.

In September 2009, National Australia Bank and credit union automatic teller machine administrator Cuscal combined their ATM networks to create Australia's second biggest but most geographically dispersed ATM network—called **rediATM** (not to be confused with reddit). Today there are over 100 financial institutions with access to this consolidated network supporting more than 3400 ATMs across Australia. Increasingly, this sort of network interoperability on ATMs will become essential. If you're going to reduce your ATM footprint, you'll need other ATMs to pick up the slack or provide continued access. This was part of the reason for rediATM's rapid success—that and the fact that customers could get no-fee withdrawals in most instances.

As cash usage declines in the later half of the decade, many banks will look to outsource their ATM business entirely. Why? The costs of managing real estate relationships, servicing the ATM hardware and keeping them cashed up, along with the interoperability angle, means that an independent, outsourced ATM network could have significant cost advantages. Smaller banks will be the first to move on this, first leveraging fees for withdrawals, and then negotiating arrangements for the outsourcing of their networks altogether.

In January, Skandiabanken was the first bank in Sweden to outsource its ATMs when it inked an agreement with Kontanten, Sweden's largest independent ATM operator. Kontanten is now managing more than 1000 ATMs in Norway, Finland and Sweden, and seeing more requests for outsourcing in Europe due to the fact that its specialisation means it can run the bank's own networks at a lower price than the banks themselves.

It is likely that as we enter the next decade the majority of financial institutions won't have their own exclusively branded ATM networks. But they may not have to lose the branding opportunities and client connections that their current ATM network provides.

It won't be long before self-service machines, digital signage and media walls combine into one platform. For the Beijing Olympics, Coca-Cola deployed an interactive touch-screen vending machine from Samsung that they called **uVend**. And future ATMs might work in a rather similar way.

RFID or facial recognition built into the ATM will recognise us and display our bank's brand as we approach. If not, it cycles through the available brands or paid-for-advertising from the banks that use the network. When we insert our cards or tap our contactless phones to sign in, the ATM becomes a HSBC, Barclays or BofA ATM in schema, branding and interface—the branding proudly displayed, and the touch-screen interface modelled to our bank and/or our most frequent ATM activities. So if we

Figure 7.7: Coca-Cola's interactive touch-screen vending machine

like to pay bills at the ATM, that's one of the first options; otherwise it goes straight to withdrawal options, for example.

As it is getting our cash ready (maximum five-second waiting time), the ATM displays related location-based shopping offers for retailers nearby which can be transferred to our phone by touching the offer. It might also, for example, give us a credit card acquisition offer and, if we accept, we touch our NFC phone to the screen and our new credit card is uploaded.

This way, the banks still get branded ATMs, and customers still get the same consistent level of service, but the bank doesn't need to own the hardware in order to provide it to them. Costs for the bank are reduced, customer satisfaction is increased, and the utility of the ATM is optimised.

I think by 2020 this type of interaction will be the norm, and the bank-owned ATM network will be the memory of a bygone era.

Conclusions

The ATM has to continue to adapt to survive, but in doing so, banks must realise they have very limited time to engage customers who are using ATMs primarily because they are time-poor. Think very carefully about the interface and the engagement method. New technologies integrated into the ATM must improve the speed with which customers transact, and not extend the transaction time frame.

While cash is still king, there are threats coming from mobile devices and smartcards which will, over time, have a deleterious effect on ATM utilisation. If ATMs can become part of the solution, then their lifespan will be extended for another couple of decades. For the more adventurous, this represents new revenue opportunities also. Cash deposit, cheque deposit, couponing and passbook updating machines have all been an important part of the restructuring of the branch to a more sales- and service-oriented front-line psyche.

The inclusion of mobile technology into the ATM machine is the next big step. Second will be the big shift around interaction and personalisation, along with efforts to source revenue from self-service platforms. Third will be the specialisation of ATM machines into essentially two form factors— cash-dispensers or full-featured self-service devices. Lastly, or perhaps in parallel, will be the outsourcing of ATM networks by banks to reduce cost.

As cash use declines, the ATM will be an essential platform to transition day-to-day interactions with the bank brand. However, keep in mind that as mobile payments become the norm, the "functionality"' of the ATM is no longer special. As a consumer I can conceivably do everything on my phone that I can do functionally on an ATM—except deposit or withdraw cash.

KEY QUESTIONS

The ATM recently had its 40th birthday and it doesn't look like it is diminishing in popularity anytime soon.

As banks seek to leverage their extensive ATM networks, what are the key drivers for use by customers? Where should ATMs best be located? When do customers use them, and what could prevent them from using a specific ATM?

The case of revenue is still a question—is the ATM a cost centre, or a profit centre? Originally designed to reduce branch load, is it doing its job?

Other self-service devices such as cash-deposit and cheque-deposit machines are also being deployed. How successful are these?

What does the future hold for the humble ATM platform?

The key to self-service is ease and speed of use. Don't get too complicated and when it comes to decisions on what to deploy, strip the process or task down to its simplest form.

How soon before cash-dispensing is the only unique functionality separating an ATM and the mobile phone? If I'm using my phone to pay, how will this reduce my reliance on cash and thus, the bank's ATM network?

Keywords: ATM, Cash Machine, Withdrawals, Account Balance, Security, Shopping Malls and Retail, Usability, Advertising, Coupons, Biometrics, Facial Recognition, Fingerprint, Convergence, Travel Insurance

Endnotes

1 Gizmodo: http://gizmodo.com/5895379/smarter-safer-and-fun-the-surprising-science-of-atms

2 http://futureselfservicebanking.com/

3 http://www.gabriellogan.com/whats-new/page.asp?page=530/Retail-Convergence:--The-Future-of-Multi.html

4 NCR Blog: http://blogs.ncr.com/ncr-banking/consumer_experience/atms-at-the-center-of-the-conversation/

5 For more information see AirtelMoney.in

6 Near-Field Communication

7 ATMIA: http://atmsecurity-pro.blogspot.it/2011/02/how-will-global-atm-growth-forecasts.html

8 i-Design and FirstData Analysis: http://www.firstdata.com/downloads/thought-leadership/fd_atm_advertising_marketinsights.pdf

9 ATM Services Inc: http://www.atmserve.com/placements.html

10 "Privacy in the face of augmented reality", Carnegie Mellon University, 4 August 2011

8 I Trust the Crowd, More Than I Trust the Brand

Social media grows up

The emergence of social media

Social media can trace its roots back to 1978 when Ward Christensen and Randy Seuss, two computer hobbyists, invented the Computerized Bulletin Board System (BBS) as a way to share information, events, announcements, and such with friends electronically. In 1993 the first internet browser, Mosaic, was launched—which would become a critical element in the growth of the web. Through 1994–1999 the first building blocks of modern-day social media emerged—including Geocities (a service allowing you to build your own website), AIM (AOL's instant messenger service), Friends Reunited (a social network in Britain designed to reunite you with old school friends)—and on 23 August 1999, Blogger, the first web log tool, was launched by Pyra Labs.

In 2002 the networking site, Friendster, launched. In just three months it had already grown to three million users[1], but its user base peaked in 2008. By 2004 AOL had 34 million users, and it spurred the launch of MySpace. It was in 2004 that Tim O'Reilly first coined the phrase "Web 2.0" when attempting to define the intersection of the web and applications that facilitate participatory information sharing, interoperability, user-centred design, and collaboration.[2]

Facebook launched in 2003, but MySpace was the dominant social media platform in the US at this time. iTV bought the Friends Reunited network in 2003 as it climbed past the 15-million user mark. It was also in 2003 that YouTube first started its video storing/retrieval service. In 2005

News Corp purchased MySpace for $580 million[3] and Viacom offered Mark Zuckerberg $75 million for the rapidly growing Facebook service.[4] In 2006 they returned with an offer of $1.5 billion. When that deal fell through, Yahoo tried a counter-offer of $1 billion—unsurprisingly it was declined. By 2007, when Apple released the iPhone, Facebook was already outperforming MySpace in terms of monthly visitors. One year later, Facebook had 200 million users, twice the size of MySpace.

In 2008 Facebook tried to buy the rapidly growing social network and microblogging service, Twitter, for $500 million.[5] In the same year, Tumblr launched.

On 15 January 2009, US Airways Flight 1549, flying from LaGuardia Airport in New York to Charlotte, North Carolina, crashed in the Hudson River six minutes after take-off. Both engines of the Airbus A320 were disabled due to birdstrike by a flock of Canadian geese during its climb out. At 3:31pm, the plane made an unpowered ditch landing in the Hudson River. At 3:33pm (two minutes later) Jim Hanrahan (Twitter handle @highfours) tweeted the following:

Jim Hanrahan
@highfours

🔵 Follow

I just watched a plane crash into the hudson rive in manhattan

3:33 PM - 15 Jan 09 via Twitter · Embed this Tweet
← Reply ⇄ Retweet ★ Favorite

In February 2008, in the run-up to the US presidential elections, John McCain raised US$11 million through campaign fundraisers[6] to support his nomination. Barack Obama attended no campaign fundraisers, but used online social networks to raise $55 million in just 29 days.[7] Twitter also gained fame following the 2009 Iranian presidential election when protests were held against the disputed victory of Mahmoud Ahmadinejad. Twitter and Facebook, for the first time, became essential tools in mobilising these protests.

Twitter also broke news of Michael Jackson's and Osama Bin Laden's deaths prior to all the major news networks. Beyonce's baby news made her the most tweeted-about celeb in 2011 at the VMA music awards, with the first twitpic of her touching her pregnant stomach on the red carpet passing 600,000 views in just six hours.[8] During the Superbowl of 2012, Twitter reached 12,233 tweets per second.[9] But that was a blip on the radar—Twitter normally deals with one billion tweets every four days. It's not like there's that much activity really…

Today Facebook is worth roughly $50–90 billion[10] (depending on their share price) after their recent IPO on the US NASDAQ exchange.

Research from Bain & Company shows that as part of a broader customer engagement strategy, social media can be an effective and cost-efficient marketing, sales, service, insight and retention tool. They found that customers who engage with companies over social media spend 20 per cent to 40 per cent more money with those companies than other customers.[11] They also demonstrate a deeper emotional commitment to the companies.

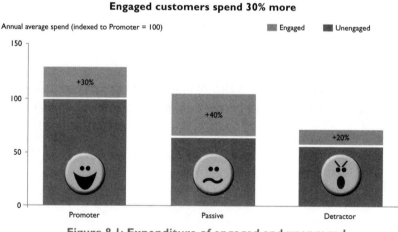

Figure 8.1: Expenditure of engaged and unengaged customers (Credit: Bain & Company)

It's fair to say that there has never been a new media type that has such a profound impact on business messaging and dialogue in such a short period of time—ever. When we put it in that light, there are many banks that should have been taking social media far more seriously for quite some time already. But perhaps they're waiting for the crash, the dot-bomb of social media—when things all return to normal?

Facebook, Twitter, Pinterest, Foursquare—when will it all end?

iCrossing in January predicted that Facebook would reach one billion users by the summer of 2012.[12] That number is pretty significant. Firstly, any corporation that can claim its customer base would make it the third-largest country in the world (behind only China and India) has a case for celebration. Secondly, it doesn't look as if its global growth will slow anytime soon. Lastly, its growth is not restricted by physical distribution or inventory constraints, its marketplace is anywhere you are.

In real terms, Facebook does have some limits on growth. Firstly, it can't have more than the population of available Internet users. Secondly, it can't have more than the population itself right? But these are constraints we wouldn't normally talk about in any realistic discussion of a company's growth curve. Already in the United States alone, Facebook is projected to reach 150 million users by 2014,[13] or very close to half of the projected 320 million population of that time. Name one other company that has grown to encompass close to 50 per cent of the population in just a decade of operating history? Even if it was ten per cent of the population, it would still be incredibly impressive. There's no brand in history that has ever come even close to this growth in terms of number of customers.

Twitter is not far behind, with 500 million Twitter user profiles created by 31 July 2012 and close to 350 million tweets a day (although Twitter

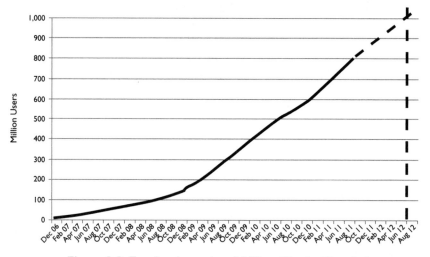

Figure 8.2: Facebook reaches 1 billion (Credit: iCrossing)

itself has said that less than one-third of its users are active on Twitter, or around 170 million users globally).[14] Foursquare, the geolocation social networking service, is up there too, with 20 million users. Then you have newer social networks such as Google Plus (Google+) and Pinterest. Pinterest was the fastest-growing stand-alone website ever to pass the 10-million user mark, which it did back in January 2012. Pinterest was ranked the third most popular social networking website in the US in the first quarter, having come from nowhere just months before.

When will it end? It won't—that's like asking when television, music, the Internet and mobile phones will end—it's an absurd question. In 2011 Facebook had its biggest growth yet, adding 200 million users in just one year. Does that sound like it's slowing? Yet, we struggle to name a Fortune 500 financial institution that has a recognisable head of social media today.

Commonwealth Bank, Citibank and ING Direct are a few of the rare exceptions with a senior executive at the helm of their social media presence. Citi has Frank Eliason (at the time of writing) and he joins a long line of distinguished Twitterers internally, such as Anna O'Brien before him, and Jaime Punishill before her. But Citi appears to be the only major in the US that has any real social media visibility or senior representation in the organisation. Given the massive influence of social media, why have banks been in such visible denial over the power and impact of social? Right now we're still hearing long debates on whether social has any ROI—as if that is seriously a factor for banks to decide whether they should be involved?

Any major consumer engagement technology or capability that has adoption rates of close to 50 per cent of the retail banking customer base should be their absolute highest priority. Yet, it barely registers in respect of both budget and organisational priority at most majors. At the time of printing, HSBC doesn't even have a Twitter account globally to engage its customer base through this medium. That is pretty much unforgivable, or just plain ignorant.

Right now, retail banks should be reorganising with social media and digital responsiveness at the core of the organisation—it is that critical. It should redefine the way banks engage with customers, but it doesn't—it is greeted at the boardroom table by a fundamental lack of appreciation that it has anything to do with "real" banking. Perhaps it is worthy of some marketing effort, but even then it's often relegated to an agency to enact or strategise.

What is it good for?

Social media is a fantastic opportunity to listen to what your customers are saying and form useful strategies for advocacy, inform product and marketing strategies based on real-time feedback from customers, and is increasingly a very powerful servicing tool. While there has been some viral marketing success on social media, if social media is classified as simply a marketing tool or channel within a bank's organisation, it means one of two things:

- The bank doesn't understand the two-way-dialogue nature of social media, and/or
- It has too many traditional marketing people in its marketing team today

So now that we know social media isn't a fad and isn't just a marketing tool, what happens next?

No Facebook allowed here, unless you're a marketer

So the first trick with social media and how it's going to affect the business is learning about how it works. The knee-jerk reaction for most banks when social media came along was twofold. The first was to try to figure out how to dump traditional advertising and PR campaigns down the pipe. The second was to shut down any access internally within the organisation because it was risky for employees to talk directly to the public, and also because it was feared there would be wholesale time wastage from staff playing Farmville and other sorts of unproductive, non-work-related tasks.

The problem with this mindset is that it was fundamentally wrong.

Primarily, the organisation was prevented from learning about the real capability of social media, and this hampered the brand from creating advocacy and engaging customers. Additionally, the reality was that employees were simply pushed away from the desktop internally to their mobile devices, and the risks that employers were hoping to prevent by shutting off access weren't prevented—they were simply pushed outside of a controlled environment.

I visited a major financial services player in January 2010 in Europe and met with the Head of Marketing with whom I discussed social media. I was told by the Head of Marketing that this brand "**didn't believe in social media**".

The logic was as follows: The institution spent hundreds of millions of pounds and dollars on reinforcing and projecting its brand into the public sphere each year, very carefully positioning its brand to potential customers. The bank wasn't ready to start talking with customers in real time on social media about its brand where an issue could potentially "hijack" the conversation and take it to places outside its very carefully crafted brand communication strategy.

The only problem was that customers were already talking about its brand and they were being ignored, which in turn was intensifying the potential for undermining the brand image. It was like a group of customers had got together and had set up a radio station dedicated to slamming this brand, and the institution simply said: "Let's ignore it, no one is listening and if we listen to it, we just give them credibility!"

The strategy shouldn't be to ignore social media, try to shut down conversations around your brand or even attempt to force employees to refrain from social media activity. In February 2011, the Commonwealth Bank in Australia tried exactly that by implementing a harsh social media policy for employees[15]—it backfired massively and the resultant press blitz and union reactions quickly caused Comm Bank to withdraw its ill-thought-out policy.

In recent times some employers have even requested access to the Facebook accounts of prospective employees/candidates—causing massive fallout from civil rights activists.

This problem is largely generational. Most banks have grown up over many years as command and control structures, not working in a networked, interconnected world as they do now. Stupid decisions that don't fit with the crowd, whether employees or your customers, are likely to receive vocal and severe pushback.

Banks need to understand they can't control social media, but organisationally they must participate. Social media strategy needs to be one of informed engagement and encouraging positive use by the employee base. The more banks attempt to control it, the more likely this strategy will end in tears, as the following examples bear out.

You can't control the crowd

Given the rate at which Facebook, Twitter and other such social networking sites have impacted popular culture, it should come as no surprise that financial service providers are seriously starting to think about integrating social media into their business. However, the path to integration of these new media tools into the institution is a tough one. It requires a commitment across the organisation, but achieving such is difficult because finding someone who can garner that broad support is a challenge.

On 11 February 2012, ANZ and Westpac became the first banks in Australia in four years to put up mortgage interest rates without guidance from the Reserve Bank of Australia. Although ANZ joined Westpac and hiked rates, the criticism was not on the rate hike itself, but on Westpac's response to those customers who were angry about the decision and chose to vent their anger via Westpac's Facebook page.

Disgruntled customers started to voice their opinion and dissatisfaction with the rate hike just minutes after the decision was announced. Clearly both Westpac and ANZ had a communications strategy in place as they were engaged with the press all morning after the release of the mortgage rate increase decision. The problem was that whoever was managing the Facebook page for Westpac, in this instance, did not get the memo.

As soon as negative comments started coming across the bow, whoever was in control of the Facebook page at Westpac started to censor those comments. Now, while it may be appropriate to censor profanities, racial comments and the like, negative comments against the brand for a decision that is unpopular with its customers need to be handled very differently.

If banks haven't yet figured out how social media works, it's about time that someone clears the air. Social media platforms such as Facebook are not about spin, control, or nuancing an audience. Despite what institutions such as Westpac might think, they don't own their Facebook page. It is a community forum to discuss the brand, on a platform hosted by a neutral third party—Facebook. In that environment, the responsibility of the brand is to talk—not to censor comments that are negative or challenging, unless they might be considered particularly offensive.

While Westpac thought that this might have been a safe option (getting rid of the negative comments from irate customers), the fact is it just served to make the whole situation worse.

It was as if customers were ringing the call centre or walking into a branch and voicing their dissatisfaction with the rate hike decision, and Westpac was hanging up on them mid-sentence, or worse, ejecting them from the branch forcibly for not being nice to Westpac in their hour of greed. That's how customers saw it, and the press jumped on it in droves.

Here were a few of the press headlines:

Westpac in Facebook Crackdown
National Nine News

Bank bashers united by social media
Business Day

Westpac criticized over social media policy after censoring rate rise comments
smartcompany

Dis-Like: Westpac the Facebook police
Smart Office

Westpac accused of censoring Facebook
Finextra

Social media experts criticise Westpac for censoring Facebook page
Ideal Path

If you are going to be a brand living in the world of hyperconnectivity today, you can't think like you used to think 10 years ago with respect to communications strategy.

Westpac had the opportunity to discuss its rationale on the rate hike in an open forum and accept that customers were not happy with the increase. Half the time when you get irate responses, people are simply looking for validation, for their complaint to be heard, to be recognised. If you can address their problem, then they're generally satisfied. That's how you earn the trust of digital natives—you engage them and you validate their voice. What you don't do is cut them off at the knees if they don't agree with your spin or brand positioning.

Westpac shouldn't feel special though. In September 2009 Ann Minch launched a very public and scathing attack on Bank of America for hiking up her credit card interest rate (APR) from 12 per cent to a "whopping" 30 per cent by posting a very clearly articulated message on YouTube. In the words of Ann Minch...

"I could get a better deal from a loan shark!"

BofA's response to Ann Minch's diatribe was fairly typical of banks confronted by this new medium—it didn't respond. Not until local media picked it up did BofA defend its position, telling Minch that it was in her credit card *terms and conditions* that it could make these sorts of changes. How did that work out for BofA? Within a few short weeks, Ann Minch had coverage on major TV networks, newspaper coverage, as well as over half a million views to her YouTube video. In the end Bank of America really didn't have a choice—it reversed its decision. In doing so, it set a precedent for the millions of BofA credit cardholders who could now cite Ann Minch's case if it tried to do the same thing to them. Yep, BofA was screwed.

Now there are some who might say that BofA shouldn't have jacked up the APR to 30 per cent in the first place, but that is not really the issue. The issue is that BofA completely underestimated the power of the consumer in the new, socially connected, viral, mobile, tribal world. When it had the chance to resolve the issue quickly, it thought like a bank—not like a customer service organisation.

Citibank took an entirely different approach to the dialogue. Citi was the first global financial institution to get Twitter accounts and start actively seeking support and dialogue opportunities. When it launched its iPad app back in August 2011, it even integrated Twitter into the app for customer support.

Social media will hurt you if you don't start responding to customers in more effective ways because social media is powered by people who have a stake in the game, individuals who believe in those around them.

There is an abundance of stats out there now that show beyond any sliver of a doubt that if you put a bank's PR machine up against social media, it will lose every time. Just ask Ann Minch, or Westpac.

But the crowd can get carried away with itself too. On 16 April 2010, ANZ announced it was dumping its m-banking WAP service. The bank sent customers a letter warning that the service would be discontinued from 14 May. Although it was going to continue to support text services and its iPhone m-portal, that was not the message customers heard. Even those who read the letter believed that mobile banking was simply being turned off. Why? Because in the letter ANZ emphasised that customers could use the Internet and phone banking to do those things they used to do on WAP m-banking.

Within just hours of the release of the letter, Twitter was ablaze with tweets such as "What was ANZ thinking when they suspended mobile banking?", "ANZ kills mobile banking", "ANZ to kill mobile banking", "What's with ANZ losing #m-banking?" What's the old saying about bad news travels faster?

The Twitter response was technically incorrect because ANZ had not killed mobile banking in its entirety. It had just suspended its old WAP portal which had been replaced by a better mini-browser and text-based m-banking support anyway. What it should have done on social media was talk about its great *new* m-banking services and, buried within that announcement, let its customers know that the "old", out-of-date WAP service was effectively redundant and thus being phased out.

If you're engaged with your audience and the crowd gets it wrong, you can at least engage and put your message out there on Twitter, Facebook, Google Plus and other channels. If you're not connected to the stream, the first you might hear about it is when it crosses over from social media into mainstream media. Considering many journalists are now sourcing news via social media, this is increasingly a major PR risk for corporations that aren't plugged in.

Most of the larger players are experiencing some growing pains when it comes to Twitter, Facebook and the like. For banks, which are risk averse and often regulated not just by bank regulators, but also by capital markets where they are listed, the risk of saying the wrong thing to the public is a pretty big incentive not to engage early in a totally transparent medium. Which is why the process of adopting social media in the first place has been so hard to sell.

The five stages of social media grief

Dealing with innovation in social media for banks is a lot like the classic five stages of grief. So here are the five stages of social media grief for banks, credit unions and bankers (it probably works for most companies actually):

Stage 1: Total ignorance

When a new innovation such as social media comes out, bankers simply ignore it because "banking has been around for centuries and it fundamentally doesn't change…"

Stage 2: It's just a fad

The justification of lack of action comes down to the risk-averse nature of banks. You think it might just blow over, so no use getting your knickers in a knot over this… "Let's not commit any money just yet."

> "There were people walking around saying the internet was a fad, and they weren't joking. They won't admit it now…Social media is not a fad because it's human."
>
> —Gary Vaynerchuk

You think, "Ok, so now it's on our radar, but it's just a fad—all the fuss will blow over soon." Right?

Stage 3: I still don't get it—where's the money?

Because of Stage 1 and Stage 2 bankers are looking at social media's incredible rise to fame and then looking at their competitors (who are mostly doing nothing) and saying, "Well, as an industry no one is making any money out of this, so let's not bother just yet..."

Does it escape these laggard banking brands that entire multibillion-dollar businesses make their gazillions out of social media today? Yet, this is not really the point—if your customers are there at this sort of scale, then you have to be there also. There's simply no excuse.

"The ROI of social media is that your business will still exist in five years."
—Erik Qualman, Socialnomics

Qualman's quote is great, but I think a better characterisation might be "your business [or brand] will still be relevant in five years".

How can you tell you are one of the organisations at this stage of development? The biggest giveaway would be that likely you have a Facebook page for the bank, but no one actively managing your social media listening post

Stage 4: The sonic boom

Internet banking, mobile banking, social media are all the same for bankers. It's like they're sitting there watching the Concorde or an F15 doing a low-pass fly-by, and not yet registering what they're seeing as significant, until the sonic boom hits them and blows them off their feet. By then it is already too late because at Mach 1 or Mach 2

Figure 8.3: The realisation of the role of social media is a lot like a sonic boom

their competitors are already way, way in front of them. This is where the message finally breaks through the ignorance! BOOM!

This is the stage most banks are hitting today.

If you work in a bank, how can you tell if you are at this stage? Your bank has just hired a Head of Social Media, albeit probably a college graduate who has a nice-looking Facebook profile.

Stage 5: The mad scramble

Excuse the vernacular, but this is the "Oh, crap" moment when bankers suddenly realise they should have been heavily invested in this three or four years ago, and the lack of preparedness is highlighting to the customer base, employees and the world just how out of touch the brand is. The mad scramble may have occurred because of a PR disaster such as those that BP experienced with the Gulf oil spill, or that Bank of America experienced with Ann Minch's debtor revolt.

This is when the knee-jerk hiring spree starts with hit-and-miss initiatives occurring throughout the bank.

How do you know when you are at this stage? The CEO of the bank is talking about social media in press conferences and how the bank is committed to reaching customers better through this medium.

Marshalling the "right" forces

So how do you stop the grief cycle within your organisation? The first thing you need to do is rethink organisational structure around the customer. Social media is a tool for reaching customers, for engaging customers. It is as important as investing in branches, it is just as critical as having a telephone number for customers to call; but more than that, it can help you transform your business internally, too. To fix your organisation to serve customers in the digital and social media age, you need to think independently of channels.

The biggest risk businesses face today is clearly reputational risk associated with a social media blowout. You need someone in charge with common sense, but also with the organisational wherewithal to actually get something done. This is not a junior role. You need a policy that encourages participation across the organisation, but that provides strong guidelines, supported by training, on how to engage customers and how to support the brand through social media. But most of all you need a mechanism to take what you hear from your social media listening post and inform strategy, change policy, and improve customer experience. That is the potential of social media that is so underutilised today.

We'll talk about the organisational capability required to support Engagement in the next chapter, but for now let's discuss building advocacy.

Advocacy and influence—the real ROI

Around 57 per cent of Internet-connected individuals in the US engage on social media platforms every single day.[16] The speed of and access to information that they've come to appreciate have made them more demanding customers. For example, many now expect real-time customer service recovery and quick responses to their online feedback. Hyperconnected individuals regularly broadcast their opinions. And they rely on their friends and social networks for news, reviews and recommendations for products and businesses.

Social media is about giving power to the people. I know it sounds corny, but it's true. Social media is more powerful than simply a voice for the humble consumer though. Social media is creating tribes, groups of friends, networks, viral onslaughts and enabling key influencers in ways that traditional companies can only dream about—or maybe should have nightmares about. If you don't believe me, just ask Mubarak in Egypt.

Social media is here to stay... in a big way.

In countries such as China, the variety of local social networking tools is just as bewildering, with sites such as QQ, 51, Xiaonei, Chinaren, Kaixin001, 5460, Wangyou, and others. Individuals who do tireless outreach to their large networks are deemed to be influencers and are now courted by corporations to help sell new products and socialise ideas. Even less-frequent commentators can serve as "citizen journalists", notifying others about their concerns or experiences with organisations.

The Chinese author and blogger, Han Han, has received over 300 million views to his blog, making him the most-read blogger in China, and probably the entire world. In September 2010, the British magazine, *New Statesman*, listed Han Han at 48th place in the list of the world's "50 Most Influential Figures 2010".[17] Han started as a writer when he was at high school, and won literary awards such as China's New Concept Writing Competition. His first novel, *Triple Door*, with 20 million copies printed, is China's best-selling literary work in the last 20 years.

Han showed a gifted understanding of social media and the broader social landscape by taking on his critics head-to-head via his blog, and engaging his audience. This approach has sometimes meant very direct exchanges with some of his more vocal critics, most of whom ended up worse for wear. In May 2009, Han posted a blog letting China know he was going to publish a magazine, and invited submissions. He offered to remunerate those whose articles or stories were published in his magazine. This was effectively a crowdsourced magazine, and within five days of his post he had already received 10,000 submissions. On 6 July 2010, his magazine, *Party*, was finally published. Although short-lived as a publication, it became the most popular publication on Amazon.cn less than 10 hours after pre-selling opened, largely due to Han's phenomenal social media presence.

Justin Bieber is another social media success. He was just starting out—singing on the street with a guitar case in front of him and entering small talent competitions—when he decided to start uploading some of his videos onto YouTube. Music producer Samuel "Scooter" Braun saw Bieber's videos and sought him out.[18]

Initially US record labels simply didn't see how they'd market Bieber and said that while his success on YouTube was impressive, no one had successfully launched their career via social media. Scooter was thus forced to take an alternate route, leveraging social media and Bieber's willingness to sing almost anywhere.

Within months Bieber had over ten million views on YouTube and was signed by Usher. After Bieber's single, "One Time", and debut album, "My World", were released, he already had over 100 million YouTube views. In the midst of it all, @justinbieber embraced Twitter. His ability to create a flash mob was demonstrated when an event in New York had to be cancelled when 5000 fans showed up to see him. Today Bieber has over 10 million Twitter followers and almost 30 million Facebook fans.

Virtual social networks work to mimic the best parts of "real" social networks, but have a few defining elements that make them more successful. One of the effects is that of "tastemakers", or specialised key influencers who popularise new fashions, trends, brands, products or technologies.

> "For a generation of customers used to do their buying research via search engine, a company's brand is not what the company says it is, but what Google says it is. The new tastemakers are us. Word of mouth is now a public conversation, carried in blog comments and customer reviews, exhaustively collated and measured... the ants have megaphones."
>
> —Chris Anderson, *The Long Tail: Why the Future of Business is Selling Less of More* (2006)

Social media is also surprisingly effective in creating long-lasting ties. Business consulting firm, Bain & Company, released a report[19] in September 2011 that concluded brands that were early adopters of social media (Dell, Wal-Mart, Starbucks, JetBlue, and American Express) have captured real economic value from their budget investments. Surprisingly, Bain concluded that most billion-dollar companies were spending less than $750,000 annually on social media, whereas the early adopters were spending tens of millions and were, not surprisingly, much more effective.

The survey of more than 3000 customers helped identify what makes social media effective. Bain found that customers who engage with companies via social media channels spend 20–40 per cent more money with those companies than other customers. They also demonstrate a deeper emotional commitment to the companies, granting them an average 33 points higher Net Promoter score.

The Bain report also gives some concrete advice for companies that are unsure about their investments and the value that social media can bring:

- Generate awareness at a fraction of the cost of traditional advertising media

- Prompt trials with daily and, increasingly, real-time, location-based promotions
- Improve the product/user experience by embedding social capabilities, i.e. social gaming/shopping
- Wow customers with real-time service response, recovery and technical support
- Capture torrents of consumer insights, and facilitate consumer-led innovation
- Build community and affinity through engagement, earning greater loyalty, spending and referrals

Forrester's 2010 Customer Advocacy rankings report[20] ranked nearly 50 financial services firms in the United States by the percentage of customers who agreed with the statement: "My financial provider does what's best for me, not just its own bottom line." Credit unions ranked much higher than the big banks, as they have in previous years, with 70 per cent of credit union customers saying their financial institutions put their interests first. In contrast, the bottom seven of the rankings in 2011 included Bank of America, Chase, Capital One, TD/Commerce, Fifth Third, Citibank, and in last place, HSBC. These bottom seven rated between 16 and 33 per cent.[21]

In the midst of the recession and ongoing sovereign debt crisis, only 29 per cent of Europeans believed their banks acted in their best interests. This matters because, as the Forrester report points out, there is a strong correlation between customer advocacy and future purchase intention.

What differentiates advocated banks from those that have poor relationships with their customer base? The top-rated banks keep things simple, operate transparently, build trust, and treat their customers benevolently. Social media is currently the best way we know for building broad customer support and advocacy. It's no coincidence that the highest advocated bank in the UK is "First Direct" and they have strong social media integration across the board, but its parent company, HSBC, has a dismal record and doesn't have a Twitter account for talking to customers.

Right now we're seeing a shift in customer sentiment in the financial services space and, specifically, in the way consumers select financial institutions based on "the crowd". Brands need strong advocacy to remain relevant in this new dialogue space, but you won't get that advocacy if you don't provide the respect to your customers that they expect and deserve in the transparent, social space.

That's what Westpac got wrong with its Facebook strategy. By trying to filter or censor the Facebook stream, it thought it was conducting damage control in the old marketing/communications sense of the word. Instead, it increased its risk of brand pushback and negative sentiment exponentially—a much tougher and longer-term issue to deal with.

Respect the crowd—they have enormous power and will be the future of your brand. Understand that the crowd can advocate your brand, that they can be a massive resource. Push them away, and you may never again get their trust.

Talk to them, even when you screw up, and they'll respect your openness and willingness to improve, adapt and engage.

Customers are powerful voices, and they can hijack your brand... in more ways than one.

Platforms for advocates to talk to the brand

In November 2011, Google Plus allowed companies to publish brand pages as a voice for their presence on the newly minted social network. Bank of America had not long before this announced the axing of 30,000 jobs, so sites such as Business Insider joked that the social media team must have been the first to get news of the redundancy, especially when a BofA parody page popped up on Google Plus within the first week of Google supporting the new corporate pages.

The Google Plus page for Bank of America thrashed the US's largest bank with a series of mocking photos, images and other posts. A series of messages satirising the bank's overall business practices appeared regularly on the site.

"Starting tomorrow, all Occupy Wall Street protesters with Bank of America accounts around the country will have their assets seized as part

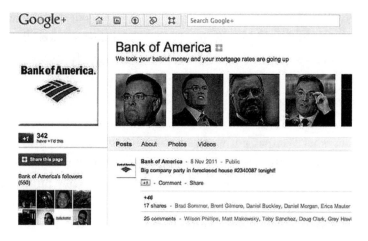

Figure 8.4: The "brandjacked" BofA Google+ page (since removed)

of BofA's new Counter-Financial-Terrorism policy," read a post dated 8 November, "You will sit down and shut up, or we will foreclose on you."

Thus was coined the phrase "brandjacking".

Now some might look at this and say this is exactly the sort of risks that social media carries as an unregulated, uncontrolled, free-for-all environment. However, what BofA really got wrong in all this is that it wasn't ready for Google Plus when brand pages became available. If it had a social media team, with a ready strategy on Google Plus, then the brandjacking simply could not have occurred. Instead it was left to try legal angles to get Google to remove the offending page. The latter was immeasurably more difficult and more expensive from both a cost and branding perspective than simply being early with a brand presence on Google Plus. The biggest cause of the failure here was not social media, but the lack of preparedness of BofA to engage on the medium.

Facebook has recently shifted brand pages to the Timeline format, just like personal profile pages. But many brands have treated Facebook just like a landing page and put static content that never changes. This is not a method for engaging advocates or the community at large either.

With the new Timeline layout, building exposure for the storefront and its products rely on frequently posting advice, promotions and deals. While a post can be "pinned" at the top of the Timeline for up to seven days, smart brands will create a daily posting plan to develop continuous awareness with their fans or advocates. Better yet, they will look for ways to encourage comments actively on their posts by asking questions, creating polls, or publishing other content designed to provoke responses and make their stream an active discussion forum. This is not a skill set readily available in most institutions today.

Customer advocacy aims to build deeper customer relationships by earning new levels of trust and commitment and by developing mutual dialogue and partnership with customers. Put simply, customer advocacy is doing what is best for the customer, even if that entails recommending a competitor's product, or recognising when you can't serve the customer's needs.

Customer advocacy programmes also enable organisations to work out how to leverage social media within community ecosystems. By identifying locations or sentiments with the ecosystem, you also can target or identify segment enthusiasts such as *influencers*, *connectors*, *authoritarians*, and *advocates*. Once you identify the key influencers, you can work out the right networks to seed key messages to get the campaign started and empowered.

It is important to select the right advocates in the crowd. First, find them where they already are. Look at the top blogs in the industry, the most helpful and knowledgeable community members in the support forums, and those who have dedicated their time to managing Facebook pages and online forums, or are active in the ecosystems.

YouTube, key influencers and the testimonial

The crux of an advocacy programme is giving fans or influencers a platform for communicating. You'll want to support their efforts by giving them a publication platform such as a group blog or community so they can tell their story. Ensure they are properly kept up to date, and that the lines of communications are always open for discussion, even when there is negative content. You should reward them, too. Whether rewards are unique access to early innovations, such as the pre-release of your latest mobile app or website, or other tangible rewards, this will keep them happy and advocating.

They key challenge is recognising them, though. If you don't know your customers' Facebook page or Twitter handle, it's going to be almost impossible for you to recognise these customers in the wild. So start by engaging customers on FB and Twitter and figuring out how to connect these social media profiles with their account profiles within the bank.

The aim is not to get "Likes" or followers, however; it is to build a community and engage. There are plenty of organisations asking customers to "Like" them on Facebook and even offering a competition or similar, and then just ignoring those customers or trying to shove more ads down their throats via the social media channels. I can't emphasise this enough: Don't treat social like another marketing channel. It's an opportunity for dialogue, and if you just try to generate ROI by broadcasting more marketing, you'll do far more damage to your brand long-term than you can imagine. Engage, build and collaborate with your customers. That generates advocacy.

The Y-Gen is far more likely to listen to their pals in the social media crowd about "good" or "bad" brands. Influence in the Y-Gen is very much subject to word-of-mouth movements—so much so that key influencers can have far more influence on your brand than advertising can to the younger segment of customers.

Take for example Elle and Blair Fowler, two sisters who post beauty- and style-related tutorials on YouTube under the handles AllThatGlitters21 (Elle) and juicystar07 (Blair). Their videos of make-up

Figure 8.5: The Fowler sisters are super influencers in the crowd (Credit: YouTube)

tutorials and clothing "hauls" quickly garnered a large audience on the video sharing site and rose in popularity. As of April 2012, Elle's videos on AllThatGlitters21 have been viewed more than 114 million times, while Blair's channel, juicystar07, has received over 189 million views.

A quick search on YouTube for "haul videos" will return more than 350,000 results of young vloggers recording their shopping hauls and giving their opinions to their peers. But in the case of Elle and Blair Fowler, their success has made them household names within their peer group, and major influencers in the choice of cosmetics, clothing and jewellery. Far more influential to their peers than TV advertising, magazine ads, in-store promotions, or any other traditional form of broadcast advertising, the Fowlers have hit on the magic formula of turning a knack with their peer group into real careers.

The best video promotion produced by Bank of America, on the other hand, has got 11,956 views and this is after BofA paid YouTube to host its video. However, that's not the most interesting stat here. A video entitled, "Why Bank of America Fired Me", made by a disgruntled former employee, has 453,006 views. This is a brand that has very little customer advocacy or connection.

If you want your brand to be trusted in the new medium of the socially advocated, transparent world of Web 2.0, you need advocates such as the Fowlers. However, the best way to get advocacy from customers or to create fans who will talk positively about your brand is to give them great service. That's tough if all your metrics are about optimising profitability and you can't tell one customer from the next when they visit your website, ring your call centre or visit a branch.

Tying in data on influencers in the crowd with a bank account or credit card number, and then ensuring the message goes down the line to the CSR, teller or relationship manager who gets the enviable task of serving that influencer, is like something out of a fantasy novel for most banks. Such a task appears impossible. But that's what you'll need to do if you don't want to screw up the opportunities that key influencers in the crowd give you.

How well is social media being measured?

Whilst there is evidence of plenty of social media monitoring—pulse-checking using the plethora of free online monitoring tools—most companies report difficulties in trying to incorporate insights derived from social media into their key product development, customer service and sales improvement processes primarily due to a fragmented set of "enterprise" technologies.

It is important to note that the journey to maturity of both companies' use of social media and vendors' development of social media "enterprise" technologies is only three or four years old. Nevertheless closing the ROI loop from measuring the engagement metrics of **Mentions, Likes, Fans, Followers** and **Re-tweets** to the incorporation of the measurement of the revenue metrics of how many of these engagements and conversations lead to new customers and additional revenues from existing customers, is turning into a key strategic objective for companies in 2012.

Right now the best thing you can do is monitor and engage. Listen to what is being said, respond positively and show openness. Why? Regardless of where social media is taking us, credibility is built only through dialogue and open communication with the crowd. If you aren't in the game already, it's getting harder and harder to get a proper seat at the table.

There's no technological fix to being able to tell whether or not people like you. There's only the ability to change the way you talk to your audience.

Crowdsourcing—use the power of the crowd

The "occupy" movement we talked about earlier is an example of how communities work in the social, hyperconnected landscape of today. However, there is a mechanism for using crowdsourcing as a mechanism for designing new products and services that are immediately advocated by customers because they were designed by the crowd, for the crowd.

Commonwealth Bank in Australia has invited the crowd to submit, discuss and vote on ideas that improve the Australian banking experience. Through their web portal, dubbed IdeaBank, Commonwealth has essentially tried to establish a new R&D department, one that turns the bank's customers into an army of brainstormers, beta-testers and budding inventors. Commonwealth Bank offered $10,000 to the creator of the best "idea". The winner of IdeaBank was Andrew Dane, a 22-year-old industrial design student from Herston in Brisbane, who introduced the idea of electronic receipts

Figure 8.6: Use the power of the crowd for good, not evil (Credit: Washington Post)

(isn't that like Square, you ask?). It's early days, however. Commonwealth is hoping to drum up more ideas along the lines of Kaching, a mobile app that lets people make P2P payments via email, Facebook and wireless phone numbers.

The concept of an idea lab or crowdsource engagement platform is hardly new. In fact, CommBank's IdeaBank appears to be a close facsimile of First Direct's "lab" launched five months earlier.

First Direct was the UK's first financial provider to exploit the power of crowdsourcing. First Direct Lab is, according to the official press release, a social platform "that will be populated with content every month such as product designs, service innovations and website concepts. Users will have the chance to critique the content through a comment facility and forum,

Figure 8.7: First Direct was the first to launch a crowdsourcing platform for regular interaction with the crowd (Credit: First Direct UK)

with the feedback collated and inputted into the product or service teams before release".

Finding out how customers interact with financial services can be tricky and expensive. Crowdsourcing appears to be an effective tool that vastly simplifies that, but only if you're an engaged brand with strong social media values. On the one hand, it makes customers feel heard and valued; on the other, it can also drive innovation very cheaply. Innovation can come from anywhere—within or outside of an organisation—and what could be better than sourcing it straight from your own customers?

As well as improving satisfaction, fostering relationships and growing engagement, Q&A communities such as this have the potential to save you a lot of money by helping to iron out product defects and scrap bad ideas before millions of pounds have been wasted in development.

In addition to the UK, there have been some solid examples of Y-Gen engagement in economies such as Singapore, with both DBS and OCBC focusing efforts on crowd engagement for product generation or testing.

In June 2010, DBS bank announced a contest entitled, "I-Designed-A-Bank".

> "Today's youth are confident, assertive and vocal. Their lifestyles and needs have evolved with the times and they no longer communicate in a traditional manner. We want them to express themselves, register their say in the future of branches and tell us how DBS can best meet their banking needs."
>
> —Jeremy Soo, head of consumer banking group, DBS Bank

The contest was divided into two age groups, 26 and under, and over 26, and there were cash prizes in each category, ranking from S$5000 down to S$3000. The bank received over 80 design entries. The contest was open to people of all ages, although 80 per cent of the entries submitted came from those under 26. The youngest person to submit a design entry was 10 years old.

The primary vehicle for submission was a specially created Facebook page.

The result has now been committed to history as a redesigned branch called **DBS Remix**.

Figure 8.8: DBS Remix branch, a result of crowdsourced input (Credit: DBS)

Not to be outdone in the supercompetitive market of Singapore, OCBC then launched its own initiative to crowdsource not just a new branch design, but a whole new Y-Gen-focused brand initiative.

The result was **FRANK** by OCBC. Frank (or *#frankbyocbc*) has been phenomenally successful in building a "cult"' brand following within their intended Y-Gen segment.

Figure 8.9 and 8.10: FRANK (Credit: OCBC)

If you want to engage customers, why not let them choose the direction for a selection of new products, branch design or engagement approaches. What have you got to lose?

A good best practice for this is, not surprisingly, from outside of financial services. A great crowdsourcing platform is also one of the hottest conferences on innovation on the planet—known as SXSW—but more formally as South-by-South-West. It is held annually in Austin, Texas.

Haven't heard of SXSW? Have you heard of Twitter? Of course… Well, Twitter wasn't launched at SXSW, but its "buzz" and rapid growth are often attributed to its appearance at SXSW in 2007. Foursquare launched at SXSW, along with a bunch of other start-ups and apps. In 2006, Jimmy Wales of Wikipedia and Craig Newmark from Craigslist were the primary speakers. In 2008, Mark Zuckerberg from Facebook took the stage, and in 2010, Evan Williams, the CEO of Twitter, was the primary personality on the interactive stage.

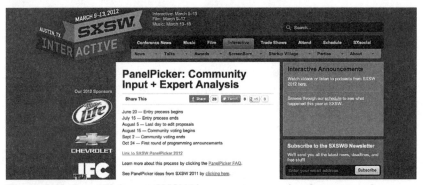

Figure 8.11: PanelPicker at SXSW is a great example of structured crowdsourcing (Credit: SXSW)

However, SXSW uses crowdsourcing to select most of the topics for its interactive week. It does this by first asking for submissions from the crowd, and then encouraging voting over a period of some months. That way, the contents that end up being selected for the event are that which are most popular with the crowd. As a result, SXSW is always extremely well supported and brings more than 20,000 people to Austin annually.[22]

Conclusions: What it all means

As social media continues to be integrated into the mainstream of business and consumer experience, banks have generally been far too slow. Customer advocacy will grow as a dominant new metric over the next few years as banks try to measure the value and popularity of their brands in the social "cloud". As they do so, they will work to improve customer referral and positive brand sentiment. Bank of America certainly found out in 2011—when Bank Transfer Day targeted its brand—that the social dialogue is incredibly powerful as a tool both for growth and for attacking a brand.

We'll start to see search engines incorporating more and more recommendations from our friends or our networks. We'll see geolocation tools starting to record brand preferences, based on our friends' "likes", married with location.

Strong social brand advocacy will become a highly sought-after goal, but it will bring with it a host of complexities. For banks of all sizes, a challenge in building and maintaining market share is delivering on the brand promise. For the first time, marketing and simple customer service will be hardwired into this new metric—having satisfied customers results in stronger brand advocacy and back again.

So there will be the realisation that the *entire* organisation is involved in improving advocacy so that it is positively reflected in social media and promoted by key influencers as referral agents. For this reason, we'll start to see retail banks create a new layer of brand management across both marketing and customer service, using tools such as Twitter, Facebook, Google+ and the like to improve brand perception more broadly.

As the realisation hits top management that everyone in the organisation is a potential brand advocate and part of the dialogue, organisations will work to develop better engagement models and policies around social media, instead of denying access to Facebook and the like within the workplace.

The "*conversation*" will be a big theme over the next couple of years. Talking to customers and solving their problems via open, transparent dialogue will be a challenge for those banks whose processes currently dictate that customers need to jump through hoops, or where support mechanisms are hardwired today into the branch or call centre. We'll start seeing customer service increasingly becoming more broadly distributed through 2012 and beyond.

There are huge advantages using social media, whether it is for support, branding, engagement or research. The biggest power behind social media is clearly getting plugged into consumers and how they see your brand. But beware, the crowd is fickle and cannot be controlled in the way brands have historically managed their customers and their brands—with brute force. Finesse and transparency are the keys to successful social media engagement.

We're starting to see banks that understand that Facebook, Pinterest and Twitter are no longer about shoving the same old messages down new broadcast pipelines. Instead, banks are understanding that social media platforms are now part of a growing dialogue about the brand, products, and customer satisfaction.

Make the crowd happy and you'll have a very powerful brand. Ignore them at your peril.

> **Keywords:** Social Media, Advocacy, Dialogue, Connection, Customer Service, YouTube, Haul Videos, Influence, Engagement

Endnotes

1 *New York Times*: http://www.nytimes.com/2006/10/15/business/yourmoney/15friend.html?_r=2&oref=slogin&pagewanted=print

2 O'Reilly Media and Wikipedia

3 http://news.bbc.co.uk/2/hi/business/4695495.stm

4 Facebook.com: https://www.facebook.com/note.php?note_id=125834784133334

5 *Businessweek*: http://www.businessweek.com/technology/content/mar2009/tc2009031_743025.htm

6 http://blog.mlive.com/elections_source/2008/03/mccain_raises_11_million_in_fe.html

7 http://articles.latimes.com/2008/mar/07/nation/na-money7

8 http://www.mtv.com/news/articles/1669903/beyonce-lady-gaga-vma-twitter-trends.jhtml

9 *Los Angeles Times*: http://www.latimes.com/business/technology/la-twitter-super-bowl-46-new-york-giants-new-england-patriots-eli-manning-tom-brady-madonna-20120206,0,1184572.story

10 Facebook (NASDAQ:FB) traded around $32.50 towards the end of June 2012, putting its market capitalisation very close to $70 billion. This was down from its opening price of around $38, and the share price has gone as low as $20 recently.

11 Bain and Company, "Putting Social Media to Work" (http://www.bain.com/Images/BAIN_BRIEF_Putting_social_media_to_work.pdf)

12 iCrossing: http://connect.icrossing.co.uk/facebook-hit-billion-users-summer_7709

13 eMarketer, as quoted on http://therealtimereport.com/2012/03/06/forecast-twitter-to-grow-4x-faster-than-facebook/

14 TechCrunch Analysis: http://techcrunch.com/2012/07/31/twitter-may-have-500m-users-but-only-170m-are-active-75-on-twitters-own-clients/

15 SocialMediaToday, 12 Feb 2011: http://socialmediatoday.com/craigthomler/269570/learning-social-media-policy-mistakes-commonwealth-bank

16 57 per cent of Americans have joined a social network, making it the number one platform for creating and sharing content (Universal McCann, 2008)

17 *New Statesman*, "50 People Who Matter 2011", http://www.newstatesman.com/blogs/2011/09/han-popular-blogger-star-china

18 *Los Angeles Times*: http://www.latimes.com/business/technology/la-fi-tn-justin-bieber-twitter-king-20120703,0,1667104.story

19 "Putting Social Media to Work", Bain & Company, 12 September 2011

20 Forrester, Customer Advocacy 2010: How customers rate US Banks, Investment Firms, and Insurers: http://www.forrester.com/Customer+Advocacy+2010+How+Customers+Rate+US+Banks+Investment+Firms+And+Insurers/fulltext/-/E-RES55483

21 "The Least Trusted Banks in America", *New York Times*, 3 February 2010

22 CNN Tech: http://www.cnn.com/2012/03/08/tech/innovation/sxsw-changing-culture/index.html

Part 03

The Road Ahead —Beyond Channel

9 Living with Continuous Technology Improvement

On 19 April 1965, Gordon Moore, co-founder of Intel Corporation, published an article in *Electronics Magazine* entitled, "Cramming more components onto Integrated Circuits". In that article he stated a law on computing power that has remained consistent for more than 40 years, a law that drives technology development today and for the near future.

> "The complexity for minimum component costs has increased at a rate of roughly a factor of two per year... Certainly over the short term this rate can be expected to continue, if not to increase. Over the longer term, the rate of increase is a bit more uncertain, although there is no reason to believe it will not remain nearly constant for at least 10 years. That means by 1975, the number of components per integrated circuit for minimum cost will be 65,000. I believe that such a large circuit can be built on a single wafer."
>
> —Gordon Moore's prediction in 1965

The term "Moore's Law" was reportedly coined in 1970 by CalTech professor and VLSI pioneer Calvin Mead.[1] Essentially what this meant was that Moore predicted *computing power would double every two years*. Since 1965, that law has held true and remains the backbone of classical computing platform development. This means that since 1965 we have been able to predict reliably both the reduction in costs and the improvements in the computing capability of microchips, and those predictions have held true.

Let's put it in perspective. In 1965 the number of transistors that fitted on an integrated circuit could be counted in tens. In 1971 Intel introduced the 4004 Microprocessor with 2300 transistors. In 1978 when Intel introduced the 8086 Microprocessor, the IBM PC was effectively born (the first IBM PC used the 8088 chip)—this chip had 29,000 transistors. In 2006, Intel's Itanium 2 processor carried

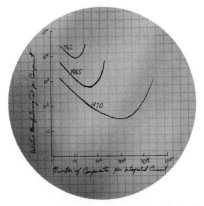

Figure 9.1 Gordon Moore's original graph predicting transistor growth (Credit: Intel Corp)

1,700,000,000 transistors. Today we have chips with over 15 billion transistors. Want a better understanding of the scale of this transition? Transistors are now so small that millions of them could fit on the head of a pin. Quite a change from a single transistor that typically measured ½ inch by ¼ inch back in the 60s.[2] While all this was happening, the cost of these transistors was also exponentially falling, as Moore had accurately predicted.

In real terms this means that a mainframe computer of the 1970s that cost over $1 million had less computing power than your average smartphone has today.

Have you ever watched the movie, Apollo 13? Remember they were trying to work out how to boot up the **Apollo Guidance Computer** without breaking their remaining power allowance? Well, that computer, which was at the height of computing technology in the '70s, had around 32k of memory and ran at a clock speed

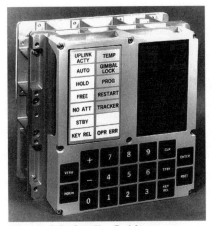

Figure 9.2: Apollo Guidance Computer (circa 1970) Credit: Draper Labs

of 1.024 MHz. When the IBM PC XT launched in 1981 it was already about eight times faster than the Apollo computer. The current iPhone 4S is roughly two million times more powerful than the Apollo 11 Guidance Computer that landed men on the moon. In fact, the first iPhone model (the 2G as it is now known) had more computing power in one handheld device than NASA had in its entirety in 1970.

Those little musical greeting cards with a chip inside them to play a tune have more computing power than all the Axis and Allied forces had combined in World War II.

In 1961 Monash University in Melbourne, Australia, purchased its first computer for the computer science department, the Ferranti Sirius.[3] This computer had 1k of memory, 3k of additional storage in cabinets, and was programmed via tape. It cost around A$50,000 in 1961, or, inflation adjusted, around US$360,000 today. It had a 1 Hz processor. The basic computer was in the form of a narrow cabinet standing on the floor along the back of a 6 ft 6 in desk. The cabinet was 4 ft 9 in high and 6 ft 9 in wide.

A typical laptop computer today (say, a Mac Book Pro or a Sony VAIO) has 250,000 times the memory, is 4–8 million times faster and costs 1/500th of what the Ferranti cost as a computing platform. It is also quite a bit smaller.

This is Moore's Law in action. Moore's Law has the same sort of impact on all sorts of devices that have a chip or CPU in them—whether it is our washing machine, fridge, tablet device, TV, mobile phone, computer, or an electronic razor/shaver.

This has resulted in advances in storage media as well. It's common for us to carry around hard disks now with 1 terabyte of storage space, or to carry phones with 64 Gb (gigabytes) of storage space. In 1995, 64 Gb of storage space would have cost around $50,000; in 1985 the cost would have exceeded $4 million (at approximately $71,000/Gb).[4] Today, the average 64 Gb SD card costs less than $100. To illustrate, in 1995 I bought a 2 Gb Hard Disk for my 486 Pentium Computer for around $2000. It means that the USB memory stick we carry around with us would have taken a room full of hard disk platters in the '70s. Today it's tough to buy even a memory stick with only 2 Gb of memory—it's simply too small.

There are other laws or principles at play here also, such as Gilder's Law[5], which says that improvements in bandwidth will occur at 300 per cent of the rate of Moore's Law. In the next five years we will be looking at devices capable of 1 Gbit/s downlink speeds.[6] To put that in perspective, by 2016 our mobile phones or tablets will be able to download a DVD-quality movie from anywhere in less than a minute.

The Singularity concept

Ray Kurzweil is credited with extending this principle of computing advances into what is broadly known as the concept of the Singularity. The Singularity, according to Kurzweil and others like him, is a point in time in the not-so-distant future when machines become vastly superior to humans in every way due to the emergence of true artificial intelligence. Computers will be able to improve their own programming, form factor and processing capability in ways we could never conceive. This will result in a paradigm shift that sees mankind coalescing with its own creations—man and machine merging into one.

> "The computer in your cell phone today is a million times cheaper and a thousand times more powerful and about a hundred thousand times smaller (than the one computer at MIT in 1965) and so that's a billion-fold increase in capability per dollar or per euro that we've actually seen in the last 40 years...
>
> "The rate is actually speeding up a little bit, so we will see another billion-fold increase in the next 25 years—and another hundred-thousand-fold shrinking. So what used to fit in a building now fits in your pocket, what fits in your pocket now will fit inside a blood cell in 25 years."
>
> —Ray Kurzweil, inventor and futurist[7]

Kurzweil's propositions are based on tracking the exponential growth of technologies on the basis of the various technology and network "laws". These technology improvement cycles are actually speeding up, so the growth curve of core technologies such as integrated circuits or the rate of Internet adoption trends upwards where they eventually reach exponential growth. Those core technologies then have an impact on a whole range of other industries or fields other than computing, such as health care and medicine. Today, faster computers have allowed us to map the human genome and there are services where you can have your own genome mapped for just a few hundred dollars, a task that would have cost a billion dollars just two decades ago.

So think about the implications of this. A computing device with the power of our current iPhone would fit inside a "nano-robot" computer the size of a blood cell in two or three decades' time. What does that mean for medical sciences? What will it mean when the device we carry around in our pocket is more powerful than the most advanced supercomputer available today? How will such technologies impact our life? Self-driving cars, computer-based personal assistants that can predict and anticipate our needs or manage our calendar without needing to ask us any questions; holographic telepresence when we're away from our loved ones; computers built into everything, from the paint we put on our walls, the clothes to jewellery we wear, to sensors in our bathrooms that can monitor our health based on our morning's ablutions…

However, one of the most significant developments Kurzweil predicts centres around the development of 3D printing and replication technologies.

> "Ten years ago, if I wanted to send you a movie, I would have sent you a FedEx package. I can now send you an email attachment. The same goes for a music file or a book. What used to be physical products can now be sent as files of information."
> —Ray Kurzweil, *Vice Magazine* interview, 2009[8]

Ubiquitous 3D printing technology means I might soon be able to email you a toaster, toast, a blouse, a solar panel or a module to build housing or transportation. What we now consider physical products will eventually become information files—email attachments.

In the past, manufacturing something made out of a plastic was generally done through a technique called injection moulding. For metal forms, components were either cut from a block of raw material, cast via a mould, or cut from steel plate. Often these methods required a very expensive mould or die that was used for that one single component. 3D printing allows new techniques such as additive manufacturing, where raw materials are used to build up the form gradually, printing one layer at a time.

Figure 9.3: 3D printers are a reality today

3D printers are advancing in capability rapidly. Already 3D printers today can print wearable fabrics, integrated circuits, blood vessels, cells and organs (a kidney, a bladder and an ear have recently been printed, for example[9]), engine components, model aircraft, etc. It currently takes around six hours to print a human kidney using a 3D bioprinter, starting with a scaffold and adult stem cells from the patient's own body so that the new organ is not rejected. While still largely in development, imagine what the 3D printer will do to the world's manufacturing sector. There will be a huge business in manufacturing 3D printers at least! Well, that is, until we can print a new 3D printer using your old one…

A great quote to illustrate the concept of the realisation of such technological advancement is one from the late science fiction author, Arthur C. Clarke:

"Any sufficiently advanced technology is indistinguishable from magic."

An iPad would certainly have appeared magical to someone living in the 18th century.

While 25 years is a long way away, let's think about the devices we'll be using in 2016, just four years away, and how those devices will enable the banking experience. The technology of 2016 should inform the type of services and technology utilisation required for banking in four years' time.

Faster, smaller, smarter

Advances in computing architecture, data storage and transmission, along with improvements in materials science, are enabling us to build computing devices that would have been considered science fiction just a few years ago.

William Gibson in a recent interview with the BBC said that it's getting harder and harder to write science fiction because the technology is moving so fast. "If I write something set 60 years in the future I am going to have to explain how humanity got there and that's becoming quite a big job," explains Gibson.[10]

In 1987, Gene Roddenberry launched Star Trek: The Next Generation[11] as a reboot of the Star Trek franchise. The show went on to attain widespread popularity and spun off major motion pictures, and three other TV show franchises.

A regular feature on Star Trek TNG was a device called the PADD™. Now this was imagined as a 24th-century computing device by the futurists associated with the show. However by 2010 the iPad effectively introduced a product that mimicked this "24th century" technology. How can you predict the future

Figure 9.4: The PADD—how *Star Trek* imagined computing to be in 2364 (Credit: Paramount)

when within just 22 years we've built a device that we previously thought would only likely be possible to build 200 years in the future?

Predicting the long-term future of computing is much tougher these days than predicting the near-term future and impact of technology improvements. We are literally getting to the point where we could build a mobile phone that is effectively too small to use practically, and where portable computing platforms would be powerful enough that I could soon duplicate the entire computing functionality of a small bank on something I carry around in my bag or pocket.

So let's discuss key areas where computing improvements are going to affect retail banking, or the behaviour of consumers in the retail banking space, in the next four to five years:

1. The "Screen"
2. Electronic Paper
3. Multitouch, Interactive Displays and Recognition
4. Network and location awareness

The "Screen"

The current iPad launched to much fanfare with its use of the "resolutionary" retina display, as Apple has dubbed its screen technology. Retina display is so described because the human eye can see detail only to a certain maximum resolution, and the retina display meets or exceeds that ability. So when you look at a retina display, the resolution is high enough that you can't discern the pixels in an image or on the screen.

Why is this significant? Technologically we're reaching the limits of human perception to discern the difference between a screen and real-world images. Conceivably, within a few generations of current screen technology, it may be difficult to discern the difference between a real-world image and an image on the screen. Right now work has begun on improving screen technology from not only a resolution and natural colour perspective, but also to reduce the weight, size and power consumption of screens.

Over the last few years, a few companies have introduced OLED or Organic LED screens into their mobile devices, TVs and laptops. The advantage of OLED technology is a super-bright, extremely thin screen that takes almost no power to run but retains the resolution, colours and capability of traditional LCDs and plasma screens—in fact, generally the resolution and quality of the image are far better than on a traditional screen. Within a few years, we'll have wallpaper-thin 60-inch TV screens that take less power to run than our average lightbulb. In fact, these devices run off 40–50 per cent less power than the most energy-efficient LCDs currently in the market. With contrast ratios of 1 million to 1, that is pretty impressive.

Sony and Samsung have thus far led the way in the commercialisation of OLED technology. In April 2008 Sony demonstrated a 3.5" display screen just 0.2mm thick that displayed a resolution of 320x200. It also recently demonstrated a 21-inch flat-screen TV that was only 1.4mm thick. Samsung, not to be outdone, has recently demonstrated a mobile phone that has a foldable display screen, manufactured using OLED technologies.

The Sony VAIO "Contrast" concept[12] features a foldable, seamless OLED for the display and a touch-screen keyboard, but the keyboard can also be hidden so that the whole thing turns into a display. It is made of high-performance, flexible bioplastic, and would be thin enough to slide under a closed door if it went into production. A wearable walkman that can be worn as a bracelet is another "Contrast" concept. The near future of this technology is called QD-OLED, or quantum dot OLED, and could be even thinner and sexier than the current OLED standards. Pretty wild.

3D displays have become common in just the last few years, with various approaches to the technology. Some manufacturers are even releasing TV screens that don't require special 3D glasses to see 3D effects. The early commercial uses of this technology included the 3DS Nintendo game device, which allows players to play games in 3D without the use of 3D glasses.

Computer software can now take traditional movies and convert them into 3D versions of the same. Recent movies re-released in 3D include Star Wars: The Phantom Menace and Titanic. How long before we see Casablanca and Gone with the Wind in 3D?

Corning has recently featured videos showing the use of embedded screens in a range of commercial glass applications, themed as "A Day of Glass". Due to Moore's Law, the cost of screens is also coming down, meaning that it won't be long before we see screens everywhere in our daily lives. In our tables, on our walls, built into the windows, whiteboards, walls and panels we use in the workplace. Sounds like science fiction? In this case you can expect to start to see media walls and in-built displays being deployed everywhere within the next four to five years. They will be commonplace by 2016–18.

Electronic Paper

Very closely related to soft-screen or OLED improvements is the area of electronic paper. This has been termed the most significant development in print technology since the invention of the printing press by Gutenberg in 1440.

It was actually in the 1970s that Nick Sheridon at the Xerox Palo-Alto Research Centre developed the first e-paper. This electronic paper, called Gyricon,[13] consisted of polyethylene spheres embedded in a transparent silicon sheet. Depending on whether a negative or positive charge is applied, the spheres would translate into a pixel that emits either a black or white appearance, thus looking a lot like normal paper.

The Amazon Kindle and Barnes & Noble Nook are both examples of implementations of E-Ink® technology. They implement a type of technology known as electrophoretic display. This is essentially an information display that forms images by rearranging charged pigment particles using an applied electric field. The Kindle and Nook devices use a hi-res, active matrix display constructed from electrophoretic imaging film manufactured by E-Ink Corporation.

However, in recent times, E-Ink has upped the ante on the capabilities of e-paper by introducing Triton Imaging Film. These e-paper displays are no longer limited to shades of monochrome, but deliver high-contrast, sunlight-readable, low-power displays that can show thousands of colours. According to E-Ink, the Triton display applications including:

- Readers—e-readers, e-textbooks, e-newspapers, e-magazines, e-documents
- Wireless devices—remotes, game controllers
- Thermostats and industrial displays
- Mobile point-of-sale units (signature pads)
- In-store signage

Already the Kindle, Nook and other e-paper devices are in widespread use. However, in the next five years, we expect e-paper to be deployed in form factors not much thicker than a few sheets of paper. Such devices will be highly portable, flexible enough to roll up, give us a modest ten hours of battery life, and be able to simulate newsprint, books, and web pages in either grey-scale or colour.

Companies such as Amazon are championing the deployment of e-paper as a cheaper, more paper-like experience to that of the iPad or tablet platforms. The advantage of being able to use the device in natural sunlight can't be ignored.

Figure 9.5: iPad

In 2009, Samsung showed an early prototype of a flexible e-paper display using WiFi technology which they called the "IN" device, short for "Innovation Newspaper". Place the device in its cradle before going to bed, set the embedded alarm, and wake up to an updated feed of news for your morning coffee. Within five years such devices should be relatively commonplace.

Flexible TFT or thin-film-transistor technology is allowing the likes of Samsung and Sony to trial smartphone, tablet and laptop designs that are extremely thin, and flexible enough to bend. Sony's latest incantation is a 4.1-inch OLED screen that is just 80µm (micrometres) thin. A human hair is a comparatively hefty 100µm.

Figure 9.6: Sony's latest screens can be wrapped around a pencil

These new screens are also very simple to manufacture. In fact, the organic components used can be dissolved in common solvents from which the screens are actually printed, instead of being assembled!

What this means is we're going to find increasing uses for screens in everyday life where screens replace paper, where they are integrated into glasses, clothing, furniture, kitchen fixtures, you name it.

Multitouch, Interactive Displays and Image Recognition

The biggest single improvement in screens and devices over the last few years, however, is obviously the integration of multitouch touch-screen capabilities. Of course, we've had touch-screen technology for many years, but not touch screens that allow us to use multitouch or multiple fingers on the screen simultaneously. Multitouch enables unique actions such as pinching, poking, panning, etc. that were not possible with previous iterations of touch screen which could only cope with one-digit interaction at a time. It enables more natural interaction, such as using an on-screen keyboard to interact with. This is a fairly recent technology and comes through the likes of the iPhone, iPad, Microsoft Surface and other devices.

More recently we've been hearing a lot about haptic touch emerging so that touch screens and devices will provide more interaction capability. Haptic feedback, for example, would allow us to use an on-screen keyboard that feels like a real keyboard in its response to our touch. It accomplishes this by using vibration technologies similar to the motors that are activated when our phone is on vibrate mode. Apple is reportedly releasing a haptic-feedback, multitouch "mighty mouse" as a replacement for its current Mac mouse series.[14]

The one perceived shortcoming on the iPhone is the poor comparative usability of the on-screen keyboard, which has an unusually high error rate compared with its RIM competitor or a standard QWERTY keyboard. While Siri is an effort to reduce reliance on an on-screen keyboard, haptics may work as a mechanism to resolve the usability issues of an on-screen keyboard. If we feel like we are using a real keyboard as a result of haptic feedback, then the theory goes that the keyboard (and the user) will behave as if it is "real", and accuracy will be improved dramatically.

This is why it is possible that the mouse and physical keyboard will disappear over the next 10 years. Screens will become the PC or laptop, our fingers will be the mouse and an on-screen haptic keyboard will be there when we need to type.

As a result, screens will get larger, perhaps as large as the entire table or desk surface area, and for "desktop" PCs, we'll more than likely use something more akin to a drafting table that sits on an angle with the screen embedded, rather than the current separate displays. As we do more things wirelessly via LAN, and as more hard disks become solid state, we'll do away with DVD drives pretty much completely, so our computing devices will be contained completely within our screen form, whether that be a tablet, a smartphone, a screen, a desk or a wall.

The iPhone started all this, but it is by no means the finish. The next seven to ten years will really produce a very significant revolution in these technologies. So as bankers, you have to be ready to use this and produce applications that leverage these capabilities.

As screens become more pervasive, one of the first broad uses will be to shove more advertising in our faces via digital screens, walls and signs. Electronics industry analysts predict that by 2015, about 22 million traditional signs in grocery stores, shopping malls, restaurants, health clinics and other businesses will be replaced with digital displays that interact with consumers in various ways.[15]

An early example of this was a vending machine produced by Unilever which gave away free ice creams when you interacted with a "smile". The technology behind it is sophisticated, but the concept is simple: consumers walk up to the machine, smile and are rewarded with a frozen treat. According to information provided by Sapient and Unilever, who collaborated on the product design:

> "When its motion detectors sense someone is near, the machine beckons them to come closer and interact. Using facial recognition technology, it can then recognize a person's age, gender and emotion, and measure their smile using a 'smile-o-meter'. If their grin is wide enough, they get free ice cream."

Figure 9.7: Unilever's smile-activated ice cream vending machine

So it won't be long before the signage in a bank branch is detecting a customer's age and offering him a student loan, a first-home mortgage, a ladies-only shopping credit card, or a retirement planning session, based simply on his face, gender and age.

Digital signage deployed today might include the likes of a 2m-by-4m (6 by 12 feet) high-definition video screen, a 70-inch touch-screen digital whiteboard, a 70-inch holographic display that shows 3D images viewers can discern without special glasses, or a see-through display that projects colour images inside a pane of clear glass.

Retailers are even experimenting with concepts such as immersive signing, digital signage, HD content, background music or sound effects and ceiling LED lighting, coordinated to respond to customers as they enter a store.

This technology doesn't need to be complex. While some use quite complex image-recognition software and cameras, others use readily available technology such as XBox Kinect units integrated with a fairly ordinary PC unit to handle image recognition. Even the recently launched Samsung Galaxy S3 has "Smart Stay" technology built into the phone so the forward-facing camera can track eye movements and determine if someone is reading a web page on his phone so that it doesn't power the screen down to save battery.

Network, location, behaviour and context awareness

Within city locations, it's becoming increasingly difficult to find locations (unless they're underground) where we don't have either mobile data network access or wireless access through WiFi. Add in the fact that most mobile devices now incorporate GPS chips, and our device will soon be connected online all the time, and know where we are.

Early innovations around the use of these geolocation technologies included the ability to tag photos with a location or check in using Foursquare, Facebook or Google+.

Context, however, pulls all of this together. The core of banking in the emerging future will be understanding how a customer needs his bank to facilitate a transaction or financial event. We'll talk more about point-of-impact marketing in a couple of chapters, but understanding how and why customers use banking is critical to developing contextual banking. We'll talk more about this in Chapter 13.

Enterprise-wide implications

So now you bankers have geeked out with me, why am I sharing such futuristic technologies and concepts with you?

The simple fact is that you're not going to stop innovations in the use of technologies that affect our banking experience day to day. If anything, you're going to see the development of such technologies speeding up—on an exponential growth curve. The time you have to adapt is shortening, and the impact to your business is increasingly disruptive. The longer you sit there telling yourself you have "time" before you have to change your approach to the business of banking, the more at risk your business is.

By correlating Moore's law, Gilder's Law, Metcalfe's Law, along with the psychology of Maslow's Hierarchy of Needs, we get an unavoidable, unstoppable, and unquestionable impact on adoption rates for new, innovative technologies. For the last 100 years or more, time to adoption rates has been collapsing. The emergence of Moore's Law led these adoption cycles to speed up, then the web again boosted the cycle. Mobile smart devices, social media, always-on IP connectivity, and wireless access have further compressed the adoption cycle.

While it is conceivable that adoption cycles can't reduce down to nothing (i.e. instant adoption), the fact is that not even the largest bank in the world could ever hope to slow adoption rates of something such as social

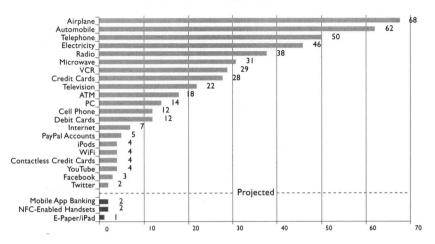

Years till 50 million users

Figure 9.8: The shortening adoption cycles related to innovation

media, mobile or internet banking. For example, when Internet commerce started to emerge in 1996 and 1997, many bankers and traditionalists in business either honestly felt that this was a fad, or they were so significantly threatened by the new "challenger" that they tried very hard to convince all and sundry that it was really a fad. And some argued it very passionately too...

> "Visionaries see a future of telecommuting workers, interactive libraries and multimedia classrooms... Commerce and business will shift from offices and malls to networks and modems... Baloney. Do our computer pundits lack all common sense? The truth is no online database will replace your daily newspaper, no CD-ROM can take the place of a competent teacher and no computer network will change the way government works... Yet Nicholas Negroponte, director of the MIT Media Lab, predicts that we'll soon buy books and newspapers straight over the Internet. Uh, sure."
> —Clifford Stoll, *Newsweek*, 27 February 1995[16]

Or this telling quote from a reformed banker...

"I thought in rural Tennessee we would not be confronted with Internet banking in my lifetime. I was wrong…"

—John L. Campbell, CEO of First Community Bank of East Tennessee, 1997

Or this classic prediction from Bloomberg in 2007?

"Apple will sell a few to its fans, but the iPhone won't make a long-term mark on the [financial services] industry."

—Bloomberg, 14 January 2007

The fact is, the financial services industry cannot keep the traditional retail banking system going with old artefacts, channels and technologies because we're facing something more destructive than the Global Financial Crisis or the "Great Recession". The industry is facing something more unrelenting in its progress than even the Internet "fad". Banks are facing a complete re-engineering of the customer behaviour dynamic and a complete shift in the way financial interactions occur at a consumer level. A world where traditional banking with branches, ATMs, cash, cheques and the same old, same old simply won't cut it. Why? Because the rate of change is rapidly speeding up, and no one is immune.

Simply put, the speed of change is disrupting first and foremost what it means to "bank".

In many ways, new organisations appear better equipped to utilise the new technologies and these fill the breach in gaps between consumer behaviour and the industry at large. Banking gets redistributed via technology, experiences and journeys. Banking evolves from being somewhere you used to go, to something you do.

Some may argue that there are still plenty of "normal" customers who like to visit a branch. Customers who still write a cheque. But those customers are in an ever-shrinking demographic. If you are catering first and foremost for this behaviour, your business will be operating in an ever-shrinking market. Then you have stats that fly in the face of those assertions. The fact that even the most loyal long-term customers aren't visiting the branch with the frequency they used to, that cheques are irreversibly in decline, and that even the oldest customers are moving online.[17]

It isn't ever going to return to "normal" folks—we are in the new Bank 3.0 paradigm. Constant and unrelenting change, based on the increasing capability and availability of new technologies, and customers who just can't get enough of these new gimmicks—this is the new world order.

Here's the complication.

For the current generation of customers coming on stream, the stuff that you consider "new" as bankers, stuff such as Facebook, iPhones, Internet and NFC is not new for the Y-Gen customers of today. This stuff is just life. It's normal. They don't have to learn the Internet, mobile, social media or multitouch—it is just the way they live their lives. So when you don't serve them this way... you're simply irrelevant.

Now, the reality is ***banks are not going to disappear***. However, their role in the day-to-day operations of the financial system will change.

If retail banks are no longer the mechanism for cash distribution and cheque processing, what is their role? Financial products, credit mechanisms, repositories of money, etc. all remain. However, the distribution system is completely disrupted by technology. As Mr Gates said, banking might be necessary, but banks...

Given that third-party players such as Square, PayPal, Simple and Movenbank are increasingly infringing on the traditional banking infrastructure—banks may have to fight for their very existence. PayPal has been a great example of this. Twelve years on and most banks still consider PayPal a new kid on the block, and yet it is the number one payments platform used on the Internet today. New start-ups such as Dwolla consider PayPal an incumbent and are already trying to disrupt its business.

So banks need to become very, very good at being virtual and digital repositories of their clients' money, allowing access to that money anywhere, at any time. Most of all, however, banks need to be great service organisations because the third-party challengers that are nipping at their heels will invariably be faster, more adaptable and more in tune with their customers and their behaviour.

Constant innovation, experimentation and testing of new ways and means to engage customers are the only things that will save banks from being replaced by more relevant mechanisms that utilise consumer will and device evolution in the coming years. If I sound like a broken record, please forgive me…

Oh and for the Y-Gen/Digital Native, I won't explain what a broken record is. Ask your grandparents.

KEY LESSONS

Technology appears to have reached a point where exponential improvements are nothing new. Adoption rates for new technologies are skyrocketing and prices are coming down so more people have access to these technologies.

New materials science such as organic LEDs, flexible circuit boards and chips are producing entirely new possibilities in device construction and design. As wireless technologies become increasingly pervasive our devices are more intelligent because of their access to networks.

New interface mechanisms, augmented reality and increasing use of technology embedded into our everyday experience will continue to make new technology advances just the "norm" of doing business.

Delivering value, but in a relevant and contextual way, will become key—not just shoving more ads at me via a digital wall, my mobile phone or tablet. Understand my behaviour, what I'm doing and why I might need a deal or a product from a financial institution, and cater to that behaviour or the evidence of a need.

Technology is no longer exceptional, nor is it an alternative choice for consumers—it is the way we do our banking in the Bank 3.0 world. It is the primary, day-to-day relationship channel for your customers now.

The branch cannot compete in any meaningful way.

What will such a future bring? How does it impact service providers in the finance space? How can they prepare?

Keywords: Disruptive, Moore's Law, 3D Printing, Screens, Image Recognition, Exponential Growth, Haptic Touch, Artificial Intelligence, The Singularity

Endnotes

1 Excerpts from *A Conversation with Gordon Moore: Moore's Law* (Intel Corporation, 2005), p.1

2 IBM: History of Transistors, IBM 1401

3 http://archive.computerhistory.org/resources/text/Ferranti/Ferranti. Sirius.1961.102646236.pdf

4 mKomo.org, "A history of storage costs" (http://www.mkomo.com/cost-per-gigabyte)

5 See http://www.netlingo.com/word/gilders-law.php

6 See Wikipedia.org articles on WiMax, 4G, UMTS, and Spectra Efficiency of long-range networks utilizing 802.11, 802.16, and 802.20 standards

7 CNET News, 19 Nov 2008,Q&A: Kurzweil on tech as a double-edged sword, Natasha Lomas, http://news.cnet.com/cutting-edge/?keyword=Ray+Kurzweil

8 http://www.vice.com/read/ray-kurzweil-800-v16n4

9 Source; BusinessWeek.com (http://www.businessweek.com/technology/bioprinting-the-3d-future-of-organ-transplants-01092012.html)

10 http://www.bbc.com/news/technology-11502715

11 http://en.wikipedia.org/wiki/Star_Trek:_The_Next_Generation

12 SonyInsider.com

13 Wikipedia article on Gyricon

14 Geek.com, "Apple has a mightier mouse that needn't be moved at all", 5 Oct 2009

15 *USA Today*, "Digital Sign Revolution", 11 April 2012

16 "The Internet? Bah! Hype alert: Why cyberspace isn't, and will never be, nirvana", Clifford Stoll, *Newsweek*, 27 Feb 1995

17 Pew Internet Research showed that the fastest growing demographic on Facebook was the above-50 generation (http://www.pewinternet.org/Reports/2010/Older-Adults-and-Social-Media.aspx)

10 A Land in the Data Cloud

In 2011 Google launched the Chromebook—a laptop that doesn't contain a conventional hard disk or hard-coded software. What flash memory is available is dedicated to simply managing the Chrome OS and some basic functionality to connect to the web. All the data lives in the cloud. The software used is accessed via the cloud. Need to work on a document or a spreadsheet? Just fire up the Chromebook, connect to the web and access the required documents virtually.

As we become more mobile, a great deal more of what we do will need to become detached from our work computer, laptop or enterprise network server. The ability to get access to our data and core applications on the move is one simple example. Restricting this data to physical devices in one specific location is not going to work. So the trend has been for laptops to get more capable so that we can carry them with us. But laptops still have to deal with access to corporate data, security issues and such, regardless of their portability.

Already, we're moving away from the laptop as our primary device. We're moving into a distributed computing paradigm at the personal level. The growth in tablet computing is ferocious—already mobile devices outsell traditional PCs; within just a few years tablets will outsell PCs too. As we move into a more mobile way of life, it will be essential that our data moves with us. Anyone who has ever been through the process of attempting to simply sync his contacts across multiple devices will know that currently this process is pretty hit and miss. Now, extend that to personal medical data, financial information, important company documents, purchase history, favourite movies, music and so forth. How do we get access to this information on the move?

Figure 10.1: All the major platforms see a silver lining in Cloud services

For this reason, Google, IBM, Apple, Microsoft and a host of other players are making various bets on what is known as *cloud computing*. Cloud computing uses the Internet and central remote servers to maintain data and applications. It allows the use of applications without installation and allows users access to their personal data and files using any device that has Internet access. Cloud computing abstracts users from their applications and data by providing those facilities via a browser, effectively minimising storage requirements and leaving processing to the cloud rather than requiring heavy local processing capability. It does, however, rely heavily on bandwidth to get expeditious results.

Although Windows still runs on over 80 per cent of PCs and laptops,[1] the fading importance of the PC means that Microsoft is no longer all-powerful in the software and platform game. While some look to Google's Android and Apple's iOS to produce a viable competitor to Windows, the fact is that with increasing reliance on mobile devices the role of the PC operating system is not a key driver in the future of computing. This is why with Windows 8, Microsoft is moving towards an operating system that is device "agnostic" and truly portable, where we can fire up our tablet, mobile, PC, gaming console or TV and see a consistent interface with access to the data we need. This is a smart move.

While there are hundreds of firms offering cloud services—web-based applications living in data centres—Facebook, Amazon, Microsoft, Google, IBM and Apple play in a league of their own. Each of these firms is building its own global network of data centres and working on a bunch of services within the cloud.

Some of the more successful cloud initiatives in recent times are simple plays around online storage, data and transfer. Whether that be DropBox™, YouSendIt™, or the likes of Flickr, the cloud of data being stored, moved and managed is rapidly growing. This is not surprising. Data storage is abundant and cheap.

We talked previously about Moore's Law, and discussed briefly Metcalfe's Law on networking and Gilder's Law on growth in bandwidth and data-carrying capacity of networks. These all add up to a time soon when our devices are likely to be connected full-time with all the capacity in terms of storage capacity, data retrieval and transmission that we'd ever need. Once that occurs, it's likely that we'll abandon most of our local storage of data and files, and move to devices always connected to the cloud. Why transfer files constantly from one device to another, or sync our smartphone every few days, when the data is shared constantly via an online store of all our personal information, our private and public data and our identity and associated artefacts? If all our devices connect with the same data in the cloud, we need never sync or transfer a file between our devices ever again.

The Players

Apple has recently started to make a foray into cloud computing in a major way. It is building a $1-billion data centre in North Carolina, possibly the largest of any in the world.[2] iCloud (previously MobileMe®) was the first of a series of online services based on cloud computing designed to create new revenue streams for the tech giant. iCloud is designed to connect all our devices and push information up and down to keep everything synced and up to date. iDisk, incorporated into iCloud, gives users 20GB of remote hard disk space for storing files that are too big to email, photo galleries, and such. Not to be outdone, both Google and Microsoft followed with their own cloud initiatives.

While Microsoft has launched Office365 as an attempt to win over cloud enthusiasts, Microsoft's poor mobile showing kept it behind both Apple and Google's Android initially. Microsoft's recent teaming with Nokia and its Windows 7 efforsts, and now Windows 8, are designed to improve integration with the cloud. Microsoft's competitive play against iCloud is a combination of Office365 with SkyDrive.

The questions remain as to what services work, and what revenue models will drive cloud computing. For corporations, the business case is simple: shifting to the cloud reduces infrastructure costs and moves platform and application costs to an OpEx (Operating Expense) model instead of CapEx (Capital Expense). In the current economic environment, this has to be promising. Distributed platform access and the benefit of data centres in the cloud also create more opportunities for more agile institution operations and different models such as telecommuting, homeshoring, portable or outreach branches and so forth.

If you are sitting there reading this right now with some scepticism about the possibilities of the cloud as it pertains to banking, think about this. Arguably the most successful cloud computing service today, with close to one billion users, is Facebook.[3] It is run almost completely through our browser or apps. It allows users to collaborate, share information and communicate online—all things that businesses want to do too...

If you are a decision-maker in the business, you need to think about whether some of your core infrastructure, platform or applications would be better placed in the cloud so that your workforce can be more innovative and productive, and so that your customers can get access to your services more widely and freely. A cloud solution can be just as secure as your own dedicated infrastructure, plus you get the benefit of distribution, agility and better-developed shared services.

The ability to rent computing and storage capacity as needs arise, as well as applications that can be used to manage accounts, deploy frontline sales staff, or just about any other function, gives CIOs the ability to help their organisations seize new market opportunities without making huge upfront investments.

One of the more interesting elements to think about with cloud computing is what happens to the role of the bank in payments. If the majority of payments processes on a consumer and B2B space are increasingly deployed within the cloud, then the need for such services to be provided by banks to their customers directly becomes effectively redundant. After all, PayPal is already in the cloud...

Thus the cloud is becoming a top priority for global financial services CIOs. Gartner reported in 2011 that in Europe, the Middle East and Africa (EMEA), 44 per cent of financial services CIOs expect that more than half of all their institutions' transactions will be supported via cloud infrastructure by 2015.

> "Early cloud adoption, especially in the FS sectors, may have been limited to non-core areas and proofs of concept, but it is set to go mainstream, moving the heart of the business, transaction origination and processing, into the cloud."
>
> —Peter Redshaw, managing vice-president at Gartner

Services that move into the cloud

Many of the international financial network systems in place today are proprietary, or have grown up around proprietary networks that existed before the interwebs were mainstream. For example, bank ATM networks exist largely on closed-loop, proprietary networks either independently for a bank, or as a "network" in the case of switching services. The SWIFT interbank payments network existed from the 70s[4], well before the IP-layer of networking technologies we see today.

Visa and MasterCard's own payments networks connected to POS devices, back-office payments engines and banks themselves. While Visa, MasterCard, Amex and others have integrated IP connectivity in recent years, these networks remain largely proprietary systems and hence the networks are still able to substantiate their "interchange" fees and so forth. The domestic or regional payments networks of Giro, the networks behind SEPA, or the ACH networks in the US, are similarly deployed generally as proprietary networks, with recent hooks via an IP-layer.

It is inevitable that most of these networks will be integrated into the cloud in the next few years. In fact, one could argue that most of these networks are already heavily integrated with IP-layer architecture. However, for networks such as those of Visa, MasterCard and even SWIFT, there is a chance that the cloud could be quite disruptive to them. It could even mean the appearance of new competitors in the mix that circumvent the traditional wires in favour of less proprietary systems.

For example, in the case of point-of-sale systems, merchant integration and card payments, there is an argument that the entire "swipe" paradigm is under threat via the digital wallet. What the incumbents are hoping for is an orderly transition from plastic to mobile, from swipe to tap. However, as the likes of Apple and Square have recently shown, there is the question as to whether one needs a "register" or POS at all.

The recent announcements by both MasterCard and Visa in respect of their digital wallet platforms are a partial admission with respect to this as both are designed to work ubiquitously across devices, applications and use cases.

However, it's likely that as banking becomes measured by the core "utility" of its operations and the ability to bank whenever, wherever required, engineering bank products, services and journeys to work in the cloud will become absolutely essential for building engaged brands. The likes of Citibank have already started on this journey.

Citi's online payments strategy has evolved into the provision of an API that can provide the processing backbone, as well as the banking licence, for the likes of PayPal and other new payment providers. Rather than building a process and a fixed interface between two partners, as has long been the industry approach, Citi has already moved to a common interface layer that any partner could access. The purpose of this is to abstract the complexity of payments integration with partners, but still retain a secure and stable operating environment.

> "The threat of terrorism is real and money laundering is real... Citi has banking licenses in 149 countries and complies with all the regulations in those countries. So we are quite slow to move sometimes but when we do, we move with a lot of power. These are things that on this side of the banking industry we struggle with daily."
> —Yobie Benjamin, Chief Technology Officer, Global Transaction Services, Citi[5]

While regulation and legacy systems are often cited as a reason for slow integration and innovation, Citi's API move could be interpreted as simply copying the approaches of progressive start-ups. The likes of Square, Twitter,

Facebook and PayPal already provide access to their systems via APIs, so if banks want to compete in the customer journey, then flexible, manageable access to bank products, processes and functionality is required. Citi made the decision, for example, to build out the likes of the entire **debit and credit card onboarding process** in an API, meaning that an approved partner could issue and provision a credit card in real time. How so? Google Wallet was the first implementation of the API layer, enabling Google both to onboard a customer and provision a card securely in real time to the end user's mobile phone, without the need for clumsy paperwork and identity verification mandated by the majority of card issuers.

In doing so, Citi was not making the process less secure. After all, the owner of a mobile phone had already provided his name, address, social security number and other data points to his network operator, and in many cases, he was already a Citi customer. There was really no benefit in restricting the issuance of new "cards" (albeit digital version of cards at this point) to a manual process that required physical paperwork or in-branch KYC (Know-Your-Customer) hurdles.

Citi realised, like others, that the future of the bank lay not in physical networks or process, but the ability to enable banking in real time as required.

When banking and payments are in the cloud

To date, most banks have been reluctant to embrace cloud computing. With some justification, compliance teams fear moving essential functions from server-based systems to the cloud will put sensitive information at undue risk. Yet the potential benefits of the model to the financial services industry are such that for banks to reject the cloud outright would be a mistake.

The biggest reason to consider a move to the cloud, however, are the very limitations of current systems. With the average customer accessing the bank via digital channels such as the web, mobile and social media hundreds of times a year, there is a compelling need to move operations to a more flexible platform.

Most banks are founded on legacy IT infrastructure developed on mainframe systems that hail from the 60s. Large banks have sunk literally billions of dollars over decades into legacy systems, so it is not surprising that there is reluctance to abandon long-held investments. The problem, however, is that these core systems were developed in a different age, an age where the transaction was at the core of what banking was.

Today, in a world where the customer is at the core, the suitability of those legacy systems is in doubt. These systems persist with their outdated hardware and software because of the expense, difficulty and risk of transferring everyday operations and the massive quantities of data to more advanced, up-to-date infrastructure.

Among the most attractive benefits of cloud banking, in particular, is being able to deploy (in an economically feasible way) the "champion-challenger" model. This adds a competitive dynamic to the way processes are improved and chosen.

As Big Data become core to the strategy of a bank in the making of risk decisions, or in engaging customers wherever they may be, more of the processes in the value chain will become data-driven, based on real-time analytics. Over time this means that human resources in the value chain are replaced with what is known as Algorithmic Operations (AOs)—virtual processes and decision making capability. For example, instead of a risk officer adhering to a manual risk decisioning process assessing individual customers for a loan, increasingly those decisions will be done on a pre-approval basis, or in real time as a lending decision is required.

As banks progressively replace human resources in the value chain with algorithms and data-driven decision matrices, their intellectual property increasingly resides in "code"—the data in the system and the ability to deploy solutions relevant to customers—not in structures such as branch networks, product divisions or trading platforms. Unless those things can be brought to bear in the cloud and leveraged off dynamically, legacy platforms become representative of a barrier to agility, competition and customer engagement.

Already some banks are making tentative steps into cloud deployment. In January 2012, BBVA announced it was moving its desktop applications into the cloud via Google Apps' platform. In the announcement of the move, BBVA made sure the market understood that this was a move to increase staff productivity, and not a move to transition sensitive customer data into the cloud. At least not yet.

> "The main goal is to promote innovation and making decisions and increase productivity. We are in a challenging market and need to make faster and more accurate decisions… mobile access to systems is also vital."
>
> —Carmen Herranz, director of innovation at BBVA[6]

However, much earlier than the BBVA move, some of the more progressive institutions were already floating the concept of moving core banking systems into the cloud for the same reasons—improved productivity, decision making, portability and speed.

In May 2010, Michael Harte, CIO of Commonwealth Bank in Australia, announced CBA's intention to set up a cloud-based operation with Amazon Web Services. Harte explained the rationale behind this move as looking to reduce the cost of purchasing IT and related infrastructure by paying for services on demand as CBA grew, especially as reliance on more digital integration and real-time engagement became essential to CBA's customer experience.

In December 2011, Deutsche Bank went live with its first phase of cloud deployment, namely its IaaS (Infrastructure as a Service) development platform. One of the imperatives at DB was faster development times for bank partners, developers and vendors, and what it called an "aggressive standardisation" attempt.

So the first driver for private cloud deployment is clear. Standardisation of employee internal applications and systems across the enterprise, and very agile platforms that can scale up and down with demand. The next obvious step would be finding applications that allow integration with customers or bank partners in real time with the same flexibility.

Other applications for the cloud

I guess it's an obvious statement, but for small to medium-size businesses, banks provide a logical partnership as an enabler for a range of bank services. Banks such as Bendigo and Adelaide Bank in Australia have in recent times been providing a range of services to small businesses beyond the traditional merchant, trade finance and credit services, including extended services such as cash-flow and accounting analysis, SME advisory, website/minisite development, telecommunications deals as a reseller, and similar services. Recently ANZ launched The Small Business Hub as a way of extending more services to their SME clients. American Express has gone one step further with its Open Forum platform as an attempt to engage the broader business community in actively sourcing solutions. Bendigo Bank has been able to facilitate community involvement through its PlanBig portal.

It has occurred to me that many of the services we're seeing in this space are candidates for the cloud. Here are a few that come to mind:

Accounting, cash-flow modelling and credit services

Plugged into an SME's basic accounting package (think MYOB, Quicken, etc.), the ability to provide some intelligent tracking of cash-flow, help businesses think about aged receivables, and the need to rightsize a credit or overdraft facility, are all very valuable tools. Extending a basic accounting facility with cash-flow analysis tools that is an extension of your banking relationship is not a stretch for corporate internet banking platforms either. A range of tools that allow SMEs to plug in their basic financial statements and get some great analysis on break-even, cash-flow, and various what-if scenarios are starting to emerge in this space too. Think of these like PFM (Personal Financial Management), but for business. Does that make it BFM?

If this could be married with basic account information, accounts and invoicing data, etc., this could give SMEs a nice tool embedded within banking to start looking at a basic overdraft facility, factoring, inventory financing and a whole range of complementary services.

Easier merchant and P2P enablement

E-invoicing is becoming increasingly important as part of the SME toolset for commercial banking. RBS has recently launched a range of services including e-invoicing and electronic accounts receivables/payables management. HSBC Net for some time now has offered Accounts Payable Integration which allows for e-invoicing, better cash-flow projections and management, etc. The name of the game here is simplifying processing, improving the likelihood of rapid payment and better bank integration into an SME's payments and receivables process.

The decline of cheque use in the UK has been widely documented. In 2000, cheques represented 25 per cent of all non-cash transactions, but by 2010 they accounted for less than five per cent.[7] By 2020 that number will be less than one per cent.

This is also where the mobile device and P2P platforms come into play. While debit cards have had big success in recent times, as credit and debit cards are integrated into our mobile phone for contactless payment capability, it is obvious that the use of cheques and cash will further decline. With the introduction of Square it is becoming increasingly simple to provide merchant type services to accept payments.

Person-to-Person or Peer-to-Peer is a huge innovation for SMEs and businesses. In 2009, financial institutions, including Bank of America (BAC), ING Direct and PNC Financial (PNC), rolled out so-called P2P technology that lets customers use the web or a mobile phone to transfer money from their account to any other account. JP Morgan Chase and others soon followed. Within the next two to three years our phones will become the payment devices of choice for paying SMEs that provide services.

Think of it this way. What's the single biggest challenge an SME business has day to day? Probably the toughest in recent years has been cash-flow. Closely associated with this is the simple challenge of getting paid for services in a timely fashion, etc. So if you enable a better or easier payments capability, the likelihood is that as an SME, I can get paid faster and quicker. No more "The cheque is in the mail" problems.

This makes cloud services even more viable as SMEs will increasingly rely on virtual platforms to effect and receive payments. The ability to augment basic banking services to capture the need for virtual P2P and payments capability is a no-brainer.

SME Community Building

There are over 1.4 million groups currently active on LinkedIn[8], many dedicated to SME forums and the like. Ecademy.com is a social networking site based in the UK, but active globally with more than 17 million members, most of whom are SMEs. A survey by O2 in the UK showed that more than 600 SME businesses were joining Twitter every day, and that 17 per cent are already actively using Twitter to support their business.

SME community building is a great way to empower businesses and is a logical extension of the already powerful network that banks have with their customer base. Banks don't use their community of clients to encourage interactions, but it makes increasing sense for bankers, as a trusted intermediary, to utilise their community to encourage internal business between their SME clients, creating a sort of private value chain within the bank ecosystem. The cloud and online communities such as LinkedIn, Ecademy and others seem like the perfect partners to kick this off.

The advantages of a private cloud

The advantages that private cloud implementations offer are the security of a private, secure system, and the agility, utility and simplicity of conventional cloud architecture.

Deutsche Bank, mentioned earlier, has also developed new modular data centre designs and elastic computing platforms, underpinned by its core identity management platforms, including a Microsoft Active Directory system and an SAP-linked Global LDAP directory.

Bank of America, in its efforts to build up private cloud capability, ran just south of 90,000 physical servers and 40 per cent of them were running in the cloud. BofA has set the target to create scaling and capability similar to that of Amazon Web Services environment too, according to Brad Spiers, Head of Compute Innovation at BofA. Interesting to note is that BofA is heavily investing in graphics processing capability, solid-state storage and in-memory databases, with large, fast processing and decision-making capability as the objective.

NAB (previously National Australia Bank) of Australia has also committed extensively to private cloud infrastructure as it has moved to a platform-as-a-service concept as part of its programmes built around what it calls NextGen. NAB's Next Generation Platform programme started as a core systems replacement, but has quickly morphed to encompass cloud capability. UBank, NAB's online direct banking brand that launched in 2010, was the first to be deployed on this platform in the market. As mentioned earlier, UBank has been an outstanding success.

Big Data

With trillions of dollars on the line, banks and financial institutions pay close attention to the emerging "exaflood" of available data about their customers and the world around them. Hugely complex markets are about to become transparent because of new regulations, the push for transparency and pricing pressure, and that means masses of new data available for analysis and utilisation. Scalable processing of that data will require outsourcing, thus giving birth to new industries. Millions of people will need to be trained to deal with all this. Data will not only be big by nature of the quantity of data in the system, but by the huge industry that emerges to support it.

Can Big Data help banks avert the next financial crisis? Could regulation resulting from the last crisis yield newly available data that could themselves become new mega-resources for innovation?

The reality is that regulation is actually part of the push towards Big Data. Over the last decade or so, financial reporting requirements around money laundering, suspicious transactions, identity management and know-your-customer data have exploded. The likes of BASEL II and III and suspicious-transaction reporting as it pertains to terrorist financing and AML (anti-money-laundering) have been as much about visibility of such data to outside agencies, as they have been about organisational awareness and readiness to respond from a compliance perspective.

However, now the likes of Google Wallet, PayPal, Square, Apple and others are attacking transactional data as if it is fair game. While many in the banking industry are extremely resistant to exposing such data, the reality is that customers are increasingly demanding more responsive banking relationships, and are prepared to trade off some of the security concerns in return for benefits such as PFM, daily deals or offers. All kinds of businesses will need to learn to work with this data, new providers will need to emerge to serve them. They have to get outside of silos—it will be a dramatic opening up. As banks won't have enough capital to build it all themselves. it will have to be an open-source model to build the infrastructure.

The problem right now is that analysis of data takes months. It requires specific programming or scenario-modelling, and then data mining projects around this can take weeks or months. By the time the data is actually available, its application or value may itself be challenged. The challenge Big Data will need to solve is extracting that data and processing it efficiently, and that will require more visibility on the data, along with outsourcing and external data-smoothing and what the industry calls "story extraction"—finding the usefulness in the data.

As we're seeing with the cloud, scalability is going to be key. Banks just aren't scalable around data. In fact, banks regularly throw out or fail to utilise terabytes of data with massive potential.

An example of this is credit card purchasing data. Banks are always struggling to ensure that consumers keep using their cards. Revolvers, or credit card customers who maintain a so-called "healthy", regular balance on their credit card, are attractive to banks because they continue to pay maximum interest rates on that money (compared with other forms of credit). In an effort to stimulate card usage, banks throw offer after offer at consumers, hoping these deals will stimulate ongoing activity. However, the simplest way to encourage usage would be to marry the customer's previous purchase activity with the available offers. If you know I've shopped at a specific merchant before, then a deal for that merchant is likely to be far more effective than pitching me an offer for a "deal" that I've never shown any interest in before.

> *"Your data is sexy... don't throw it out."* Sean Park, Anthemis Group, at SIBOS Innotribe in 2011

This type of data gets discarded or ignored frequently by even the biggest banks. When you start reviewing the masses of transactional and behavioural data that banks have with respect to our money and life, the argument to have the ability to match that data to new use cases that help customers in real time is extremely compelling. Imagine using geolocation data on top of that layer of data to figure out how to deliver an offer for a specific merchant in real time based on the customer's location and proximity to a favoured merchant. That would make for a very compelling offer.

The argument may be that privacy is a reason for dragging the organisation's feet on the Big Data side, but I believe that is largely an excuse for putting the brakes on in recent lean years. There are, however, two sides of Big Data that are consistently discussed in the industry as having strong business benefit. The first is the ability to make better trading decisions, and the second, the ability to connect with customers in the retail environment.

In a trading environment, the financial benefits of Big Data appear extremely compelling. The ability, for example, to understand trading cost analytics, capacity of a trade, performance metrics of traders, etc. could be massively profitable to a trading business. How do you create alpha opportunities to outperform, based on that data? The ability to create algorithms that forecast prices in the near term and then make trading decisions accordingly is what will likely drive the profits of banking and trading firms in the near term. Speed of execution is, of course, another key platform capability to leverage this learning and has spawned a raft of low-latency platform investments designed to capture the value of these so-called "alpha" data points.

On the retail side of the business, the ability to sell to a customer remains paramount, especially as acquisition and cross-sell metrics take a dive in the physical space. The ability to test small offers quickly, then ramp up, will be key in leveraging data and converting behavioural patterns into revenue.

> "Don't confuse data content management with big data. Dealing with big data requires mining through massive volumes of data to find trends and reveal insight."
>
> —Mike Atkin, managing director of Enterprise Data Management Council[9]

A key element is building a relationship with a customer who has no interaction with the branch, but still connects regularly via direct channels.

We'll talk about engagement in the next chapter, but key to engagement modelling will be the data we bring to bear on the problem.

Unfortunately for banks, but fortunately for the Big Data industry at large, collaboration will be the key to leveraging these types of opportunities: collaboration with retailers, network operators, daily deals providers, mobile search providers, and so forth. There is no way that banks will be able to do this in a closed-loop internally, within the confines of the current bank systems, and there's no way that banks will be able to stay competitive without collaboration and offering delivery in this way.

Big Data analytics break down the barriers between traditional, structured information that is typically stored in a data warehouse, and unstructured information and content—video, voice, text, images, etc.—that are now part of the digital landscape. We have vast amounts of unstructured customer data in our organisations, such as application forms, telephone conversations, email dialogues, transactional history, etc. Bigger still are the masses of content and data that are generated by customers on the web at large in the form of blogs, forums, wikis, tweets, Facebook posts and the like. Is there a way to bring this data together to serve the customer better?

Behavioural analytics are a subset of these efforts. The likes of FICO are using behavioural data to detect fraud both from a third-party and first-party perspective.

In the age of social media, your customers are already sharing attitudes, opinions, intentions and behavioural information by the petabyte in the public domain. Mining this data to gain insight into how your customers (and non-customers) act, feel and talk about your brand, products, service, and pricing, could represent massive competitive advantage. There is even the opportunity to monitor your brand and interact with customers in the social media domain in real time that you didn't have before.

Then the question arises as to how you'll use all this data.

The first obvious area is to utilise data to produce better targeted marketing offers. However, increasingly banks will be deploying solutions that overlay key data on the natural environment so that they can change consumer financial behaviour or influence decisions in real time.

Augmenting our environment with the application of smart data will be an intriguing and highly profitable business over the next decade.

Augmented reality

Something that is a little bit out there, but interesting to think about, is the emerging technology around image recognition and data overlays in the real world. We've had OCR or Optical Character Recognition for many years now, but there have been recent improvements in image processing and matching. Recently Google has developed search engine technology called "Google Goggles" that allows users to search based on images taken by their camera phones. It is currently in beta with some reasonable search support for books, DVDs, landmarks, logos, contact info, artwork, businesses, products, barcodes, and text.

Augmented reality (AR) is the term for real-time, digitally enhanced interactions with the physical real-world environment, where real-world elements are merged with (or augmented by) virtual computer-generated imagery, touch or positive feedback, sounds and even possibly smells. The resultant mixed reality is what we call "augmented". The term "augmented reality" is believed to have been coined by Thomas Caudell, an employee of Boeing, in the early 1990s.

Augmented reality is changing the way we view the world—or at least the way tech users see the world. Picture yourself walking or driving down the street. With augmented-reality smart displays, which will eventually look much like a normal pair of glasses, informative graphics will appear in your field of view, and audio cues will provide information or feedback on whatever you see.

Applications of smart glasses could be anything from an equivalent of our current laptop display while we are on the move, to simply a Bluetooth plug in our app phone showing us in real time a virtual HUD (head-up display) with key information from our device (Caller Id, local weather, e-alerts or appointments, etc.). Incorporating image and facial recognition software, along with RFID technology, smart glasses could remind us of the name and details of a key business contact, an old school friend who passes us by while we're chilling out at the mall or the current price on

Figure 10.2: Where's my nearest NY subway station? (Credit: Apple)

Figure 10.3: Augmented reality aims to contextualise data in new ways (Credit: Google)

Amazon of that book we're looking at through a retailer's window. The possibilities are far-reaching, and just a little freaky.

In any case, within just five years, we could have access to such devices married to our app phones, watching a movie or receiving a video phone call. That is all pretty amazing. Glasses could become the next iPhone-type fashion accessory.

Right now both iPhone and Google Nexus phones incorporate some AR applications that are very simple to use and very, very cool.

Combining this type of technology with digital cameras or camera phones is one thing, but there is an emerging technology that might change the way we see our environment and the things around us in an entirely new manner.

Google Glasses

At Sony's 2009 CES (Consumer Electronics Show), Tom Hanks appeared on stage with Sir Howard Stringer, CEO and president of Sony Corporation in the US. Sony was parading its new high-definition video glasses that are currently under development—these HD specs have a widescreen 16:9 HD-quality image projected onto the lens. In the show version, they also had in-built cameras.

In 2003 MIT published a paper on the concept of smart glasses they called "The Memory Glasses".[10] These memory glasses used both cameras and FLIR (Forward-Looking Infra-Red) for image recognition and a HUD system for visual cues. The prototype glasses were interfaced to a large database of objects that could be recognised by the glasses. Facial recognition software could be used in tandem with the glasses to help us recall an acquaintance's name or specific details. MIT experimented with both overt and subliminal cues for proactive memory support using the glasses, showing the application for those suffering memory loss, Alzheimer's, or amnesia.

Recent advances in nanotechnology applications have enabled the creation of prototype contact lenses with a built-in pressure sensor using a novel process that etches tiny electrical circuits within a soft polymer material. In other research, scientists at Boston Retinal Implant Project have been developing a bionic eye implant that could restore the eyesight of people who suffer from age-related blindness. The combination of these various technologies leads to the conceptualisation of some very interesting technologies.

Google is expected to launch its Google Glasses commercially within the next year or so, but officially launched Google Project Glass to its developer community late June 2012.

Some of us might be excited by the idea of an incessant stream of data floating in front of our eyeballs, but there are just as many others who might recoil at the thought. For one thing, how can we interact authentically with the world around us when everywhere we look we're prompted to check in, reminded that we have a meeting in 30 minutes, or fed instructions about which path is the best walking route to take?

Figure 10.4: Would you wear Google Glasses? (Credit: Google)

In Google's concept video the man wearing the glasses meets a friend in a bookstore by following the most direct walking path to where his buddy had checked in.

The problem is that in doing so, he might have missed out on a couple of interesting books had he taken a more circuitous route. Google Now is the data and interface platform that will underpin Google Glass technology, and it's definitely a work in progress.

Of course, the concerns with all that data being fed into our line of vision are well founded. Distracted driving as it relates to making phone calls and texting pales in comparison with what could happen when people use AR glasses in their everyday lives. Cities such as Fort Lee in New Jersey have taken these concerns one step further in recent times by imposing a law that issues offenders who text and walk at the same time an $85 fine.

Most of us have probably been bumped into by pedestrians walking their dogs, people window-shopping, fast walkers looking to the other side of the street, slow walkers trying to navigate an unfamiliar neighbourhood, kids running around aimlessly, men in a hurry looking at their watches, women looking in their bags, girls browsing their iPods for a new album to play, kids playing a portable game console, and other similar scenarios. These are not uncommon. The problem with banning an activity such as texting is that suddenly a precedent is set where any of those other activities are just a step away from being challenged as illegal also.

Until AR technology also helps us avoid collisions with fellow pedestrians, it might be a problem in transition.

CONCLUSIONS

As already borne out by our review of technology adoption, along with social media, the smartphone phenomenon, and so forth, customer experience is now in a state of gradual, but constant change. What is going to happen next to the customer experience? The explosion of data is going to change a customer's expectations of how he connects with his bank in real time.

The way we receive, prioritise and review information will have to change. We are simply getting too much of this information now to deal with it the way we always have.

The amount of data we have to deal with is staggering, so the real art for banks will be in processing, sifting and applying all this data in helpful, creative ways to serve the customer better, or to help the business make more timely and accurate decisions.

Secondly, the way we all interact with technology is going through an evolution. Touch screens are allowing our fingers to replace the mouse and keyboard, and new ways of accessing data, user-interface approaches and application platforms are opening whole new ways of organising, processing and prioritising key content. Augmented reality is changing the way our devices will interact with our environment.

Lastly, the core platform technology to enable this will have to be highly flexible, agile and open to collaboration. Increasingly the cloud and APIs will come into play so as to connect various players in the customer ecosystem to provide better real-time problem solving and real-time solution offering. Banks that stay within their own data boundaries will be severely hamstrung by not being able to integrate with partners that are enabling customer connections every day.

Keywords: Big Data, Collaboration, Cloud Computing, Minimising Storage Requirements, Augmented Reality

Endnotes

1 w3schools: http://www.w3schools.com/browsers/browsers_os.asp

2 See Wired: http://www.wired.com/wiredenterprise/2012/08/apple-maiden-construction/

3 955 million registered users as of the company's quarterly financial call; 26 July 2012

4 SWIFT History: http://www.swift.com/about_swift/company_information/swift_history.page

5 Finextra.com, "Citi slaps down Bank 2.0 rivals in Innotribe face-off", 22 September 2011

6 BBVA Press Release

7 UK Payments Council: http://www.paymentscouncil.org.uk/media_centre/press_releases/-/page/943/

8 LinkedIn.com

9 Bank Technology News, "Defining Big Data", 20 January 2012

10 See http://www.media.mit.edu/wearables/mithril/memory-glasses.html

11 Engagement Banking: Building Digital Relationships

The era of customer engagement

With contributions from Alex Sion, Global Vice-President, Financial Services Centre of Excellence, Sapient, and Geoffrey Bye, Fellow of the UK Chartered Institute of Marketing

Mein Name ist...

Watashi no namae wa...

Je m'appelle...

When it comes to engaging a customer, the single most important piece of information you can know about that customer is his name. His name is everything when it comes to engaging a customer.

If you don't know my name, then you don't know me, you can't know me. Right? If you don't even know my name, then how can we possibly have a relationship?

Think about this for a second... does anyone at my bank actually know my name? I don't mean just having it filed somewhere on a database, having it show up truncated on a piece of direct mail, or displaying in full formal detail (first, middle, last) every time I log in to online banking. I mean, does anyone at the bank personally *know* my name? The kind of *know* that defines a relationship of some sort. Is there someone I can call at the bank today who will know who I am and what relationship I have with the bank?

For most customers, this would be a fantasy. For a private banking client, or potentially, for those classified as an affluent customer, there might be a relationship manager in the bank who knows him. But if that relationship manager leaves, often the relationship migrates with him. The bank no longer has a relationship with him when that happens. The *Asian Banker Journal* reported in 2007 that 60–70 per cent of customer relationships went with a departing private banking relationship manager when he changed institutions. When institutions are looking for experienced private bankers to join their team, they will ask for them to bring a "book of business" with them—this is the key measure in the hiring decision.[1] So even at the coveted private banking level, relationships are very tenuous things.

Here's the flip side. Do I know the name of anyone at my bank? According to a recent SapientNitro survey, 70 per cent of bank customers don't know a single individual at the bank they regularly use.[2] Every bank claims that it wants a relationship with us. But do we want, need, or even value a relationship with a bank brand?

The bank says customers need a "relationship" with their brand, but the reality is that what we need more often is simply great service, advice and problem-solving. We need a bank that understands us, our financial needs, our financial position, and tailors recommendations and advice based on that knowledge. A relationship starts with knowing the person.

In this new digital age, however, the trick is not just knowledge, it is how a bank uses that knowledge to engage us. Engagement, in this sense, is the ability to connect in rich immersive ways through a digital and multichannel experience. Fundamentally, it's about using technology to create personal, meaningful relationships.

Using technology to drive personal experiences

Technology creating personal relationships? That seems counterintuitive. Everything we know about technology today seems to indicate that it is impersonal, cold, hard, functional elegance—but not a relationship creator.

Then again, think about Amazon, the most transactional of websites. If we're regular users of Amazon, I doubt we'd have any question on whether or not it knows us by name. It knows our names, our reading habits, the way we like to pay for things, where we want things shipped, how we want things packaged, the things we might like, the things we might need related to the things we've bought, and they can even provide insight from folks (like us) who might help us make purchasing decisions. It wouldn't be a far stretch to say that Amazon is perhaps the most personal shopping experience of all. And one without any of the elements that we normally would normally associate with a personal shopping experience— storefronts, check-out counters, people walking the aisles, shelves, aisles.

While banks spend most of their time and budget trying to sell products through the public website, Amazon spends most of its time trying to sell customers products behind the login. This allows personalisation, faster fulfilment and provides results that make the average bank's online revenue really wanting.

Think about Facebook, too. Facebook creates, strengthens and restores relationships. Think about long-lost friends rediscovered through Facebook; relatives whom we haven't spoken to in years, suddenly reconnected; old school buddies, friends we've just met, friends of friends, and more. Facebook, and much of social media today, creates relationships that are just as tangible, if not more real, than a relationship that could be created over the counter of a bank branch. In that light, we might wonder how a relationship created in a bank branch could ever compete with a relationship conducted through Facebook.

Facebook is such a human technology that it also has dramatic power over very real relationships, sometimes in a negative way.

The Daily Mail reported in December 2011 that Facebook is becoming a major factor in divorce cases, according to lawyers.

> "The social networking site was cited as a reason for a third of divorces last year in which unreasonable behaviour was a factor, according to law firm Divorce-Online. The firm said it had seen a 50 per cent jump in the number of behaviour-based divorce petitions that contained the word 'Facebook' in the past two years."
>
> —*Daily Mail*, "The Facebook Divorces", 30 December 2011

When technology has such definitive power to connect people, how is it that we think of it as inferior in building relationships with a brand like a bank? Clearly, the previous chapters show that today it is far more likely that our day-to-day relationships will be formed, managed and shaped via technology than it will in the increasingly rare instances we visit a person or a bank branch.

So, what does engagement for banking look like? How can you build constructive, meaningful relationships with customers via digital channels today? The Amazon metaphor is actually not a bad one at all.

Amazon has a transactional mission just like banks. The difference is that Amazon packs its transactional experience with context and things that it has learned about us along the way. Amazon makes sure that the transaction we are making is well informed, simple, and smart. If this is engagement for retail, why does engagement for banking have to be any different?

Mobile takes the engagement capacity for day-to-day banking to a whole new level. With mobile banking capability and mobile payments on top of that, you have the ability to deliver transactions and context at the most relevant point: when the customer is about to use, is using, or just after he has used his money.

Making smart personal financial planning decisions while we're doing online banking after dinner on our desktop is one thing. However, making smart spending and saving decisions while we are using our money to buy things every day completely elevates the notion of context. Thus, *engagement* for banking has the potential to go well beyond anything conceived even in the retail space. It has the potential to redefine people's relationships with, and connection to, their money.

Which, after all, is what a bank branch was supposed to do, but has failed to deliver, as banks have dismissed real relationships in exchange for profits and cost savings.

Money "moments of truth"

Creating delightful engagement experiences is all about timing. It's about reaching customers in the right place, at the right time, with the right kind of service or message. The holy grail is to engage customers at key "moments of truth", where money and life connect, and consciousness about personal finances overall is raised.

In the past, the industry has often focused on "life events" as key moments of truth—when we get a new job and move, when we have a child, when we retire. These moments are important but infrequent, and the fact that many banks tend to organise customer relationships around life events is much of the reason customer engagement is low in general. Most banks are only set up to "get to know you" when we've got big life events going on. But if we think about the customer experience of money for everyday individuals, perhaps the most frequent moment of truth happens nearly every day: when we are purchasing something at a store.

When we're doing this, all of a sudden the abstract concept of money becomes quite real. We're making a small financial decision which, depending on the nature of the purchase and its size, can raise our financial consciousness significantly: Can I really afford this? Is this the best way, time, place to buy this? Does buying this mean that I'll have to forgo buying other things on my wish list?

Where is my bank at these moments of truth? Other than enabling the payment itself, banks are typically nowhere. Silent. Indifferent. The only feedback we might get from a bank at the time of payment is a rejection of our card if we've used it too much, if we've hit our limit, or if we're transacting at a merchant that's outside of our established behavioural norms and hence flagged as an anomalous transaction.

Mobile transforms customer engagement

With mobile payments at the point of sale, the game changes. The potential for banks or other kinds of providers to capitalise on this most frequent "money moment of truth" skyrockets. What happens when consumers have easy access to information and intelligent help via their mobile devices in the aisle? The implications in respect of what he buys, but also as to how he buys it, are tremendous.

Mobile payment at the point of sale has the opportunity to connect individuals with their money like never before because it has the ability to do two things:

1. Provide smart context on everyday financial transactions
2. Reach people at a point of heightened money consciousness.

From a bank's standpoint, how we buy things is also a large brand decision in and of itself. Banks and cards companies spend billions in advertising to influence our choice of payment at the point of sale. Banks and card companies spend a ton of money to get us to remember their names at the point of sale. But what's in it for the customer?

The point of sale is where consumers are perhaps the least informed of all in respect of their money—unaware of the basic characteristics of the bank product and the transaction itself: rate, balance, impact on near-term or long-term needs and goals. Making selections based on brand recall, "top of wallet" proximity, fear (the "Which one of these haven't I maxed out?" decision), or rewards programmes. Yet, for every purchase there is a logical way—a *right* way—to pay for it. A way that's best for us, that optimises our finances, our preferences, our rewards, and the ability for us to meet our current and future goals. So, banks invest a lot for us to know them, but how much, really, do they know about *us* at this particular moment of truth, and how much do they share?

Generally banks have developed a methodology that is not about sharing with us the right information to make the right decision. In fact, banks have got used to encouraging us to use our credit cards as much as possible because of the income they earn off interest, or using a debit card when we don't have enough cash so that they can charge us an overdraft fee at exorbitant costs. Neither of these approaches is right for the customer.

What if a mobile payment/mobile wallet was smart enough to know the right way to pay? What if it knew how much we had, how much we owed, when cash was expected to come in and when it was expected to go out, what our future goals were and when we sought to achieve them, and how all of this was impacted by the purchases we make every day? What if our bank knew all that information? We'd certainly have a different, more engaging financial services world. All this boils down to intimacy, knowledge and trust—banks knowing their customers and customers trusting their banks at key moments that matter. It's not just a payment at a store anymore, it's an engagement opportunity that builds a relationship, every single time.

So, what's in a name? When it comes to the future of retail financial services, the future of mobile money, and the future of the everyday banking client experience, the answer is simple: everything.

Engaging in the dialogue

2012 is the year that companies, including in the retail banking sector, need to get themselves seriously organised for engagement with their current and future customers. Why? Because their customers are already well advanced recapturing the marketplace conversation, engaging in digital word-of-mouth to define a brand's reputation with simple actions such as "Like", "Recommend", "Share", "Tweet" and "Follow".

Consumers are already experts in talking amongst themselves in social media, comparing brands, commenting on their services and influencing one another's purchase intentions, both favourably and unfavourably, but it seems that many in the retail banking sector seem frozen in their response to the conversation.

Javelin Strategy & Research's recently published report, "Banking and Social Media: Easy to Say, Hard To Do" (January 2012), analysed how effective three of America's biggest banks—Bank of America, Wells Fargo and Citi—were in resolving customer complaints on Twitter across a period from 20 September to 10 November 2011—5489 public Tweets in total.[3]

The report's overall findings showed that these brands were generally not at all effective, and my guess is that this wouldn't be a surprise for most customers, who broadly see banks as notoriously poor at resolving customer complaints, regardless of channel.

So what is holding back this level of quality engagement with the end customer? One of the key problems is that today the dialogue is 24/7 and not the predominant "9-to-5 and not including weekends" bricks-and-mortar branch distribution or call-centre model. But is it more than just hours of business? Do many retail banks also have a "bricked-in mentality" that institutionally and instinctively precludes them from adopting an effective approach to engagement? A mentality that the customer is a target, a segment, a line item on a profit and loss statement, or an entry in a database—but not someone you would engage with one-on-one when it comes to a valid discussion on the brand's performance or on the future of the business? After all, a bank can't honestly be expected to engage with every one of its customers surely?

Are banks better or worse than other industries?

It is fair to ask the question of whether the retail banking sector performs better or worse than other industry sectors in their approach to customer engagement in the social media world? Singular and ad hoc examples of best (and worst) practices have been blogged and showcased, but it has been notoriously difficult to date to find cross-industry surveys comparing relative approaches from an engagement perspective.

However, two recent surveys, spanning the Atlantic, are shedding some light on how companies across various industries are starting to get to grips with social media and real-time customer engagement.

The UK Chartered Institute of Marketing (CIM), supported by Ipsos ASI and Bloomberg, published Wave One of its new "Social Media Benchmark" research report in March 2012.[4] The longitudinal survey looks into how UK national, multinational and global companies are adapting to, investing in, and drawing value from social media. The research, to be conducted and its findings reported in successive six-monthly reports, canvassed opinion and social media practices from 1295 marketers across B2B, B2C and B2B2C sectors. Respondents varied in seniority, from practitioners (26 per cent), to managers (38 per cent), to heads of department and above (36 per cent).

On the US side of the Atlantic, the research-based advisory firm Altimeter Group in its report titled, "Social Business Readiness: How Advanced Companies Prepare Internally", published in August 2011, surveyed 144 companies, all with 1000 employees or more, and conducted 63 interviews or briefings with corporate practitioners and social business software, service and solution providers. The report examined how companies "advanced" in social media usage prepare themselves internally to become a socially engaged corporation.

Both these reports highlighted the significant challenges companies face in adding in an "effective layer of Social Media Intelligence".

> "Some organisations still aren't convinced about the benefits to their business or sector; others don't know how to get started or worry that once they do, they won't be able to keep the pace."
>
> —Russ Shaw, non-executive director, Game Group plc

Who's doing what and why?

The CIM Social Benchmarking Report findings highlight that whilst companies' adoption and usage of the core social media platforms—Twitter, Facebook, Linkedin, YouTube—is starting to trend above 50 per cent, social media management is inconsistent at best, **with only 4 per cent of**

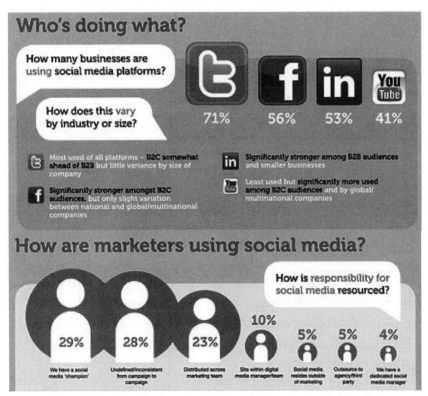

Figure 11.1: How businesses and marketers use social media
(Source: "Social Benchmark Wave One Report", March 2012, reproduced with permission of UK Chartered Institute of Marketing)

companies reporting that they have a dedicated Social Media Manager, and 39 per cent having some sort of Social Media "Champion".

Only 27 per cent of respondents report using social media platforms as a core part of a campaign, with the remainder reporting that they are just experimenting or using platforms because customers and competitors are using them—or as a last resort because it is just expected of them.

The CIM Social Benchmarking report identifies the "barriers" to effective adoption of social media as:

- A lack of senior management understanding
- A lack of clear rationale and strategy around "home for" and "usage" of social media
- A lack of a dedicated social media manager
- A lack of skills and competencies within companies

The home for an engagement hub

Social media is an emergent medium, one that is accessible and already used as a personal tool by many employees within companies. However, from an organisational perspective, social media management needs to be housed, orchestrated and have a cohesive strategy developed that can be measured, and for which the organisation can be held accountable.

Unmonitored and non-engaged "favourable" customer conversations in social media may well represent "opportunities lost" to the company, but unmonitored and non-engaged "unfavourable" customer conversations can lead to substantial "reputational loss".

The Altimeter Group subheads its Social Media Readiness report "Social media crises are on the rise, yet many can be avoided through preparation", and highlights the need for companies to organise themselves internally to reduce risks from social media crises, whose occurrence are on the increase—whether due to exposure of poor customer experiences via social media, poor influencer relations, or violations of ethical guidelines, or simply rogue employees.

The importance of potential reputational loss and the need for crisis management and preparedness lead one to the conclusion that a company's Engagement Hub or Social Media Centre of Excellence needs combining support from the marketing and corporate communications teams and product teams, with elements of the customer-facing teams.

A dedicated engagement team

In this Engagement Hub, companies need to employ and empower a dedicated Social Media Manager, with an authority level of VP/director, as the champion of social media and consumer engagement throughout the organisation. This champion needs to be a strategic thinker, comfortable and experienced at translating corporate objectives into brand, customer service, product development and operational goals across different parts of the business.

The dedicated Social Media Champion needs to be a seasoned professional with the experience and gravitas to manage persuasively the executive suite, business division heads and a department's individual employees towards alignment of a company's goals and best practice in social media. Gone are the days when social media was farmed out to anybody who could "Tweet'", or to a fresh university graduate who is "really good with Facebook". Personal use of social media and youthful appearance do not translate into the ability to take the lessons from the dialogue with customers, and push the organisation to change process or behaviour to serve customers better.

Would you put a fresh graduate in charge of your PR department, your call centre, or your brand identity? No? Well, social media engagement is all three of those and more **in one very strategic engagement funnel**. By putting anyone other than a seasoned, innovative and flexible senior executive, you are exposing your organisation and brand to risk. The real risk is not competently handling customer engagement, rather than the minor risk of screwing something up online.

Ironic, isn't it, that risk aversion is the reason many would cite for not pursuing a social media strategy, when the reality is that *not* pursuing that same strategy is far more risky. In fact, core risk to the brand voice, integrity and advocacy is a massive incentive to get active fast on social media as a business.

Avoid building another silo

Social media isn't something that can be owned by any one "team". Whilst, for reputational risk purposes, there is an element of brand hygiene best facilitated by professional marketers, social media management belongs everywhere, right down to the individual employee level. It should not sit in an independent silo. In effect, every department that produces a product, or has contact with end customers, should provide support for this team. That means every product team, every channel team, every cost centre in the business, should have a resource that is the go-to guy or girl who liaises and interfaces with the engagement team.

The engagement team should encompass cross-functional team members with a primary remit to establish social media governance policies and to educate and train company personnel in how to (and how not to) use social media in the context of a professional—building a clear separation between what people can do as individuals and what they can do as employees.

Making social media strategic to your business

The transformation of a company into a social business and adding a social engagement layer of excellence is not an overnight fix. For a corporation, this involves the identification of skills and competency "gaps", the realignment of roles, policies, processes, objective-setting, investment, analytics, measurement of ROI and the education and training of hundreds to thousands of employees.

It is easy to see why many companies become immobilised or indecisive in their approach to the management of social media.

The need is to develop a sound engagement strategy and evolve, organise, or acquire a highly skilled team that is vested with the appropriate social monitoring (listening and engagement) and analytics (data and intelligence) tools to measure the impact of customers' interactions with the company, and the impact of the company's own interactions with its customers of today and tomorrow.

The Altimeter Group survey mentioned previously identified 18 companies that were "advanced" with respect to social media readiness, such as eBay, Intel, Dell, Cisco (not one of the 18 was a bank), in order to define the common attributes these "advanced" social engagers shared.

All had empowered a senior-level Social Media Strategist and all had established a cross-functional Centre of Excellence (COE) that served the company as a shared resource across the corporation, providing social media governance, education and training, research, measurement frameworks and vendor selection.

According to the survey, the common attributes of these "advanced" companies' Centres of Excellence included:

Table 11.1: Attributes of "advanced" companies' Centres of Excellence
(Credit: Altimeter Group)

Centre of Excellence Duties	Best Practice Attributes of Advanced Companies
Provide leadership from a dedicated and shared central hub established at corporate or divisional level	Establish cross-functional, scalably organised in hub-and-spoke formation Centre of Excellence with a Charter Document clarifiyng the business goals and purpose of COE. Provide expert resource on vendor selection, monitoring, analysis and measurement across the company.
Establish baseline governance and reinforcement policies	Publish and reinforce corporate media policies that clarify how employees can participate in social media in a professional and acceptable manner that legally protects both employees and the company.
Establish and cascade company-wide workflow and response processes	Publish social media workflow and response processes to allow social media practitioners across the company to know "how" and "when" to respond to customers in social media. Establish social media crisis response plan that outlines roles, responsibilities and actions.
Provide ongoing education and best practice sharing	Governance education through e-learning programmes, continuous ongoing education through internal collaboration tools (intranets) and internal conferences, brown bag lunches, etc.

The survey also asked respondents to report on how many full-time equivalents made up their dedicated Engagement or Social Media Hub and found that the average size of a corporate social media team was 11 full-time employees. Their roles and responsibilities are defined and described in the diagram and table below.

Average Size of a Corporate Social Media Team: 11

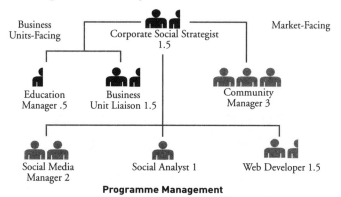

Programme Management

Figure 11.2: Composition of a Social Media Team (Source: Altimeter Group)

The most common roles that were employed in these teams staffing the social media or engagement function of the business included:

Table 11.2: Role of social media team members

Role	Description
Corporate Social Strategist	Programme leader for social business, responsible for overall vision and accountability towards investments. The strategist is primarily internally facing, rallying and coordinating with business units.
Social Media Manager	Coordinates with business units to launch social media initiatives. The social media manager may straddle internal and external communications, direct resources and formulate programme plans.
Community Manager	Primarily outbound and customer-facing, serving as a trusted liaison between the community and the brand. The community manager spends more time with the community, rather than with internal stakeholders.
Social Analyst	Using brand monitoring, social analytics, web analytics, and traditional marketing tools, the social analyst is responsible for measurement and reporting across the entire programme, and for individual business units.

Role	Description
Web Developer	Provides dedicated assistance to help plan, brand, configure, and integrate social technologies as stand-alone efforts, or into existing systems.
Education Manager	Serves multiple business units and rank-and-file employees in planning and organising social media education, including policies and best practices.
Business Unit Liaison	Serves as an internal conduit to coordinate efforts with other business units in order to provide them with resources, as well as ensure consistency.

Risk mitigation versus ROI

There is something in the organisational psyche of banking that mitigates against the rapid adoption of new distribution and engagement channels and their underlying technologies, including social media and mobile platforms. I've previously characterised that as inertia, and underlying friction around existing processes and policies.

Certainly bankers do not lack intelligence or creative thinking. There is no dearth of ideas floating around banks, or bankers talking about the need to innovate at global conferences, but there are powerful organisational flaws that result in a poor track record in bringing game-changing innovation to market.

Some inertia comes from an insistence on hard, demonstrable ROI numbers before an innovation gets a project go-ahead. This is the case because most banks have operated on thinning margins, increased regulation, and increasing requirements to be able to explain decisions around capital deployment, and how much risk the organisation carries. Additionally, coming off the back of the global financial crisis, budgets are tight and banks retreat to safety—so new channels, products or innovations are seen as "risky" at a time when banks want to be anything but risky.

By definition innovative products lack comparisons so estimating the ROI for an innovation is inevitably difficult and this rubs against the short-term demands of C-Suite (highest-level) executives who are measured and held accountable on a short-term (quarterly) basis and are incentivised to boost near-term performance at the expense of the long-term benefits.

As such, the C-Suite executives are often unwilling to sponsor innovative initiatives that they see as offering only short-term pain (bottom-line costs) in return for undefinable long-term benefits.

If the *i*s are not dotted and the *t*s not crossed on the pre-sign-off ROI analysis, innovative ideas are not so much killed, as more often placed into life-support in the guise of poorly funded and poorly staffed "pilot projects". Project team members, often only part-time, then get themselves "bricked-in" by the organisational mentality of having to prove uncertain ROI. Also having to work to IT-defined "integrated release schedules" and "change control standards", they bog themselves down in details whilst trying to strive for the "perfect ROI provable launch" that never happens.

However, these "pilot projects" do allow the C-Suite executives to continue talking innovation in their company reports and at conferences and it is why banks seem to have pilot programmes all over the place. As Chris Skinner, in his Financial Services Club blog has said, "Banks have so many pilots they should become an airline."

For banks to innovate in the area of social media readiness and customer engagement, the CEO needs to be the real champion. The CEO needs to hire the strategist who reports to him, and this strategist needs to have:

- Adequate budget not at risk
- Freedom to hire a full-time team, and hire the appropriate external communications partners
- Publish the governance policies, education and training programmes and build the monitoring and analytical tools to establish KPIs and measure influence and emerging advocacy
- Freedom to experiment
- Freedom to engage without legal and compliance roadblocks

Engaging the overwhelmed prosumer

Many of the top 10 jobs in 2012 are jobs that didn't even exist in 2000. For example, here are a few jobs that mostly didn't exist 10 years ago:

- iPhone Application Developer
- Facebook Game Developer
- Mobile Wallet Security Consultant

- ◻ Data Analytics Manager
- ◻ Head of Social Media
- ◻ Head of Mobile
- ◻ VP of Private Cloud
- ◻ Digital Identity Specialist
- ◻ Digital Behavioural Psychologist
- ◻ Social Networking Architect
- ◻ Data Communication Analyst

We are preparing students now for jobs that don't yet exist. Much of what they are taught will probably be redundant or out-of-date by the time they graduate. The US Department of Labour estimates that today's learner will have had 10–14 different jobs by the age of 38. Web 2.0 is changing the dynamics of how we live. It's not just with our work either. One couple out of every eight who married last year in the United States met online.

Each day we receive more and more information to process as a result of the Information Age. The number of text messages sent daily exceeds the total population of the planet. Indeed, during the 2011 Chinese New Year in China, more than 26 billion text messages were sent in the space of just one week.[5] It is estimated that a week's worth of the *New York Times* newspaper contains more information than a person was likely to come across in his lifetime in the 18th century. As a result of all of this content, more than 5 exabytes (that's 50,000,000,000,000,000,000 bytes) of unique information was generated in 2011 alone.[6] This was more than was collectively generated in the preceding 5000 years of human history. To top it off, the amount of technical information generated globally is now doubling every two years. Where is all this content coming from?

Introducing the **Prosumer**—a Producer and Consumer of information. The prosumer is us—a web user that creates and uses available content and information on the web. The Web 2.0 phenomenon is responsible for the creation of user collaboration that makes social networking, virtual worlds, networked applications and other such tools work. Today, we are no longer just a consumer or "reader" of content—today, we are producing and consuming content at an incredible rate.

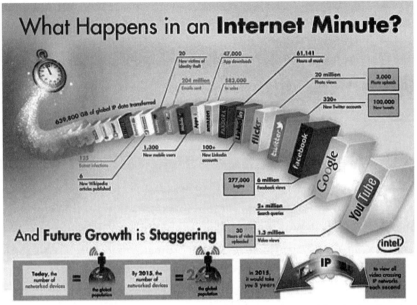

Figure 11.3: **What happens in an Internet minute** (Credit: Intel)

Here are a few stats of the prosumer in action from Intel. In just 60 seconds every day on the Internet, the following amazing things take place:

- 8 new Wikipedia articles are created (that's 3.1 million per year).
- 55,000 apps are downloaded.
- 2.3 million searches are conducted on Google.
- 30 hours of video are uploaded to YouTube—that's a 50 per cent increase on just three years ago. But there are 1.3m videos viewed in that same minute also.
- 100,000 Tweets are made on Twitter.
- Approximately 10,000 songs are illegally downloaded (mostly from areas where legal downloads of the same are not possible), while 61,000 songs will be listened to over services such as Pandora.
- By the time anyone reads these statistics, they will already be out of date because growth in each of these areas means the data do not stay static.

Today there are as many devices connected to the Internet as there are people on the planet. With the expansion of mobile and tablet technologies, along with smart cars, fridges, media players, game consoles and other devices, within just three years there will be twice as many devices connected to the Internet as there are people. In fact, it has recently been said there are more IP addresses in the world than stars in the observable universe![7]

We can't look at the above information and not realise that our world has dramatically changed because of the Internet and the 921 petabytes of information that we exchange every year. With the pure amount of information we have to deal with, we need to find new tools and media for organising this information. Ironically, the Web 2.0 phenomenon created the tools both for generating this content, as well as managing it, in many instances, e.g. YouTube.

This shift means that banks and other organisations need to be delivering content through this new medium or they become irrelevant. But right now, surveys show that more than 50 per cent of banks are so threatened by this new phenomenon that they have banned the use of social networks at work.[8] Customers are very willing to collaborate with their banks and other service organisations to improve the whole experience— but by not participating in these forums and networks, banks are missing out on these opportunities. This is simply further proof of how out of touch with the Bank 3.0 paradigm most banks are.

Getting personal

The **client experience gap**—that divide between customers' retail banking needs and technology experiences and today's retail banking client engagement model—is widening. Banks should realise that this gap is in danger of becoming an insurmountable barrier. Think about it. What is the emotional state of the financial services customer today? Confused. Untrusting. Troubled. Feeling disconnected from the "economy". Feeling abandoned by financial services companies. And seeking control.

At the same time, customer behaviours and expectations are changing with every technology innovation. Customers seek experiences that are informational, engaging, maybe even entertaining. They are mobile— perhaps even social in their digital lives. They expect personally relevant interactions in both work and play. In contrast, what does the current retail banking experience deliver? Branches, ATMs, call centres, mail, and online bill payment—increasingly generic and transactional experiences that are impersonal to the customer and don't reflect ever-changing reality.

Where are you headed? Towards rich and personal online experiences, a mobile wallet, social media, "branches of the future," touch-screen ATMs, personalised digital marketing, and more. The channels and tools customers use to manage their financial lives are dramatically changing. Technology, which has improved efficiency and convenience, often at the expense of customer intimacy, now has the power to engage customers like never before. Are you ready?

Keywords: Dialogue, Engagement, Social Media, Relationship, Digital, Smart Context, Prosumer, Risk Mitigation, ROI

Endnotes

1   See http://news.sfoa.efinancialcareers.com/News_ITEM/newsItemId-23752

2   Sapient Nitro Engagement Banking Survey, September 2010 (http://www.businesswire.com/news/home/20100901006310/en/SapientNitro-Unveils-Engagement-Banking-Concept-Interactive-Report)

3   Javelin Strategy & Research: https://www.javelinstrategy.com/brochure/237

4   Chartered Institute of Marketing, "Social Media Benchmark: Wave One", March 2012 (http://www.smbenchmark.com/the-benchmark/results-wave-one/)

5   *China Daily* (http://www.chinadaily.com.cn/china/2011-02/16/content_12021489.htm)

6   Eric Schmidt from Google estimates "we create as much information in two days now as we did from the dawn of man through 2003" (http://techcrunch.com/2010/08/04/schmidt-data/)

7   Mashable (http://mashable.com/2012/06/07/now-there-are-more-internet-addresses-than-stars-in-the-universe/)

8   Sophos Security Online Survey

12 Mobile Payments, Digital Cash and Value Stores

Mobile payments refer to the grouping of alternative payment methods to cash, cheques or credit cards. Increasingly widespread in the US, Asia and Europe, these alternative methods are particularly effective for micropayments. Instead of paying with cash, cheques or credit cards, in a mobile payment scenario a consumer can use a mobile phone to pay for services or goods.

There are seven primary models for mobile-enabled payments:

- SMS-based transactional payments
- Direct mobile billing
- In-app payments
- Mobile commerce and/or web payments
- Peer-to-peer payments
- Virtual currency payments
- Contactless payments

Figure 12.1: Models for mobile payments

We started playing with mobile payment services way back in the 90s (I'm feeling old saying that right now, but it was 20 years ago). Sonera, a mobile operator and services provider based in Finland, started to offer mobile payments back in 1997. The first payment options included the ability to purchase soft drinks from Coca-Cola vending machines (in Helsinki first, reportedly[1]). Then in 1999, Payway piloted parking meter payment in Stockholm. Next, Sonera (now TeliaSonera) launched Sonera Shopper in 2002, featuring WAP-enabled payments on a range of products and services.

Are mobile payments mainstream?

If we believe the pundits, mobile payments are still years away from being mainstream.[2] But that's not at all an accurate assessment of the state of the industry.

Firstly, a mobile payment can be many things, as characterised by the models above. As of today, it appears that around half of the developed world has already made a mobile payment of some sort in the last 12 months—at a minimum, purchasing an app or making an in-app purchase from a smartphone or iPad would qualify. Put that in perspective, more people made a mobile payment globally in 2011 than wrote a cheque![3] In fact, across the EU the average person writes approximately 10 cheques a year, but they're likely to download around 80 apps annually, most of which are purchased via the mobile application store.

Would we call cheques mainstream? Of course. So how can we not call mobile payments mainstream based on that simple metric?

A recent study[4] from ACI Worldwide and Aité Group—where smartphone usage in 14 countries was put under a microscope—identified a group of consumers for whom mobile payments behaviour is the norm. This group was classified as "Smartphonatics".

According to this research, 80 per cent of Smartphonatics have used their smartphones for mobile banking; just one-third of non-Smartphonatics report doing so. Seventy per cent of Smartphonatics have used or intend to use their smartphones for mobile payments in 2012; under 25 per cent of non-Smartphonatics have. Smartphonatics are generally younger consumers also: 36 per cent of Gen Yers (between the ages of 20 and 31) are Smartphonatics as are nearly one-third of Gen Xers (ages 32–46). The number drops significantly among both baby boomers (ages 47–65) at 18 per cent, and seniors (66+) at six per cent.

"Smartphonatics enthusiastically use their smartphones when they shop for products and services as well as when they interact with their banks. It is quite clear they are an emerging consumer force. Smartphonatics are driving the adoption of mobile banking and payments and will be an agent for change. Financial and retail institutions will need to adapt or risk being left behind."

—Ron Shevlin, senior analyst, Aité Group

The ACI/Aité research indicated that globally around one in four consumers (25 per cent) counts as a Smartphonatic, with higher numbers found in India and China than in the United States and Europe. This makes sense because in markets such as India and China, mobile payments are competing head to head in the growth of payment alternatives such as cards, which are still quite new for most of the population.

In Asia, mobile payments have been mainstream for the best part of a decade. **Japan sets the benchmark for m-payments** with 47 million Japanese adopting tap-and-go phones.[5] In China alone, there will be 169 million users of tap-and-go payments in 2013. Between 500 million and one billion people will **access financial services by mobile by 2015**, depending on which estimates you read. The mobile financial services market will be dominated by Asia, driven by mobile, operator-led initiatives in developing nations to bank the unbanked. Remittances and transfers by mobile are growing three times faster than m-banking.[6] Mobile remittances are a form of mobile payments, essentially P2P.

A study released in May 2012 from MasterCard[7] found that although the United States is ready for mobile payments, nine of the 10 countries most prepared for the technology are in Africa, the Middle East and Asia. Ironic, isn't it, that in Kenya 50 per cent of the population sends money by SMS regularly, but in the US most consumers still write cheques! Who said the US was an advanced economy?

In South Korea, there are more than 60 million contactless phones in use.[8] Most use the FeliCa standard, but already more than five million NFC-enabled phones have been purchased in South Korea by eager consumers.

In 2012 almost a third of South Koreans bought music, videos, ring tones, online game subscriptions and articles from newspaper archives and other online items and charged them to their mobile phone bills regularly every month. This amounts to total mobile transaction revenues of 1.7 trillion won, or approximately US$1.4 billion in 2008 alone. In 2012, there will be 21 million Koreans watching TV via Mobile Digital Multimedia Broadcasting (or T-DMB as it is known). Forty per cent of cellphones sold in South Korea have the capability for users to watch free-to-air TV in this manner.

T-money™, electronic cash stored and refilled in SIM cards, and phone chips can be used to ride the subway and bus, or buy snacks from a 7-Eleven store, vending machines or cafeterias at school. Instead of giving their children cash, Korean parents now transfer money to their kids' T-money account.

Figure 12.2: T-money contactless application for public transport and payments (Source: *International Herald Tribune*)

> "If I leave my wallet at home, I may not notice it for the whole day. But if I lose my cellphone, my life will start stumbling right there in the subway."
>
> —21-year-old Kim Hee-young, Sookmyung Women's University (*New York Times*, May 2009)⁹

In Japan, e-Money and mobile payments started in 1999 and usage is growing exponentially. e-Money and mobile payments are today already an important and big part of Japan's economy. Japan leads the way in mobile commerce today with 72 per cent of the population on an internet-enabled mobile phone or smartphone and more than 40 per cent of Internet users having made a purchase on their phone.¹⁰

In 2003, SONY's FeliCa IC semiconductor chips were combined with mobile phones to introduce the first "wallet phones" (*Osaifu keitai*). Today, the majority of mobile phones in Japan are wallet phones based on this standard.

The two parallel systems in Japan today are **Edy** and **MobileSuica**. Edy stands for Euro, Dollar, Yen, expressing the hope for global success— Intel Capital believes in this success and has invested in the company that runs Edy: BitWallet (backed by SONY). MobileSuica (also known as FeliCa) is a service for Osaifu Keitai mobile phones, first launched on 28 January 2006 by NTTDoCoMo and also offered by SoftBankMobile and Willcom. Initially used for commuters travelling on Japanese rail networks, today mobile ticketing payments are used by more than 90 per cent of Japanese commuters.

Electronic money became popularised around 2007 in Japan when two major retailers, Aeon and Seven & I, started their own versions of electronic money. The transactions by Aeon and Seven & I still account for roughly 50 per cent of all transactions in Japan today.

Just to highlight how huge the e-money market is in Japan: Transaction volumes at Edy, the country's biggest prepaid e-money issuer, nearly doubled in 2010 to 1.4 trillion yen (US$15 billion). PayPal did $4 billion in mobile payments globally last year, and won't top Japan's volumes until 2013 at the earliest. So Japan is the clear leader globally in mobile payments.

Figure 12.3: FeliCa technology underlies NFC applications with SONY/DoCoMo solutions

Between Edy and Suica, more than 84 million mobile contactless payment transactions take place every month[11] through around 450,000 merchants or outlets. Between retailers AEON, PASMO and NANACO (Seven & I), another 120 million mobile contactless payments are made every month, at another 300,000 merchants.

Mobile payments behaviour

On the broader vision of mobile financial services, the move by Visa to invest in disruptive payments start-up, Square, and its recent acquisition of mobile financial services company, Fundamo, should be seen as strong moves towards mainstream. One of the key challenges of using mobile devices for point-of-sale payments is the change in consumer behaviour, shifting from plastic cards and POS devices to a mobile-to-mobile transaction.

Figure 12.4: The Square device turns any smartphone into a POS terminal

If Visa could drive mass adoption of the Square reader, the market would be quickly taken through a perception change as they witness an increasing number of merchants using a mobile phone, therefore building confidence over time in the technology, and creating a more sustainable stepping stone for consumer adoption of mobile as a payment instrument.

Once the phone becomes a primary mechanism to take a payment, then logically, it's only a matter of time before the plastic card is replaced by a mobile service, whether it be NFC or an app in the consumer's handset, creating a mobile-centric point-of-sale experience, and more importantly, a behavioural norm shift.

To take the technology to its logical conclusion, a consumer would wave his NFC-enabled mobile phone to access doors, and where necessary, additional authentication is requested of the user in more security-sensitive situations. This therefore removes the need for the work-issued security card and, instead, the employee's electronic ID in his mobile is registered and used as the primary means for identifying who he is, a key concern for regulators focused on KYC, identity theft and AML. The same can be used to access our home, and while we're at home, our house recognises our home and adapts to our preferences, turns on the heater, switches on the TV to the news with items specific to us, similar to our Facebook or Twitter account, creating contextualisation in the physical world.

The reality is, all the technology to do this exists today. NFC is now standardised, door readers exist in a large majority of corporate buildings, 900 million of us have Facebook accounts and another 400 million have Twitter. Secure USSD PIN requests can be sent to a low-end mobile phone authenticating at a physical level that we are who we say we are, we have our registered SIM card, we are using the same mobile handset and we are located in a place that suggests we are actually the person requesting the service. With multiple industries all driving the adoption scale of mobile, our most personal device is destined to play an important role in the future of consumer services.

So if all this already exists, why are we not seeing the wide adoption of innovative ecosystems to enable this?

The primary answer is an uncertain convergence of industries. The NFC guys aren't openly talking to the door security companies, who aren't advising their customers to adopt an open authentication. Banks are not yet completely understanding mobile, let alone embracing its true power for payments. And no one has really looked into utilising the power of Facebook or Twitter fully as a global means to identify someone and their preferences in a mobile payment. PayPal and Chase have tried some simple pay-a-friend functionality, but there's still no social media integration at the bank level—i.e. there's no link within our bank between our accounts and our social media profiles. Thus, there's no efficient way to use a social media profile to originate or receive a payment, unless we go with Pygg or TwitPay, and then bank integration is poor.

The landscape of the consumer payment industry has historically been shaped at least in part by public policies. Historically, governments have had monopolies on the manufacture of money. Any form of payment clearly requires trust on the part of both the seller and the buyer, and the government must establish and enforce laws to secure this relationship. More controversial is the issue of whether, and to what extent, government is also needed to protect the market in private-sector payment systems.

This is one of the key reasons we see fragmented success. In Kenya, for example, where regulators took a more relaxed approach, M-Pesa mobile payments quickly dominated the landscape. In South Africa, on the other hand, where the regulator insisted on cash-in and cash-out functions being handled by banks alone, mobile money has not grown anywhere near as quickly as Kenya.

Which approach is right? By the measure of financial inclusion alone, then Kenya has shown a far more constructive and socially responsible approach to the community. It has also produced more positive economic activity, reduced crime (with respect to cash) and increased the savings of participating constituents. What has the South African approach done? Well, it has reduced the risk of disintermediation of the banks, and reduced the risk of possible fraud in the mobile payments space. I would argue that the Kenyan approach is therefore far more positive for the economy and individuals.

The emergence of the mobile wallet

This is what Visa and MasterCard already know: that mobile payments and the behaviour required to drive mobile payment adoption are already widespread. The mass market loves the ease of use and modality of a mobile payment compared with plastic, cash and cheques. While debit card usage is growing, cheque usage is rapidly declining and cash usage is declining in most developed economies. In the US, prepaid debit cards were the fastest growing form of electronic payment in 2011 with over $200 billion in utilisation.[12] Combine prepaid debit cards and smartphones that allow us to pay at the point of sale (with NFC or some other cardless method) and we have the perfect storm for disruption.

In the last 12 months, Visa and MasterCard have both been accelerating their moves to replace all existing merchant POS units with PCI-compliant alternatives that also facilitate NFC mobile payments. What Visa and

MasterCard realise is that if they don't push NFC as if their very lives depended on it, with the mobile quickly becoming the dominant payment device, payments will shift away to alternative "network" rails. The only way to ensure their current payment networks stay a part of the mix is to ensure they can support the behavioural shift to mobile (regardless of whether that is NFC or some other solution).

NFC is the only viable solution that allows Visa to support both legacy card transactions at the POS, and mobile payments. This makes for an orderly transition, and requires only a POS terminal swap out. The alternative would be new point-of-sale systems such as those offered by Square and PayPal. For larger retailers and merchants, this would require a considerable investment and could be risky, but not impossible. The last thing card issuers want right now is a major retail chain announcing a deal with Square, PayPal or Dwolla that renders them obsolete.

If Visa and MasterCard don't convert their networks to phone-capable in the next 24 months, I fear Square, PayPal, iTunes and a myriad of others are just waiting in the wings to circumvent their rails. Argue all you like about NFC adoption, but that's not what you should be watching. The tipping point is the behavioural shift on the mobile phone—that is what will kill plastic, and it's already happened.

Ask yourself this: what constitutes a mobile payment? Surely a mobile payment is simply a payment made from or via a mobile phone.

By that measure alone, anyone who has a smartphone and who has bought an app or downloaded digital content via his phone is already in the habit of making regular mobile payments. Some 25 billion apps were downloaded in 2011 on the Android and iOs platforms—a 300 per cent increase from 2010.[13] In the US, that represents 44 per cent of the population, with the 50 per cent tipping point estimated sometime in 2012.

In reality, 67 per cent of consumers flagged their intention to make a mobile purchase of real-world goods and services in 2011 (source: PayPal), and we have hard data to show that 47 per cent used their smartphone to make a purchase in December 2011[14] alone (digital content such as songs/music, e-books, ringtones, images, movies, TV shows, etc., being the most common purchases).

At the recent Digital Money Forum run by CHYP (Consult Hyperion) in London, Visa Europe disclosed that they expect 50 per cent of all payments volume to be mobile by 2020.

Here are some common mobile payment methods that are off-the-chart successful already:

PayPal

In 2009 PayPal processed just $141 million in mobile payments. However, last year that jumped to a whopping $4 billion, and PayPal recently disclosed that in the first quarter of 2012 they were on track to deliver roughly the same volume of payments they did in all of 2011—putting 2012 estimates at somewhere between $10–14 billion in mobile payments[15] just through the PayPal network. PayPal classifies a mobile payment simply as a payment across their network from one party to another. However, by attacking the mode of payment, PayPal has created an electronic payment method that is simpler, faster and cheaper than ACH (Automated Clearing House) and wire transfers offered by banks—the only viable bank alternative to cheques from within the banking system.

Starbucks

In just over one year, the Starbucks Card, powered by a mobile application, accounted for a quarter of all Starbucks purchases in-store across North America. That's 42 million mobile transactions in 15 months. The usage of the mobile app has doubled in the last 12 months on a run-rate basis, going from 1.4 million transactions per month in January 2011 to 2.9 million transactions per month last December. Remember, this payment method didn't exist a year ago, but today 25 per cent of all in-store payments are made via this method. If you're prepared to argue that 25 per cent of Starbucks' customer base doesn't represent mass adoption or mass consumer acceptance of a new form of payments, I think you're either very brave, or just plain crazy.

Square

Both the Obama and Romney campaigns used Square to take campaign contributions in the lead-up to the 2012 elections. Square, which launched in May 2010, at the time of press has more than two million merchants using its app to take payments on mobile smartphones. Considering that there are only eight million merchants in the US, this means that 25 per cent of merchants in the US use a mobile smartphone to take credit card payments—that's in the space of less than two and a half years. Now, you might argue that Square is not a "real" mobile payment because plastic is still involved, but think back to my assertion about changing behaviour. Once a small retailer or local merchant is regularly using his phone to accept "swipe" payments (such as with Square), it's then a very simple shift for the merchant to accept payments via a consumer tapping their phone (instead of a swipe). Technology such as PayPal and Pay with Square even allow payments just using our phone number or name—no physical interaction required. Once the merchant is accepting payments via a smartphone, there's virtually no ongoing barrier to entry—i.e. the merchant doesn't need to invest in a sophisticated POS terminal and such.

PayPal has already deployed its supposed "Square competitor"—the triangle—and is aiming to compete in this phone-to-POS space in the near term. In Europe this has spawned iZettle—an EMV equivalent of the Square device in the United States. In October 2011, iZettle raised $11m in a Series A financing deal, supporting its growth plans.[16] iZettle is based in Sweden. But there are other competitors also, including the likes of iCarte, Erply, iMag, and others looking to enable NFC in the same way.

Dwolla

Unlike Square and PayPal, Dwolla works completely independently of the existing payment networks beyond cash-in and cash-out functionality. Dwolla's main strategy is to attack the current transaction costs of moving money around. If a transaction is under $10, the transfer (or payment) is free, if over $10, there is a capped $0.25 fee. Dwolla has around 70,000 customers today (including 5000 merchants or retailers[17]) and it already processes around $1m a day through its network. Dwolla argues that its network is safer for consumers and merchants alike because it doesn't send sensitive credit card details across the network—just a secure ID and the transaction details. Dwolla is more than a payment network, however, because it (like PayPal) stores your balance in your account—it is a proxy for a debit card with none of the fees, and none of the card fraud risks. The majority of its payments are transacted through Dwolla's mobile app.

Dwolla has recently launched a bank-to-bank initiative that is designed to replace the ACH function used broadly in the United States. Think of this as P2P through and for banks, but person to bank, and then bank to person instead, using Dwolla's technology. The key advantage Dwolla has over traditional ACH is simplicity. When sending money, we don't need complex bank account identifiers, we only need the intended recipient's mobile phone number or email address. Consistently we see the biggest threat to banks and the payment networks in respect of moving money around and paying at the POS is the complexity (lack of simplicity) in the current systems. This is why there is disruption—friction.

Who will win the wallet battle?

When you read about mobile wallets and emerging NFC technologies, especially as they are framed in the US market, there's always the question of who will win the battle for the mobile wallet over the next five years, as use of mobile eclipses first cheques, then cards, and eventually cash.

The reason for this perspective, particularly in the US, is that right now US mobile carriers are attempting to restrict mobile wallet operations on their networks. Ultimately, these current attempts are likely to end in nought for any number of reasons, but mostly because the mobile payments market will continue to fragment. The number one reason, however, is that, unlike the credit and debit card industry, historically, the barriers to entry are extremely low. Let me explain.

When MasterCard and Visa emerged in the 70s and 80s, they had a whole infrastructure to build. Merchants didn't have point-of-sale capability to capture credit card payments. In those days there weren't even networks to process those card payments. I'm sure many of us remember those

Figure 12.5: The height of credit card acceptance technology in the 70s

so-called "flatbed manual imprinter" machines. These were known in the old days as "knucklebusters" by many merchants because of their design.

It wasn't until the late 80s that electronic networks enabled swiping of a card into an electronic point-of-sale device. In 1988 MasterCard also acquired Cirrus, the largest ATM network in the world at the time, giving users of cards global access to cash. In those days they needed bank partnerships, access to highly proprietary networks, and the ability to issue secure cards to get into this business. This is why there were only ever a few players in the space—Diners Club, Visa, MasterCard, American Express, and later Discover and China Union Pay.

As we move into the mobile wallet space, however, the only infrastructure required are customers with mobile phones and IP access. This is why new payment models such as Dwolla, Venmo and others don't need Visa's and MasterCard's blessing to start playing in this space. They don't need to hook into an existing network that's proprietary. They don't need some special contractual relationship to issue cards.

There's virtually no barrier to entry for creating a new virtual wallet based on IP-layer technology today. Of course, the consumer needs to cash in and cash out, or top up and pay out of a wallet, so that, in itself, requires some level of cooperation and partnership at the back end to enable this capability for consumers. However, given the intense competition and lower margins in the payments and banking sector today, the players are all scrambling to embrace new revenue streams, partnerships and collaborations like never before.

> "No longer will consumers have to flip through leather wallets and purses for plastic cards; instead, they'll access the wallet app on their phone, wave it or tap it on a POS device and quickly and efficiently complete a transaction. In theory, it opens up new payment opportunities and opens the door for new entrants to a market that has long been dominated by a select handful of major card brands."
> —VeriFone White Paper 2011,
> "NFC Payments and the Point-of-Sale"

This is what makes the concept that network providers, such as the partners in ISIS, or Sprint with Google Wallet, can "lock -up" the payments market quite absurd. Putting aside the fact that anti-trust rules in the US would most certainly prevent barriers to competition in this way, the fact is that it will become untenable very quickly. First and foremost, mobile operators are there to provide mobile as a platform, and one of the biggest emerging uses of mobile as a platform will be the ability to pay for stuff. Thus, by restricting this type of activity on their platform, mobile operators will fast become uncompetitive. It will only take one provider to break ranks, and the rest will have to follow to stay competitive.

The first opportunity to break the back of this duopoly in the US will, of course, be the Apple iWallet or **Passbook™**[18] as it is known. Apple's next generation iPhone will be embedded with this payments technology, based on the integration of their existing iTunes virtual wallet and linked to NFC technology. For AT&T or Verizon to attempt to restrict the use of the Passbook on their networks would be commercial suicide.

This excludes banks that logically will also want to offer their own wallets embedded in mobile banking apps. One of the key value points in mobile payments will be the fact that I can see in real time my balance reflected before and after a transaction. The problem is that, at least initially, we won't be able to do this with Google's or ISIS' Wallet. A key selling point for consumers will be spending control and transparency.

A lot of dissatisfaction at the lower end of the debit card market right now is on overdraft fees, charged when a customer uses his card for a purchase and goes into a negative balance scenario. Banks are milking this lack of information to the max. So there will be huge value to connecting our balances to the payment device to avoid poor spending decisions. Again, mobile carriers won't have much success restricting banks from deploying these apps with a wallet capability built in.

Lastly, both Visa and MasterCard have introduced their own wallets. MasterCard's PayPass Wallet and Visa's V.me are both aimed at creating virtual wallets that can exist online, in an app for mobile commerce, and integrated with NFC phones for point-of-sale payments. MasterCard and Visa have to certify the devices used by the mobile carriers on their payments rails, i.e. at the point of sale. So if mobile carriers refuse Visa and MasterCard use of their networks, then Visa and MasterCard could restrict access so that the mobile operators' proprietary wallets (such as ISIS) wouldn't work with the traditional card networks.

Then you have the operating systems play. Undoubtedly Google Android, Apple's iOS and Microsoft Windows 8 will all have some wallet capability built into the operating system to support in-app payments and the like. It's logical to extend that same wallet capability to point-of-sale payments via NFC as soon as the phones and networks support it. Clearly neither mobile operators nor card issuers will have a credible shot at restricting the handset OS providers from deploying wallets in their phones.

It's a free-for-all!

So who will win the Mobile Wallet battle?

No one can. It's going to be an even more fragmented affair than the current cards business. The complication for banks will be that the mobile wallet provider won't even need a bank account to provide a competing mobile wallet in the retail space. Increasingly we're going to see the likes of retailers such as Walmart and BestBuy launching their own closed-loop, in-store gift cards enabled in a mobile app. Just like the immensely successful Starbucks App, these will be mini mobile wallets that work within specific stores. Again, it would be impossible for mobile operators to restrict these apps from working at the point of sale.

The challenge here is who owns or provides the value to the consumer? What is the value of a mobile wallet? This is where we have some unique opportunities.

Unlike the existing cards business, the value of a mobile wallet is not just the payment. Google worked this out very early in the process, and this understanding drives its entrance into the mobile wallet space.

Google sees the big picture

Google's wallet based on NFC technology is not about payments modality alone. It's not simply the shift from chip and PIN or contactless plastic to contactless mobile payments. It's about what the mobile phone can do as a payment device that a plastic card can't—*it can give you context*.

For example, the number one enquiry to retail banking call centres today is still **"What's my account balance?"** By combining that one key piece of information with a payment device you give the consumer a very powerful context for everyday personal financial management.

If, as a consumer, I am focused on a savings goal, you can show me the potential negative effect of making a big-ticket purchase.

If I am at a retailer about to use a competitor bank's credit card, you can offer me a no-interest payment plan through my bank.

You can tell me that if I purchase that big flat-screen TV, I won't be able to make my mortgage payment due in the next three days.

You can offer me a really great deal at a retail outlet that I just walked into or am walking past.

Google has worked out that the context of payments is perhaps the biggest advertising market to emerge *ever*, far more impactful and lucrative than search-based advertising. This is about offering us consumers compelling, relevant and timely messages that improve our service experience in-store. This is about positive behaviour on the part of our service providers that produces extraordinary loyalty through relevancy, and responding to our behaviour in a way that benefits us day to day, not just when we go to the bank to ask for something.

The future won't be written by banks and marketing organisations that are passive. It won't be written by marketers that broadcast message after message hoping we'll remember a brand when we want to make a purchase.

The future will be written by organisations that know us so well that they anticipate our needs, make it very simple for us to capitalise on the relationship, save us money, and respect our time and privacy. Trust can be earned back, but it is about me trusting you enough to receive your offers and you not burning that trust with irrelevant direct mail, newspaper ads and TV commercials.

Messages wrapped around the context of a payment are the future and Google wants to own that space. It doesn't look as if there's really anyone ready to challenge Google on that front as yet. ISIS isn't thinking quite the same way about payments, and it certainly doesn't have the capability that Google does to bring marketing offers to the consumer. Apple's Passbook is probably closer to Google Wallet in this respect, but is going more for a combination of loyalty and payments, although Apple have flagged their intention to integrate the iAd platform into the wallet.

Whatever we think of Google Wallet, it's clear it probably has the most compelling business case of all for pursuing NFC payments, and this has nothing to do with competing with banks, but everything about owning the customer payment experience.

Virtual currencies

A payment system that almost brought down the yuan?

Hey friend, could you spare a QQ or a Bitcoin?

There has been a great deal of debate recently about the revaluation of the yuan (RMB). But how many of us know that perhaps the greatest risk to the yuan in terms of competing currency in the last two to three years actually came from a local online currency known as QQ coins. QQ Messenger is still one of the most widely used instant messenger programs on the planet, despite the fact that it is only mostly used in China. QQ Messenger's creator, Tencent, however, is also famous for the virtual online currency it created for paying for goods through cyberspace. The online currency, QQ coins, was used for everything from paying for avatars, downloading mobile ring tones, to even online gaming.

This illustrates the real value of online currency and payment systems, something that traditional bankers (cash-focused) have been critical of due to the absence of regulatory control. While some regulators, such as the HKMA (Hong Kong Monetary Authority), have taken action to regulate electronic payment solutions such as the Octopus smartcard, particularly in respect of deposit-taking, there are precious few rules regarding virtual currency in cyberspace.

For instance, take this possible scenario. Our boss decides to pay part of our salary in QQ coins or Bitcoins. Could the tax man come after our virtual revenue if we only spent it online and didn't exchange it for real currency? Oops. Don't tell the IRS I gave you that idea...

This from the Asia Times...

> "The so-called 'QQ' coin—issued by Tencent, China's largest instant-messaging service provider—has become so popular that the country's central bank is worried that it could affect the value of the yuan. Li Chao, spokesman and director of the General Office of the People's Bank of China (PBOC), has expressed his concern in the Chinese media and announced that the central bank will draft regulations next year governing virtual transactions.
>
> "Public prosecutor Yang Tao issued this warning: 'The QQ coin is challenging the status of the renminbi [yuan] as the only legitimate currency in China.'"[19]

Currency speculators trade QQ coins, World of Warcraft Gold, Linden Dollars, Ven and Bitcoins via forex engines enabled for virtual currencies. In China, the players have gone one step further, with online vendors hiring professionals to play online games earning QQ coins as currency. Some even use hackers and other methods to steal the coins. They then sell the virtual currency below its official value, at a rate of 0.4–0.8 yuan per coin.

The Chinese government initially tried placing capital controls on QQ coins, but that just led to scarcity, driving up their real-world value by 70 per cent in a matter of weeks. Considering the QQ Instant Messenger platform has over 900 million subscribers, can this phenomenon be stopped?

Virtual economies are becoming increasingly important, says Wharton legal studies professor Dan Hunter, adding that they could redefine the concept of work, help test economic theories and contribute to the gross domestic product. "Increasingly, these virtual economies are leading to real money trades," notes Hunter, one of a handful of academics closely following this trend.

Bitcoin is an experimental new digital currency that enables instant payments to anyone, anywhere in the world. It uses peer-to-peer technology to operate, with no central authority, managing transactions and issuing money are carried out collectively by the network. Bitcoin is also the name of the open-source software that enables the use of this innovative virtual currency.

Over the past few years, the peer-to-peer currency it has created has gained a surprising foothold in the global market.

There are now multiple Bitcoin-processing apps for Android and the iPhone, as well as an online payment system similar to PayPal. Instead of enabling merchants to process credit card payments from Visa or MasterCard, Bitcoin bypasses the system entirely in favour of device-to-device transactions using near-field communications technology.

Bitcoin's new currency doesn't require a third-party processor or a plug-in dongle. Because of this, Bitcoin can afford to charge users much less per transaction. At the moment, the average Bitcoin transaction fee is 0.99 per cent, while Square and PayPal's processing apps charge 2.75 per cent and 2.7 per cent per swipe of your credit card.

Like any currency, Bitcoins can also be exchanged for US dollars through a processing service. As of 11 April 2011, the going rate was round $4.90 per Bitcoin.

In Africa, where inflation is out of control, many merchants are choosing to hang on to their Bitcoins so that they don't have to push around wheelbarrows full of $100-billion notes. They're looking at a rival currency to hold their assets, and it isn't always the US dollar or euro.

There's been a lot of discussion around the fact that Bitcoin's anonymity enables the facilitation of illegal activities, money laundering and the like. Admittedly it is well suited to such abuse only because it is a totally open and community-regulated currency. However, suspicious transactions will still get flagged by the traditional banking system when cash is put into or taken out of the Bitcoin economy.

So what's holding Bitcoin back from shaking up the global economy and becoming a true rival currency, especially in the digital payments space?

Security is the main concern. Unlike your credit card or existing bank accounts in the system, Bitcoin currently provides no protection or compensation in the event of fraud. Recently, a hacker managed to raid several Bitcoin accounts around the world and got away with $228,845.[20]

While current technology would enable tracking of IP activity around trades and the flow of Bitcoins, in the current instance of fraud, the weak link was the Bitcoin exchange, which didn't have the monitoring tools in place to track the hack.

The other issue raised by sceptics is how "decentralised" this digital currency really is. Though Bitcoin claims that the protocol is now mandated by community consensus, the fact is that the original developers still have significant control over the system.

Additionally, there's the problem of balancing the economy. In the US, the Federal Reserve handles the printing and regulation of the dollar. If the Bitcoin is to become a widely accepted global currency, in theory a regulating agency more complex and thorough than the Fed would be required: a global regulator or agency–something that doesn't exist today.

While undeniably innovative, Bitcoin still needs to mature before it can replace any real-world currency currently in operation. However, the biggest vote of confidence would be continued adoption by merchants and consumers alike. We could just find ourselves with a Bitcoin economy in the billions of dollars in the next few years, and that would make it a force to be reckoned with.

Mobile P2P payments

Peer-to-Peer (P2P) payments are rapidly accelerating in usage. Already PayPal, a 12-year veteran in the space, processed more than $118 billion in P2P payments in 2011, a 29 per cent increase from the previous year.[21] What is more interesting is the increase in mobile payments. With $4 billion in 2011 and an expected $10–14 billion in 2012, PayPal is shifting to mobile.

We're seeing the likes of ZashPay, ClearXchange, QuickPay, Venmo, Dwolla, and others get in on the frictionless P2P market. I call it frictionless because these providers capitalise on the current friction of sending money from one bank account to another. The current wire and

ACH systems in markets such as the US that require a routing number, a bank account number, a branch code and address, etc. before sending money from one person to another, are inordinately complex, given the instantaneous communications afforded us through email, text/SMS, Facebook messaging, Twitter, etc.

Banks have been slow to innovate in the payments space because of complicated interbank agreements, cross-border restrictions, legacy systems and the like. This is why we've seen a new P2P infrastructure built on top of banks to improve the flow of cash. This has impacted developing economies too.

As we identified in Chapter 6, remittance payments via mobile phone are experiencing explosive growth. According to the World Bank, today there are 215 million migrants sending over US$440 billion annually.[22] From that amount, developing countries received $325 billion, which represents an increase of six per cent from the 2009 level. In 2010 migrants sent back to India $55 billion—a source of foreign exchange that exceeds revenues generated by the country's highly regarded software industry.

This $1.5-trillion industry and opportunity have been largely missed by banks which decided migrant workers were too low margin to be an attractive customer group. This was the case in Kenya where the four Big Banks have 3.5 million customers between them, but M-Pesa, the mobile payments solution, already has 17 million customers and that's in just six short years.[23] This is the fastest "banking" of an economy, or the fastest consumer take-up of a basic bank account capability, ever seen in the history of banking. Ironic that it was achieved by a mobile operator and not a bank, though!

More traditional banks have jumped into the mobile payments fray in recent times. Mercantile Bank of Michigan announced in November 2009 that they had launched a mobile payments solution for their customers, incorporating technology from S1 and utilising PayPal.

> "This deal reflects the growing functionality of the mobile channel and is a strong signal to banks of where customer expectations are headed," said Bob Egan, global head of research and chief analyst

at TowerGroup, a market research firm based in Needham, MA. "Given the near-ubiquity of mobile devices and fast adoption of smart phones in particular, we can expect an increasing convergence of trusted banking relationships, personal payments and mobile."[24]

The payment solution allows Merc Bank customers to send money via the PayPal network to any individuals who have an email address or mobile phone number. If they don't have a PayPal account, they will have to create one before they can receive the funds.

CashEdge released a service they call **POPMoney** in 2009. From within either online banking or a mobile banking app, customers can send money to recipients by using their email address, mobile phone number or their bank account details. If we are a customer of a subscribing bank receiving a payment, then the payment goes straight into our nominated bank account. If not, we simply go to the POPMoney website, register and give the bank account details of where we would like it deposited, and POPMoney uses the SWIFT network to finalise the transaction for us.

Chase launched **QuickPay** in 2010 as a competitor to the likes of PayPal, primarily driven from a mobile phone app that enables P2P payments. Barclays, not to be outdone, launched **PingIt** in 2011— specifically via mobile. In neither case do we need to be a customer of the bank.

In 2011, JPMorgan Chase, BofA and Wells Fargo upped the ante by forming ClearXchange, designed to facilitate a future P2P capability between three of the largest banks in the US—only 11 years after PayPal launched the same.

As money becomes more abstracted, then the digitisation of money will lead to an interesting intersection of change. Mobile payments will be ushered in, value stores will be abundant, and the concept of a currency will be harder to enforce. Imagine if Facebook credits suddenly can be used to buy goods and services at a Walmart using a mobile wallet on our iPhone?

The risk for banks is that they own only one small piece in the infrastructure—the underlying account. Telephone companies and mobile operating system platforms, on the other hand, are much more pervasive when it comes to the end consumer. Regardless, over the next couple of years, there will be lots of fussing about partnerships and trying to leverage the emerging MasterCard and Visa wallet solutions.

How is NFC going to impact the P2P space? Well, ultimately if I can take my phone and tap it to another person's phone to send him money wirelessly via NFC, I don't need a point-of-sale device, a card or even a bank account. This is the truly revolutionary piece of NFC that not everyone sees as yet. Imagine splitting the bill at a restaurant, paying the gardener, babysitter or pool cleaner, or tipping a busker in the local marketplace by tapping your phone. Who needs cash? Cheques are gone very quickly too. The ability to pay person-to-person remotely and in real life are going to be the two biggest disruptors in the modality of payments since the creation of the cheque itself.

However for NFC to be commonplace and become the backbone for phone-to-phone payments, we'll still need to be able to pay with our phones at a point of sale for this technology to be viable. To leverage NFC and emerging payments capability, there will need to be significant investment in infrastructure at the point of sale.

Point-of-sale evolution

Often lost in the NFC discussion and speculation is the role of that ubiquitous device that is needed to make it all possible: the payment-acceptance device sitting on a merchant's counter.

At the moment, POS units are dramatically underutilised from a customer experience point of view. I've never seen my name, an offer, or any other personalised information appear on a POS terminal. Even at Starbucks, when they swipe my Starbucks Card, it doesn't say, "Hi, Mr King, welcome back for your tall, skinny, no-whip hot mocha..." It would be pretty cool if the POS, the barista or my phone was able to do that, don't you think?

The technical side of the requirement is that these POS terminals need to integrate with NFC technology, talk to apps as they present themselves at the POS, or as they enter the store (via geolocation), plus merchants need to integrate in real time with the bank or retailer's system and give us that feedback. As for the checkout experience, the days of waiting in line to make a POS transaction may be numbered.

> "The way you change that is a new terminal," says George Peabody, director of Emerging Technologies Advisory Services for Mercator Advisory Group. "That is a surmountable hurdle. It's not going to happen next year, but it could happen in the next seven to eight years."[25]

Whatever replaces the legacy POS terminal will undoubtedly be based on mobile technology, and will likely use NFC, Internet protocol, or both.

> "Today, if you used RFID [or NFC] in its purest form, you could walk into a store, load your cart and walk out without talking to anybody, because they would know who you are."
> —Randy Carr, vice-president of marketing for Shift4

Ironically, the US is probably going to be last in line for these changes. Why? Largely because of the huge investment already made in legacy POS telephony and equipment. The shift to IP and cloud-based technology in POS is already on the way, but both American merchants and card providers are reluctant to make the shift from magnetic-card and dial-up systems. Thus, consumers in the US will probably be amongst the last to make the switch to the new generation of technologies emerging for retail payments.

Phase I: Chip and PIN (Current evolution)

Smartcard-based credit cards, otherwise known as Chip and PIN, are based on the EMV standard for interoperation of IC cards or "Chip cards", and IC-capable POS terminals and ATMs. The name **EMV** comes from the initial letters of Europay, MasterCard and Visa, the three companies that originally cooperated to develop the standard. Europay was absorbed into MasterCard in 2002, and in 2004 JCB (formerly Japan Credit Bureau) joined the organisation. American Express finally relented and joined EMV in February 2009.

In the UK, Chip and PIN was initially trialled in Northampton and was rolled out nationwide starting in 2004, with advertisements in the press and national television touting the "Safety in Numbers" slogan. As of 1 January 2005, the liability for signature-based transactions in the UK was shifted to the retailer. This was designed to act as an incentive for retailers to upgrade their POS systems.

The introduction of Chip and PIN through the EU decreased card fraud significantly. The year 2011 showed the lowest figure for UK card fraud in more than 11 years, and was the third consecutive year with a decrease (17 per cent decrease in 2011 alone).[26] Estimates by UK Payments claim the introduction of EMV Chip and PIN in the EU has resulted in a 50–75 per cent reduction in domestic card-not-present fraud.[27]

The US now appears to be the odd one out as Canada, Mexico and most of Europe and the developed economies of Asia are already rolling out the standard. If Brazil, Mexico and Turkey are adopting the standard, one would think it was time for US card companies to fall into line. The issue in the US is the legacy POS infrastructure. Without the regulator mandating a new standard, it is unlikely that US cardholders will see the new technology anytime soon. Thus, many US travellers abroad are now finding their plastic useless at retailers, transit stations, ATMs, and so forth. It will take some consumer lobbying to make this happen in the US, I think. Until then, some US consumers have taken to travelling with two cards—their mag-stripe card and an upgraded smartcard.

This disparity has prompted such stellar blog and media headlines as "American credit card users are cavemen in a Chip-and-PIN world", "U.S. credit cards becoming outdated, less usable abroad", and "U.S. magnetic stripe credit cards on brink of extinction?"

The US has been pushing a possible contactless standard as a replacement for magnetic cards. But with the rest of the world already rapidly adopting Chip and PIN, it looks like the US will have to admit defeat grudgingly and start the roll-out of new POS technology sooner or later. Either that or the US market will need to skip the whole Chip and PIN phase and move on to Phase II.

Phase II: Mobile integrated payments

Workarounds for smartphone integration with credit cards and POS systems are already underway. The issue with the integration of these with POS terminals is twofold. Firstly, how does the app phone communicate with the POS terminal, and secondly, how does the consumer authenticate or provide proof of identity.

There are two current technologies in place that would enable app-phone payment. The first is NFC, which means that the phone contains the IC (Integrated Chip) or smartcard that enables it to be used identically to the Chip and PIN credit card. The next iPhone is going to be the true disruptor with regard to this technology.

Based on the iPhone's massive popularity, this will quickly end the debate on whether NFC-enabled handsets are going to be ubiquitous or not in short order. Cards become redundant overnight almost. What about the required infrastructure? Imagine how quickly merchants will be scrambling to accept payments via iPhone. Major retails will deploy new POS technology with a velocity such as we've never seen before. Suddenly Chip and PIN is not an issue for the US as it skips an entire generation of technology and goes straight to mobile-enabled POS.

Ironically, the second viable technology utilising either an application IP-based or call-based solution is workable right now today, without any development of a supporting platform. There are already providers in the market that supply secure authentication utilising both methods without even the need for a POS terminal at all. We've discussed Square, PAYware, PayPalHere and others such as QR-code-based payment options already.

Which of these two methods, i.e. NFC or phone-based, or application/call-based will come out on top?

Neither. It will be a combination of the two, but over time the simplicity of NFC will win out for real-time interactions at the retailer's store or at the train station, for example, whereas application technology will work for virtual stores.

QR/Semacodes and other such methods could also be used, as could a Google Glass-type technology with our camera in our app phone, where we take an image of an advertisement we see on a billboard and have the option of purchasing that item or product through the mobile internet.

Phase III: Cardless, phoneless, personalised?

In Minority Report, we see Tom Cruise's character interacting with advertisements that speak to him about his last purchases using only retinal scans to identify the customer. While the futuristic technology from the movie may be decades away, the likelihood of some adaptation of this technology making its way into the retail experience is not that far-fetched.

POS terminals that use directed audio or send notifications/alerts to consumers via location-based messaging are highly probable. In fact, existing technology could enable us theoretically to walk in, select the items we want at a store and walk out again, without our ever having to engage a cashier at all—the charges would just be automatically made against our wallet embedded in our phone. We could then receive an instant receipt on our mobile phone also.

While Phase I and II deal largely with the evolution of the payment device (i.e. mag-card, IC card, NFC and smartphone), Phase III requires an evolution in the POS and store environment itself. Once again cloud computing could be the vehicle that breaks this platform right open for greater collaboration and more interesting application.

The most likely short-term improvement is that we could have roaming advisors or cashiers in the store with a hand-held payment terminal that can process our payments in real time. Apple already uses this methodology and most customers never even see a cash register in the Apple Store at all.

Square, on the other hand, has already turned iPads into next-gen registers (without cash). I don't need a card, cash or a smartphone as long as I'm already registered with Square. I just give my name and Square can accept the payment from my Square account to the merchants. PayPal is working on a similar solution with the likes of HomeDepot that has already signed up to integrate PayPal at the checkout.

The trick will be to integrate biometrics on our personal mobile device so that no checkout is required at all. The additional component will be integrating the likes of the daily deals technologies of Groupon and LivingSocial into attracting potential purchasers into a store. This will close the loop on point of sale, changing the retail space environment from one that requires a specific payment interaction, to one where the payment is seamless. While this is a massive evolution for the in-store experience, the option of the self-checkout store experience is likely to gain rapid momentum over the next decade.

The biggest evolution in payments is, in fact, when the modality of the payment itself disappears. There may still need to be some authentication methodology, but the key is all about getting rid of the friction. This is the path payments are taking, and ultimately why cash, cheques and even cards are doomed in the retail environment.

Conclusion: Mobile payments and quickly

The conclusions are inevitable. If we all thought Internet banking take-up was rapid, wait till mobile payments really take off. Banks and credit card companies are used to owning the infrastructure for payments processing. However, what we are seeing is a deleveraging of the retail payment experience from the back-end banking system. That is, banks are simply no longer going to be necessary when it comes to point of sale, neither are credit card companies.

Does anyone remember payment by installment, lay-aways or lay-bys? My kids have never heard of them, and I can't remember seeing them for at least a decade, but they used to be a pretty popular method of getting us through the Christmas credit crunch in the old days. But lay-aways have mostly disappeared because credit cards were a better idea. Just like lay-aways were under threat from a new payment mechanism, physical credit cards may also be on their way out due to mobile payments.

The other poignant issue is that credit cards are a risky business for banks in the post-financial crisis world. So a shift to debit cards is good business because it promotes less consumer debt, and it's a risk-averse strategy for banks. It does take a rather sizeable chunk out of their retail earnings and profits for banks though, because the margins and fees are significantly lower. Debit card usage is set to rise considerably over the coming years, making up almost 50 per cent of all transactions by 2015. As the debit card merges with our app phone and POS systems to allow us to use our phones to pay, it will be impossible to continue to support physical plastic cards. It might even be good for the credit ratings of our debt-laden economies.

As cloud computing and new IP-enabled retail POS devices allow for more and more retailers to accept payments from our phones without their having to plug into Visa, American Express or MasterCard, who will be in control? The consumer and the retailer! There simply is no real value provided by SWIFT, Visa, MasterCard and others when P2P payments and cloud computing-enabled POS systems hit our stores.

As long as these new systems or solutions provide expedient means for payment, are secure and yet flexible, then as consumers, we'll adapt. What could be more convenient than waving our iPhones over a contactless pad at a retail outlet, ordering our pizzas through our Movenbank-enabled mobile phones, or squirting some cash through the ether to our local gardener who just mowed our lawn? Especially if we don't need to carry extra plastic, jump through hoops to qualify, or pay 27 per cent interest per annum.

If banks, merchants and card companies don't move very, very fast—they will find themselves out of the loop on this one.

Keywords: EMV, Chip and PIN, NFC, Near Field Communication, PayPal, Square, Dwolla, Bitcoin, QQ, M-Pesa, Mobile Payments, Mobile Wallet, Google Wallet, ISIS, v.me, PayPass, Amex, Visa, MasterCard

Endnotes

1 Dave Birch (Consult Hyperion), "The Mobile Payment Horizon" (https://www.chyp.com/media/blog-entry/the-mobile-payment-horizon/)

2 http://www.itbusiness.ca/it/client/en/home/news.asp?id=67838

3 Ten cheques per capita across EU, Irish Payments Services Organization (http://www.ipso.ie/?action=statistics&sectionName=EUStatistics&statisticCode=EU&statisticRef=EU13) versus 83 apps per user per year (http://allthingsd.com/20110711/average-iphone-owner-will-download-83-apps-this-year/)

4 Aité Group/ACI "The Global Rise of Smarphonatics" (http://www.aitegroup.com/Reports/ReportDetail.aspx?recordItemID=931)

5 MobiThinking (http://mobithinking.com/mobile-marketing-tools/latest-mobile-stats/f)

6 While payments can be a part of mBanking, often they are distinct and separate. Some mBanking apps also don't allow mobile payments or P2P. So while mobile payments are thought of as part of mobile banking, that's not always the case.

7   MasterCard: http://newsroom.mastercard.com/press-releases/mastercard-says-early-days-for-mobile-payments-adoption-with-no-two-markets-the-same-2/

8   NFC Times: http://nfctimes.com/report/south-korea-takes-global-lead-nfc-rollouts-millions-phones-and-sims

9   "In South Korea, All of Life is Mobile", *New York Times,* May 2009, at http://www.nytimes.com/2009/05/25/technology/25iht-mobile.html?pagewanted=all

10 MobiThinking: http://mobithinking.com/guide-mobile-Web-Japan

11 eMoney in Japan: http://www.epiport.com/blog/2012/02/01/e-money-in-japan-its-everywhere-and-more/

12 "A Look at Why Consumers Are Using Prepaid Debit Cards", *New York Times*, 12 April 2012

13 http://www.readwriteweb.com/mobile/2011/11/mobile-app-inflection-point-25.php

14 ComScore, Inc.

15 PayPal: http://www.mobilepaymentstoday.com/article/197691/PayPal-expects-mobile-payments-to-more-than-double

16 http://techcrunch.com/2011/10/18/europes-square-izettle-raises-11-million-for-mobile-payments-technology

17 http://bucks.blogs.nytimes.com/2012/01/23/using-dwolla-to-send-and-receive-money/

18 Passbook™ is the new embedded Wallet service built into iOS version 6

19 *Asia Times Online*, 5 Dec 2006, at www.atimes.com

20 http://arstechnica.com/business/2012/03/bitcoins-worth-228000-stolen-from-customers-of-hacked-webhost/

21 PayPal: https://www.paypal-media.com/about

22 World Bank, "Migration and Remittances Factbook 2011" 2nd edition

23 Safaricom and thinkM-Pesa.com (http://www.thinkm-pesa.com/2012/04/every-business-should-have-m-pesa.html)

24 Mercantile Bank press release, 3 November 2009

25 "What will credit cards look like in 25, 50 or 100 years?", Jay MacDonald, December 2009 (CreditCards.com)

26 "Credit card fraud falls to a 10-year low", *The Telegraph*, 7 March 2012

27 Retail Payments Risk Forum Working Paper, Federal Reserve Bank of Atlanta, January 2012 (http://www.frbatlanta.org/documents/rprf/rprf_pubs/120111_wp.pdf)

13 Point of Impact: The Contextualisation of Banking and Messaging

Going, going, gone...

This shouldn't be a surprise, but for many of the traditional marketers in our midst, the first reaction to the following data and analysis could be scepticism or outright denial. But if you Google these statistics, you'll find they are all too real.

The fact is that in most banks today, the marketing department is completely misaligned to the reality of the marketplace. The skills are wrong, the methods are wrong and the people are wrong. It is the one department that needs to be dramatically re-engineered with immediate prejudice. Advertisers still talk about **media** and **interactive** (or digital) like they are two separate advertising universes. Marketers talk about **offline** and **online** as if never the two might be equal. These are 20th-century classifications in a 21st-century Bank 3.0 world. The only advertising spending that has increased significantly in the last decade is online and mobile; all other traditional methods have seen double-digit decline.[1]

In 2008 the Internet surpassed all media except television as the primary source for national and international news[2]; this has taken its toll. In March 2009, the 146-year-old *Seattle Post-Intelligencer* or the "PI" as it was known, closed down, citing rising costs, falling revenues and declining circulation. Since just January 2008, 53 regional newspapers in Britain have folded at last count.[3] Of the top 25 newspapers in the US in 1990 (the year newspaper employment peaked), 20 of those newspapers have seen declines (on average reporting circulation down by more than 30 per cent), and two have been closed down or declared bankrupt.[4] *New York Times* reported a 6 per cent fall in print advertising revenue in 2011 alone, contributing to the $88-million posted loss for the year.[5] In November

2009, the *Washington Post* announced the closure of all its remaining US bureau offices (New York, LA, and Chicago) outside of the capital—in addition to Miami, Denver and Austin closures in recent years.

A lot of people are asking the question—how do we save the newspapers? Unfortunately for those asking that question, it's not just newspapers we have to worry about.

In 2009 TV advertising revenues in Australia fell by more than 12.6 per cent in the first half of the year.[6] In the first quarter of 2009, the US recorded losses of more than 23 per cent in TV ad revenues in normally stable locations such as the Bay Area and New York. Declines of 27 per cent and more were recorded in radio ad spend for the US for the first half in 2009, even worse than the decline in TVCs (TV commercials).[7]

In France, TV ad revenues dropped around six per cent in the first half of 2012.[8] UK TV ad revenues were down 12–14 per cent in 2009, and Sir Martin Sorrell's Group M predicted[9] a decline of more than £350m in the UK during 2012 (a decline of around 6.3 per cent), despite the hoped-for windfalls generated by Euro 2012 and the London Olympics. While many attribute the further decline of traditional media to the global financial crisis, it doesn't explain the trending over the last decade as new media shifts have started to bite. A recent report commissioned by OFCOM forecast the value of TV ads in the UK could fall from £3.16 billion in 2007 to just £520 million in 12 years' time. That's a projected 83 per cent decline.

> "TV shows and movies are not optimally suited for survival on a two-way network. The most familiar types of electronic content must adapt to survive in the new networks. Linear one-way programs will be transformed into a two-way dialog between creator and audience. In order to compete with made-for-the-medium fare, static fixed-media content must become responsive and interactive. Likewise, the locked programming schedules set by TV executives have been replaced by instant on-demand access chosen by a consumer from a menu or playlist. Channels and programming blocks have been dissolved by search, linking and viral syndication. Today's empowered consumer has usurped the role of the programmer."
>
> —Robert Tercek, *Collaborative Creativity*

More interestingly, for the first time ever in the US, a drop in sales of TV sets was recorded in 2010. What happened to drive this incredibly significant shift? People's viewing habits have started to change. Now we're watching media on our iPads and our laptops instead of on just the television screen. In fact, research shows that tablet users are using their tablets about 30 per cent of the time while they're watching TV. In fact, according to recent research by Nielsen Group, 88 per cent of tablet users have used their device while watching TV.[10]

Free-to-air TV support has been waning for the best part of a decade due to cable and satellite TV, but for the first time in the last couple of years, we've started to see cable TV decline. This is primarily due to the modality by which we watch our favourite TV shows and movies. Increasingly we're shifting to an on-demand model for content. Think I'm talking BS? The US Consumer Electronics Association recorded that in 2011 only eight per cent of US households relied on free-to-air TV. Cable TV growth is slowing, and digital downloads are ramping up fast.

Gary Shapiro, President and CEO of the Consumer Electronics Association, says, "It's time we accept this shift away from over-the-air TV as an irrevocable fact of the TV market. The numbers tell the story."[11]

There can be no doubt that the future of advertising is going digital—traditional media is quickly being replaced by online. Televisions are now coming with internet connectivity that allows consumers to download content and consume media in a new way, minus TVCs. This is probably one of the reasons TV ad spend declined 2.3 per cent in the fourth quarter of 2011.[12]

Newspapers, books and magazines are increasingly being consumed on electronic reading devices such as phones, tablet PCs and e-readers, and radio is increasingly irrelevant in an age where music is consumed and acquired whenever, wherever, by consumers through services such as Pandora, Spotify and others like them.

"Digital Natives", the Y-Gen and younger users of technology are spending greater time online more quickly than their predecessors, and they are changing the way in which they consume and access news and entertainment through a myriad of devices. They don't think of TV or newspapers as traditional sources of content—they think of browsers and mobile devices as "traditional" media. They don't think of offline versus online—they think of content, downloads, media streams, P2P, blogs and networks.

The digital age has transformed society, which has evolved from media-fed masses who get blasted with broadcasted messages to content-seeking individuals who want interaction.

There are some commonalities. Viral videos, for example, are still potentially made like television commercials (and in some cases cost just as much)—and have only given advertisers an outlet to play with more creative and abstract ideas. Banner ads and some forms of website advertising initially started like a combination of traditional television commercials and print. It takes some time for newer, more effective forms of advertising and engagement to evolve.

Today mass media is **social,** and journalists, consumers and bloggers alike can all have a say. When presented with social media, advertisers have often given in to the temptation to populate these new channels simply with more broadcast messaging or, at best, some segmented advertising. However, putting marketing teams in charge of social media strategy misses one absolutely critical point.

Much of what we see on social media currently is dealing with consumers directly—more akin to customer service or technical support than traditional advertising mediums. Thus, when an advertiser sends a message out, an individual in the social space deems this as a communication to him/her personally, and not an "ad". The advertiser has to watch what he says, and how he says it. Broadcast has no place here.

Context is king

So how does context work in the banking arena?

Some banking products are highly contextual. In fact, many day-to-day banking products are. Here are some examples of the context of core retail banking products:

1. Mortgage (at a potential home or with a realtor)
2. Car lease or loan (at a car dealership or when purchasing a car)

3. Credit card (potentially at a mall, or getting ready for a trip overseas)

4. Travel insurance (when booking a holiday, or at the airport)

5. Student loan (when enrolling at college or university)

Context awareness originated as a term from ubiquitous computing[13] or so-called pervasive computing, which sought to deal with linking changes in the environment with computer systems which are otherwise static. Today we can determine the location of someone's phone (and hence the person), and increasingly we can gather context from data through, for example, the use of mobile search, check-ins[14] and from real-time app use (i.e. using Yelp to look for a restaurant or using an airline app to download a boarding pass).

The opportunity lies in using this data and extrapolating a customer opportunity with respect to banking. This requires you to know your customers well enough at a minimum to know what offers are relevant to them, and what merchants, locations, etc., they frequent. This data can, of course, be gleaned from existing card usage analytics, and cross-referencing with mobile data.

There are a bunch of start-ups emerging right now that use such context data to target consumers with ads that are highly relevant. However, matching this to previous card usage data or to purchases such as an airline ticket for future travel makes the pool of data available from within a bank highly sought after. I've often wondered why banks, privacy concerns aside, haven't figured out that consumer purchase data is an absolute gold mine of potential marketing offers.

Say a customer has previously used his credit card to shop at Macy's. A bank might pitch him a discount on his next purchase at JCPenney instead. He won't need to print a coupon to redeem an offer, he'd just swipe his existing credit or debit card, and receive

Figure 13.1

the discounts as a statement credit after he makes a purchase. Serve™ by American Express currently deploys a similar technology although one has to register for Serve and nominate the types of offers one would like to receive. There are privacy concerns potentially with this type of messaging approach, so it's critical to be able to offer customers the ability to configure or turn such offers on and off.

The location-based offers and services present a new revenue stream for banks, given that most vendors' programmes are paid for by participating merchants and share a fee on each offer that is redeemed with the banks. Such services are expected to generate $1.7 billion in annual revenue for card issuers by 2015, according to a report last year from Aité Group. Some of the providers of this technology, such as FreeMonee, actually charge the bank and merchant a 5–10 per cent success fee on the purchase, instead of charging upfront for the platform or marketing.

Cardlytics is a well-known provider in the space. Cardlytics essentially provides an offer-matching capability and mines card data on an aggregated basis to match merchant codes with offers that might be of interest to the bank customer. This, of course, requires that the bank have a relationship with multiple merchants so that offers can be successfully served to a customer. However, the ability to match a merchant where a customer has shopped before, or offer him a deal at a competing merchant where he might shop, given an incentive, means that customers are getting clear value from this type of messaging. It also means that banks are starting to understand that if they want us to use their credit card or debit card, they have to offer us a promotion that is not going to be simply unsolicited spam. Mobile context needs to be respected.

Right now, PayPal, Square and others such as Google Wallet are amassing incredible data and building broad merchant relationships for this exact purpose—to be able to market to customers to stimulate or influence a purchase. With mobile wallets emerging as the next big thing, banks will soon be struggling to get customers to use their "card" embedded in a mobile wallet. Offers at merchants, tied in with a specific financial institution, will be a strong influencer in the early days. For most banks, the problem will be that they have to pay PayPal, Square, Google or others to get those messages to their customers. Think about that. Better you start building that capability independently, and understand which merchants you need to start partnering, and who, with the bank, is going to manage those partnerships and offer delivery strategies.

Others have taken a more tactical approach specifically designed at stimulating bank interactions and usage. Bank of America is using a mobile advertising campaign to increase awareness, and hence downloads, of its mobile banking iPhone application.

The ads walk users through the app's features and educate consumers on Bank of America's mobile banking. The ad campaign runs off Apple's iAd network. Now if a customer isn't a BofA client, this ad is probably not of much use, but if he is a BofA client, then he might take advantage of this promotion as he is mobile. Serving an ad that says viewing your accounts is "as easy as buying milk" when you're at the local convenience store is a good messaging strategy.

Figure 13.2 Example of a simple mobile strategy

> "Mobile provides us with a targetable channel to reach on-the-go consumers with relevant products, and iAd allows for a richer mobile ad experience, offering more opportunity for brand interaction."
> —T.J. Crawford, senior vice-president, media relations, BofA

Now, you know that online customers want convenience—the number one driver for mobile and internet banking adoption. But critical to the early success of internet advertising and e-commerce was the fact that often they could get great deals online. Preferential pricing, discounts, or perceived advantages of an online or real-time purchase stimulated by an offer are powerful motivators.

"Our customers have told us ... they are looking for better
deals when they shop... They don't want to do it in a way that causes
them to jump through a bunch of hoops or clip a bunch of coupons."
—Aditya Bhasin, senior vice-president, consumer marketing
and online/mobile banking, Bank of America

Relevance again comes through as a key driver here. Give me a deal, but
make it quick, simple and fast to execute. If you need me to register first, or
print out some coupon, you're missing the point of the power of contextual
advertising and offer management.

Banner blindness, SPAM and TiVo

Traditional advertising has been about eyeballs—the more eyeballs you
reach the more frequently, the more chance you have of brand recall when
the purchase decision is being made. In the early 1900s, consumers were
faced with few choices of brands, and advertising was limited to mostly in-
store promotion. By the mid-1930s, radio has resulted in consumers facing
exposure to hundreds of products a year. These days, the average consumer
is confronted by thousands of advertising images on a daily basis alone.
The result is that advertisers are trying to shout louder for our attention,
and we are increasingly finding ways to reduce this impact.

Our browsers now have pop-up blockers, our email has spam filters,
and we have tougher privacy laws so advertisers can't exchange our contact
information; we have do-not-call lists for outbound telesales, and we have
DVRs where customers simply fast-forward and skip ads. Has anyone ever
noticed how the judges on American Idol are all drinking Coke these days?
This is the advertising industry's attempt to keep us looking at products
when it is clear we're not watching TVCs anymore.

Hollywood Reporter revealed that Coca-Cola, Ford and AT&T forked
over roughly $35 million each for the opportunity to be featured in
America's most-watched TV show in 2008, American Idol.

"Apple products appeared in 30% of the 33 top films in 2010.
Nike, Chevy and Ford in 24%. Sony, Dell, Land Rover and Glock in

15%. Product Placement is a $25 billion industry now. In fact, the next James Bond movie will cover one-third of its budget with $45 million in product placement revenue."

—OnlineMBA.com[15]

In a world where the broadcast style of advertising is increasingly failing to get results, banks will be forced to adopt a much more personalised, contextual approach to marketing. When customers come to a branch, you will need to know with a high likelihood what they will need, so they don't have to wait. If they want to apply for a loan, you'll need to be able to approve it instantly—no forms, salary records, bank statements needed. It's all about removing the friction.

The days of direct mail campaigns, newspaper ads and billboards will largely disappear as you dedicate your marketing team to customer intelligence, predictive and permission-based marketing, and better, smaller segmentation methods.

When push comes to shove...

One-to-one marketing and targeting key influencers in social marketing settings are vital for the future of bank engagement—not traditional direct mail or mass market marketing. Let customers make the decision on what information you can send them. The customer will let you know either explicitly or behaviourally (i.e. looking up a website or searching on Google) when they want home equity offers or the opportunity to assess a new health plan offering.

Call this new commitment **intelligent, non-intrusive, permission marketing**. Give customers an alert configuration engine that allows them not only to dictate what they will see, but also through what channels. Give them the ability to choose how you mine their transactions and previous interactions with the bank and retailers to provide a better service.

Use Twitter to provide awesome customer advocacy experiences which demonstrate the brand's commitment to customers. Integrate instant messaging capability right onto your websites and mobile apps so you can generate leads in real time through the contact centre.

When your customers are out and about, use location-based messaging capability to target them with relevant offers from retailers that they have purchased from before. How can you tell? Use their credit card history and trawl that to create the relevant offer pool preloaded with the network operator's CRM tools.

Guess what. Most banks are still doing none of this right now.

YouTube is the world's second-largest search engine today. How do you get your customers talking about you on YouTube so that when potential customers search, they find great messages about your brand performance?

Banks today are competing against 21st-century players, stuck in a 1970s marketing paradigm. Banks must evolve—fast. There is no downside—with 90 per cent of transactions taking place through self-service channels, how could you imagine that new media such as YouTube, Facebook, Twitter and other such media are going to continue to do anything less than grow? The only real question is: why aren't you already doing this?

Point-of-impact journeys

A bad sales experience can feel very much like we've been used or abused. Persuasive sale is the technical art of selling someone something that he doesn't necessarily need, but convincing him long enough to get his commitment to sign. Indeed, when presented with enough pressure, customers will often commit, just to terminate the sales conversation. Once bitten, twice shy when it comes to this approach. When we get pushed into a buy, we don't usually come back.

A good sale, however, feels like the brand has done something right by us. Even better, a good sale can feel like we've been done a great service. In fact, when we get great service and we feel like we came out on top in the sales conversation, or we got exactly the right solution—we normally come back for more because it was a great experience.

Combining this basic tenet with the concept of permission marketing, and better customer analytics, you would realise that push won't work in the Bank 3.0 paradigm. Indeed, marketing organisations instinctively have to understand customers so well that they can anticipate their service needs whenever possible. When an organisation gets this right, the subsequent message or offer will not only feel like a *good sale* to the customer—it will be perceived as great service.

This is why push-based message marketing needs to change to pull-based, point-of-impact, service selling.

Phase I: Distributed Applications @ Point of Impact

Right now, your bank could be doing a lot more to reach customers at the point of impact. The point of impact goes beyond simply the point of sale. It includes wherever the sales journey might be initiated with a possibility of closure. With internet technology this is very simple. In future, with more integrated wireless capability and improved handset bandwidth, anywhere your customer interacts with a vendor or sale process, your bank can integrate into that experience either from an offer point of view or a payments perspective. From web to mobile to IP-enabled point of sale, distributed application technology will become standard practice in the next five years.

A few such examples of technology capability to get to the user at the point of impact would include offering travel insurance within the online booking engine of say, Cathay Pacific's or British Airway's website, offering an instant pre-approved mortgage quotation on a property website, or offering a special car loan proposition on a dealer's website. But speed and targeted placement will be the critical factors in all of this, so you will still need to integrate this with a customer profile—this is not just about third-party banner advertising.

Figure 13.3: Point-of-impact selling strategies

Phase II: Predictive selling or triggered offers

Customer analytics also enable you to predict, anticipate or respond better to opportunities for target clients when these present themselves.

Here are some examples:

Table 13.14: Event-triggered offers

Event Type	Event	Event Description
Significant Balance Change	Investment Needs	• Customer's account holdings increased by large or significant amount ($200k to $500k, $500k+). • Lead delivered to banker next day who contacts customer with offer e.g. a financial planning appointment.
Large Transactions	Withdrawals/ Deposits	• A transaction out of the ordinary for that customer, e.g. greater than average for last three months. • Lead delivered to banker next day who contacts customer to identify and fulfil changed needs .
Personal Tax Loans	Redraw request/ Payout request	• Call centre receives request for redraw or payout. • Lead delivered to banker next day who contacts customer to identify and fulfil changed needs .
Term Deposits	Renewals/ Upgrades	• Maturing lead delivered to relationship manager. • RM contacts customer to renew or increase deposit, perhaps offering better rate through a structured product or something similar.
Home Loans	Fixed rate Rollover	• Banker contacts customer to offer various options, including home equity draw down, line of credit options, etc.

This is where the customer dynamics team comes into play. It has to create a list of these target opportunities and possible event triggers so the offers are ready to go when the event occurs. Without this vital element, these events will just pass us by.

Think of this approach from a customer point of view. If you were contacted as a result of one of these events, wouldn't you likely perceive that as *great service*? You wouldn't necessarily think of it as a sale process at all!

Phase III: Precognitive Selling

As IP-enabled technology continues to progress, point-of-sale equipment will also migrate to the cloud or integrate with our app phone's capabilities, as we've already discussed. In this environment, banks will be able to respond with an offer on presentation of the card/chip/phone for payment.

That offer may include other options for payment, for example, from an offset account, or an offer for a line of credit that is at a much lower rate than the credit card—or an interest-free period. The customer presents his fingerprint to verify his identity and accepts the offer as payment at the point of sale.

Let's illustrate it this way by comparing today's approach versus the precognitive opportunity:

Figure 13.5: Retail purchase event—credit card promotion

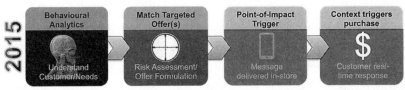

Figure 13.6: Precognitive event results in point-of-impact message

Technically we are very close to being able to offer this sort of message and service capability to the end consumer.

Conclusions

Segmentation and customer intelligence through behavioural analytics is the key to this type of messaging capability. More than simply segmenting customers, banks will need to understand how customers behave, what they do, how often, and through which channels. Currently banks don't even understand which transactions go through which channel for existing customers. Marketing must understand the why and how, and ask customers what they want. Some banks probably imagine that they do this already, but most of them certainly don't use that data effectively to sell or match offers to individual customers.

Banks will also need to deliver marketing messages in very different ways. In fact, in many ways banks will have to reinvent the marketing function moving forward. Branding will continue to be critical, but general campaigns will be replaced by messaging that is a lot tighter, and rapidly actionable. Traditional methods of campaign promotion through direct mail, radio, TV, newspaper, classifieds, outdoor and so forth, will need to be abandoned completely in the near term. While some of those media *may* still be used for branding, promotion and campaigns will no longer be cost effective enough to remain at the core of acquisition methods. As messaging and customer journeys become contextual, the old broadcast methods will simply no longer have the granularity to produce measurable success.

Your marketing team needs to change NOW!

If you haven't figured this out by now, your current marketing team is probably going to find the Bank 3.0 transition very difficult to master. The temptation to send off a brief to an agency to produce some creative output for a print campaign is a hard habit to break.

That's why new thinking will be required and new skills invested in. Half of the marketing team over the next five years needs to be focused entirely on what advertisers fondly call "interactive" or digital, but the biggest innovations in marketing need to come from mobile search, journeys, digital and social advocacy. If you are a marketer in a bank and you find yourself shaking your head at this assertion, then you might need to think about a change in career—preferably before your boss decides to make that change for you. However, if you've looked at the numbers and you've come to the same conclusions, then get on board—there is plenty of scope and room for converts in the point-of-impact discipline.

Start by building stories around customer journeys and looking at opportunities for contextualising banking. Don't limit yourself to thinking about a message that drives a customer to "apply"; start understanding why they apply, where they are when the need emerges, and how you can get a message to them when and where they need a solution. Great customer journeys are the future of the marketing domain, and it will require a very different skill set from what we see in the marketing department today.

Keywords: Ad Spend, TV Commercials, Banner Blindness, Point of Impact, Journeys, Predictive Selling, Events, Triggered Offers, Behavioural Analytics, Precognitive Selling

Endnotes

1 Duke University Business School CMO Survey, Feb 2012, http://cmosurvey.org/files/2012/02/The_CMO_Survey_Highlights_and_Insights_Feb-2012_Final.pdf

2 *EIAA Mediascape*, Nov 2008

3 "53 regional newspapers close" (http://www.guardian.co.uk/media/greenslade/2009/feb/19/local-newspapers-newspapers)

4 Huffington Post (http://www.huffingtonpost.com/2010/04/26/top-25-newspapers-by-circ_n_552051.html#s84768&title=1_Wall_Street)

5 http://www.nytimes.com/2012/07/27/business/media/the-new-york-times-co-posts-a-loss.html

6 FreeTV Australia via http://www.theage.com.au/business/tv-ad-sales-fall-less-than-expected-20090721-ds37.html

7 "Radio Advertising Spending Declines for the 10th Quarter in a Row" (http://bocpartners.com/2009/11/23/radio-advertising-spending-declines-for-the-10th-quarter-in-a-row/)

8 http://www.hollywoodreporter.com/news/french-tv-companies-report-ad-354884

9 *Guardian*: http://www.guardian.co.uk/media/2012/jul/03/tv-press-ad-revenues

10 NielsenWire Blog: http://blog.nielsen.com/nielsenwire/online_mobile/double-vision-global-trends-in-tablet-and-smartphone-use-while-watching-tv/

11 CEA Market Research Analysis Brief at http://www.cesweb.org/shared_files/ECD-TOC/CEACordCuttingAnalysis.pdf

12 Kantar Media Research at http://kantarmediana.com/intelligence/press/us-advertising-expenditures-increased-08-percent-2011

13 See Wikipedia for details

14 See Foursquare, Path or Facebook Check-In

15 http://www.marketingtechblog.com/product-placement-infographic/

14 The Road Map to a Better Bank

Your critical path checklist for Bank 3.0

Banking has already pivoted due to a fundamental shift in day-to-day banking behaviour. This shift is resulting in increasing disruption, failure points and new models that threaten the established status quo. When presented with similar disruptive behaviour, most industries stick their heads in the sand and embrace the inevitability of defeat. How can you know whether or not you are ready to shift, or whether you're likely going to go under?

Broadly speaking, the smaller the institution, the more likely this disruption will bite hard. Primarily this is because the cost of changing the behaviour of the company represents a significantly higher percentage of the annual budget/spend for a smaller institution. I think the danger zone is probably for institutions under $1 billion in assets.

How do you know you're in trouble or you're not making the shift? This checklist is designed to measure the preparedness of your core executive team and your overall bank strategy with respect to dealing with the coming onslaught of the Bank 3.0 reality. Let's see how ready you are:

1. **Do you have branches with under $15 million in assets?**
   Recent FIS research suggests that 18 per cent of branches in the United States lose on average $200,000 a year with under $10 million in assets.[1] As the impact of the customer behavioural shift around digital continues to bite, this will force around half of the branches in the US to close by 2020.

If you find this hard to believe, go back to the Chapter 3—Can the Branch Be Saved?

2. **Do you still require a signature card for account opening?**

At least half, if not more, of new customer acquisitions over the coming decade will be branchless—that is, customers will open new accounts all the time via online or mobile. If you still require a signature card, you're in bad shape for this transition. Keep in mind that since the early 2000s, there are very few regulators in the world that have required a signature card. This is just organisational inertia at play.

3. **Do you still call your primary account type a checking/current account?**

The cheque as an artefact itself is rapidly in decline, and it does not describe the day-to-day behaviour of a bank account today, where the debit card and other methods are used far more frequently than the cheque book. By calling an account a *checking* account, you are set to alienate a whole new generation of banked consumers who don't ever want to use cheques.

4. **Do you have a distinct Head of Social Media in an executive role?**

Facebook grew to 955 million customers in just over eight years, the largest consumer service business by customers ever. Instagram grew to 100 million customers in a few months, and was acquired for $1 billion in April 2012. WeiXin in China grew to 100 million customers in just six months. If you think social media is just an add-on to the IT or marketing function, you are completely disconnected from the reality of the consumer market today. Social media is more vital to the future of your business than your call centre, your ATMs or any of the branches in your network. If you don't believe me, then go back and re-read Chapter 8—I Trust the Crowd More Than I Trust the Brand.

5. **Did you invest more on remodelling, opening, staffing or marketing branch-related acquisition than in the internet, social networking and mobile in 2012?**

If you answered yes, given that the branch represents such a small fraction of your transactional activity and soon will be subordinate to the Internet channel in respect of revenue generation, you are no longer serving the interests of your shareholders or your customers; you are simply serving inertia.

6. **Does the Head of Branch Distribution hold a more senior position than the Head of Internet?**

If you answered yes, given the mix of business in the bank today, and given the increasing importance of the Internet and mobile channels, why wouldn't you have these critical leaders closer to the Head of Retail or the CEO so that bank strategy can be better informed? Your customers are going to use the digital channels 250 times a year more than the branch on current metrics.[2] Digital will be more effective at building your business moving forward than the branch can possibly be. So why is the guy looking after real estate in a more senior executive role than those who own the future of the business?

7. **Do you have a Head of Mobile, and do you have apps already deployed for your customers?**

If you answered no to either of these two questions, then you are in very serious doo-doo. Mobile is the fastest growing banking channel *ever*. To not have a senior executive in charge of this super strategic channel is a major mistake in judgement. By 2016 the majority of your customers will be using mobile banking 20–30 times a month to access banking. That's four years away. How are you going to take advantage of that? How are you going to provide personalised, high-quality service through a channel that the customer carries with him virtually every minute of the day? Why wouldn't you put your most senior retail guy on that right now??

8. **Do you have a working plan for how you are going to phase out cheques with retail customers?**
   If you answered no, then put the team on to it now.

9. **Can your customers make P2P payments, regular transfers and pay bills from their phone today?**
   If no, then this has just become the highest-priority project for the retail bank this year.

10. **Are your CEO, Head of Marketing and Head of Customer Advocacy on Twitter?**
    If no, then who is telling them what customers are tweeting about your bank?

11. **Do you prevent customer-facing staff from using Facebook and Twitter during work hours?**
    Are you going to start installing metal detectors to stop employees bringing their smartphones into the office too? You haven't merely stopped staff using Facebook by blocking access on the network, you've just destroyed the one opportunity you have for exercising some positive control over the way staff use social media to contribute to the brand.

12. **Can you approve a personal loan application for an existing customer with a salaried account in real time, instantly?**
    If no, then you are most likely missing two key components in your basic systems infrastructure today—straight-through processing, and automated credit risk scoring and assessment.

13. **Do you know what percentage of your visitors to your bank's homepage click on login versus other sections of the website?**
If not, then how do you know what part of your website budget should be focused on influencing existing customers with cross-sell opportunities?

14. **Do you know which products are the most popular in your market when it comes to new internet revenue? Or do you know which products you sell more of online than through the branch today? Do you know which products are sold online, but fulfilled in the branch?**
If not, then what about what products that sell better through the call centre or through the ATM, rather than via branch or direct selling. I'm not talking about monthly MIS reports or a report your channel guys can compile over the next ten days—I'm talking about you tracking these day to day, quarter by quarter across the entire customer journey. Don't focus on the destination, understand the journey!

15. **Do you have someone measuring sentiment, crowdsourcing new approaches, and trying to build customer advocacy for your brand?**
If you don't know what any of these means, then your bank is not plugged into the future of revenue and core drivers for acquisition moving forward. If you're still wondering how you're going to get customers back in the branch, then this is the answer, although this is more about how you're going to get customers back to the "brand". Your brand is now subject to ongoing discussion, dissection, debate and hijacking by individuals, consumer groups, and advocates. Make sure you are part of the conversation, and enabling the right type of discussion.

I could put a bunch more questions up here, but I am afraid this would make a mockery out of the process. These are serious questions that lead to the sort of reflections the CEO and Head of Retail of the bank need to be asking today. Let's discuss the possible action plan or "road map" for the next five years.

The Checklist

Here are the critical developments organisationally and intellectually your bank has to make over the coming couple of years:
- Digital competency is core
- Deleveraging branches to a supporting role
- Banking is about context and journeys
- Customer dialogue informs strategy
- Agile IT might be in the cloud

Digital competency is at the core

Three years ago when I wrote *Bank 2.0*, you still had the flexibility of having the "Internet" and such functions as a supporting cast. No longer. Today digital is the DNA of a modern retail bank. Why? Customers are using digital as part of their banking DNA—it is their everyday experience that matters now. Banking has evolved to tasks, utility, functionality and capability that enable the life of a customer when and where he needs banking. In this respect, even the branch is a part of the digital experience.

Increasingly you're going to be building experiences that anticipate customer needs or personalise the experience every time a customer interacts with the brand. Predicting those needs, pre-assessing risk, flagging a service opportunity and fulfilling it in real time won't be exotic applications of technology, they will be hygiene factors.

Future bank growth over the next decade is inexorably tied to servicing customers for whom digital is nothing new. Digital natives and the Y-Gen don't think of the internet, mobile, tablets, social media and such technologies as "new". They think of them as normal. The more you try to force a signature card, application form or outmoded process on them, the more that translates to pure friction in the customer experience and risks your becoming irrelevant to a whole new generation of customers.

Digital should not be regarded as an add-on to the bank. It is at the very heart of day-to-day banking delivery today. Restructure your executive team, your budgeting process and your core capability on that basis.

Deleveraging branches

The branch has long been at the core of retail banking. In fact, this has been the case for more than 700 years already. Today, however, that is rapidly changing. With branch visitation activity at its lowest point in three decades and rapidly shrinking further, with branch numbers declining, with transactional activity shifting to mobile and the Internet—the very real question of what happens with your branches needs to be tackled hard and fast.

While eliminating all of your branches overnight would be a ridiculous strategy, so would keeping your branch network overstocked and overstaffed the way it is right now. So start thinking about unwinding your brand gradually over the next five to six years from the most unprofitable branches. If you have branches with under $10–15m in assets, then these will be the first to go. Critical to this assessment is also accurate branch profitability measurements. Don't assume a product is sold in-branch when it was actually sold online and compliance processes forced the customer into the branch. Start measuring the entire journey, and understand profitability as a whole.

As you reassess, figure out which locations need to be your flagship brand locations, and which need to be simple points-of-presence that service the core psychological need of a branch—that is, a place I can go if I have a problem related to my money. These satellite points-of-presence might be as simple as a bank officer with an iPad, a desk and a couple of comfortable chairs. As such, some banks will retain branches at strategic locations to provide ongoing service to valuable and profitable customers. However, there are going to be just as many new "banks'" and non-bank FIs that will be competing with your bank without the distribution cost you are currently saddled with.

To remain cost-effective and competitive in the medium term, most large retail banking organisations will have to consolidate their branch network by 30–50 per cent over the next decade.

You might not believe this scale of adjustment is necessary. However, you need to start scenario-planning for this as a very real possibility because the cycle of deleveraging from current branch real estate is typically three to four years long, and this is just when mobile and mobile payments are going to be doing their most significant damage day to day to your behavioural assumptions about banking.

Banking is about context and journeys

Most marketing organisations, including retail financial institutions, still have not optimised their marketing approach to digital and interactive media. Marketing teams are heavily geared towards broadcast or, as Seth Godin characterised, "interruption" marketing.

While so-called traditional media have largely been in decline for most of the decade, "new" media have often been considered a plaything or an add-on for campaigns targeting pimply students and Warcraft-playing geeks. Interactive just wasn't taken that seriously. With management demanding stronger accountability and strong metrics which demonstrate return on marketing investment (**ROMI**), marketing departments are struggling with rising CPM (cost per impression), dwindling response rates, and traditional advertising mechanisms that are rapidly losing their effectiveness.

What invariably happens today is that, due to a deficient skill set within the marketing department, rather than coming up with original and innovative approaches to utilising social networking and digital technologies, most marketing departments are stuck and simply find themselves trying to retrofit traditional campaigns onto new media, with limited success.

Today banks need to target customers with pin-point accuracy, with offers only directly relevant to their needs. Any brand that continues today to force irrelevant offers using the broadcast or shotgun approach to lead generation or customer acquisition such as direct mail, will see the effectiveness of those methods reduce down to zero.

The organisation will need to adapt to this pressure by creating a team that focuses on constant optimisation of customer propositions through segmentation analysis, behavioural analytics, just-in-time product layering and permission-based marketing. This will be supported by systems that will anticipate the sale based on behavioural patterns, triggers, geolocation data and advocacy mechanisms.

Customers will perceive this shift not as *marketing* per se, but as providing a *service* because the resulting "point-of-impact" messages will be individual, unique and integrated seamlessly into their daily lives when and where they need the bank.

When I am shopping, my bank will offer me a line of credit to use to purchase the bedroom setting I am considering buying. When I am booking travel online, my bank will automatically provide me with travel insurance coverage at an agreed set rate, or offer me the option of purchasing the trip as a travel loan instead of using my credit or debit card. When I get a salary increase, the bank will automatically offer me an upgraded Platinum credit card with an extended credit limit.

Insurance on my home, my car, my boat will be integrated into a central policy, automatically updated unless I nominate otherwise—I will only be asked the first time. I will be offered bundled products that are constantly optimised.

The customer is the primary focus, and brand recall is only relevant to customers who can be serviced in this way. The marketing team will be a true revenue generation platform, not through advertising, but through channel, customer and offer management.

Customer dialogue informs strategy

As an industry at large, the banking sector has been guilty of blasting ahead based on the needs of shareholders, the requirements of regulators, and the legacy of antiquated mainframe transactional banking systems. The global financial crisis and subsequent lessons around new fee structures (such as post-Durbin efforts) taught most banks that they could no longer afford to blast on without nuancing the dialogue with customers. What is different?

Social media and real-time engagement have empowered the customer.

From choice driven by search, to the ability to talk about your performance as a bank in real time, customers have been given a voice like never before. With the power to overturn dictators, governments and reverse poor decisions (BofA debit card fees, anyone?), social media has added to the mix.

This is all about not underestimating the power of those customers you claim to serve. Customers are reasonable, they understand you are in a business and need to make a profit. However, they are increasingly only prepared to fund those profits if you provide real, transparent value in return. Trust in banking is all but gone today. No longer can bankers charge a premium because they have a lock on the taking of deposits.

For many bankers and marketers alike, the prospect of customers talking openly in the social space about their brand is terrifying these days. There are the likes of Westpac and others that have tried to stifle the slightest negative responses in the social space, only to find it backfire savagely. There are the likes of major brands such as HSBC, which at the time of this book going to press still don't have a Twitter presence out of fear of giving customers a further platform for voicing their opinions of the brand in an uncontrolled environment.

This can be threatening, or it can be incredibly useful and informative. Banks such as OCBC, First Data, DBS and others have embraced social media and the customer dialogue to form strategy, whether on something as simple as the design of a debit card, or as complex as a new brand design. With positive engagement, customers feel a sense of ownership of the brand and they're increasingly willing to participate in discussions on how to improve the brand's connection to the broader customer base. Remember, mechanisms such as crowdsourcing are amongst the cheapest and most accurate forms of research today, and a great way to test or validate the needs and concerns of your customers.

The dialogue isn't something to be terrified of. It is a platform for building your business. Empower customers, involve them, and you'll also be building advocacy.

On the whole advocacy issue, make sure those customers who are delighted with your service or performance get the opportunity to talk about it. By restricting your social media presence you might marginalise negative customers who want to complain about the teller who served them in the branch last month, or the way the credit department handled the way it informed them of their rejected loan applications, but you'll also marginalise customers who want to champion your brand, your products, and those moments of service excellence that are so critical.

Allow your best and happiest customers a platform for promoting great interactions, and get the word out as frequently and as broadly as you can on YouTube, Twitter, Facebook and through blogs, etc.

Nothing says you are a great bank that deserves new business like a delighted customer.

Agile IT might be in the cloud

Increasingly, building all of this technology capability, integrating with Big Data and having scalable solutions that respond to a dynamic customer base, are not only going to be extremely expensive, they are also going to push the competency of your technology team to the brink. Thus, it might be time to consider a partnership strategy that brings you elements of these capabilities over the coming years as you adapt.

Increasingly, partner or vendor choice is going to be critical. Does that vendor have the ability to adapt? Are they deploying solutions in the cloud? Are they working with other partners and vendors in the space that have best-of-breed solutions, or are they insisting on mediocre, proprietary solutions in-house?

No one core systems provider or vendor is going to be able to solve all of your needs as you move forward. The requirements are just far too complex.

The other thing to contemplate is whether you are part of a group of banks or credit unions that are facing the same issues. You might have potential collaborators who aren't competing geographically for the same customers in the same markets—other banks just like you that might consider pooling resources for an overall solution for your collective customer base. Solutions such as Kasasa, RediATM and others are examples of how the collective customer base is better served by cooperation across the industry when it comes to technology or service platforms.

The cloud is potentially the platform that enables this ty[industry collaboration.

Conclusions

Bank 3.0 is about change. Change that is inevitable, change that is speeding up, and change that is extremely disruptive.

You may not agree with all the predictions in this book. You may not think that cheques, credit cards and cash are under threat from new technologies. You may not feel that the marketing team needs to change its approach significantly because it has worked so well in the past. You may feel that the bank is in a strong financial position, so this is simply "much ado about nothing".

However, you may also agree that customers seem to be changing the way they engage banks at an annoyingly rapid rate. You are probably amazed at how many people are carrying around iPhones, iPads and Android devices. You might be amused at how many people are discussing Facebook and Twitter.

In any case, I hope that the evidence and thinking presented in this book are enough to produce one thing—a groundswell of support within your bank to innovate and try new ways of reaching, engaging and communicating with your customers.

If you are a banker and you do nothing else as a result of reading this book, just keep asking customers and listening to customers about *how* they want to engage with the bank. When these customers talk about mobile, the Internet, social networks and so forth, take it on board and figure out how you are going to provide customers with utility, accessibility and functionality on the right channels at the right time.

But most critical of all—*innovate* and *experiment*. Things move so fast technologically these days that you can't wait until a trend is three years into its cycle to adapt. Why not? Because by three years into the adoption cycle, the next big thing will already be on its way and you're now potentially five or six years behind.

Create a team that is both an advocate for customers and enabling advocacy by customers. A team dedicated to creating the right offer, across the right channels, at the right time—great customer journeys. Give these resources huge support—because they are your new front line.

Technology is a means to an end, but it is also increasingly becoming a means to profitability. Channels are increasing in complexity, not decreasing. You need to manage the customer, agnostic of any one channel he chooses. The branch is no more important than any other channel—it is also not going to be the most profitable channel in the future. So any business case you present is going to have to figure out how to tackle this channel/resource conflict sooner or later.

Understand one thing: Customers are not going back to the old ways of banking. They are moving forward. If you are not moving forward with them, then they'll pass right by you—at warp speed.

These changes are not new for many customers you are serving today. For your newest customers, the Internet, mobile, social media and such are not innovations; they are just a way of life. When you stick a signature card in front of them, insist they come into the branch, or try to sell them a checking account, you're demonstrating your irrelevance.

Build great customer journeys, and banking becomes a solution to the problems every day for your customers.

Remove the friction from the processes, because if you don't, Movenbank, Simple, Dwolla, PayPal, Square, and others will, and they'll increasingly take market share away from you.

Empower your customers and your customer-facing teams to come together. Start listening to and observing your customers. Don't assume that because it worked 30 years ago, it still works today. Don't assume your customers aren't changing the way they bank every day, if you haven't seen them in action. Don't tell me your customers don't use mobile banking when you haven't got a mobile app for your customers. Don't tell me your customers don't interact with you via social media when you don't have an executive tasked with enabling discussions via these channels.

Banking is fundamentally shifting. It is moving away from products, processes and places to a capability for customers when and where they need it.

Bank 3.0 is about enabling banking day to day. Banking that is no longer dependent on a place, but enables your customers every day to live their lives integrated with the fulfilment and capability of a bank. It is about journeys where banking facilitates a need, whether that need is buying a home, buying a car, going on a trip, shopping, sending our kids to college or saving for retirement.

Banking is no longer somewhere your customers go, it's something they do. Your mission as a banker is to build the "do"; the capability to let banking work for them day to day, when and where they need a solution to a problem life throws at them. As bankers you've been more inclined in the recent decade to become the problem, thinking that banking is unique, special and requires hurdles or qualifications before a customer is allowed to avail themselves of your products and network. This friction will kill your collective industry unless you get back to the core of what banking should be about—helping and serving those customers that are your lifeblood.

The shift in consumer behaviour is speeding up like never before. It's time to get on board, or get out of the way.

Thanks for listening.

Endnotes

1   FIS Consulting, "Shifting Investments in Legacy Branch Networks—Finally": http://bankblog.optirate.com/wp-content/uploads/2012/02/FIS-Shifting-Investments-in-Legacy-Branch-Networks-%E2%80%93-Finally.pdf

2   Refer to the estimates in Chapter 2—specifically Figure 2.1 Estimated Retail Banking Channel Interactions for 2016

Glossary

Adoption Rate: How quickly it takes new technologies to be adopted by the public at large.

ACH: Automated Clearing House

AOs: Algorithmic Operations

API: Application Program Interface

AML: Anti-Money Laundering—the efforts through legislation, regulation and through systems to track, identify and stop the laundering of illicit funds into the mainstream banking system.

Android: An open mobile phone platform developed by Google and, later, the Open Handset Alliance. It consists of the operating system (on which everything runs), the middleware (allowing applications to talk to a network and to one another), and the applications (the actual programs that the phones will run).

App: Short for application—a program or piece of software, especially as downloaded by a user to a mobile device.

App Phone: A phone that provides open application support not limited to the phone handset, manufacturer's operating system and applications; most common instances are the iPhone, Droid and NexusOne.

Augmented Reality (AR): The overlaying of digital data on the real world.

Avatar: A computer user's representation of himself/herself, or alter ego, for use on computer systems.

B2B: Business-to-Business—as in intraorganisational communication, collaboration and commerce; normally electronic, and usually using websites and/or web services.

Basel II and III: The second and third of the Basel Accords, which are recommendations on banking laws and regulations issued by the Basel Committee on Banking Supervision.

Big Data: Data sets the sizes of which are beyond the ability of commonly used software tools to capture, manage, and process within a tolerable elapsed time. Big data sizes are a constantly moving target, and as of 2012, range from a few dozen terabytes to many petabytes of data in a single data set.

Bitcoin: A type of P2P digital currency.

Blog: A contraction of the term "web log"—a type of website usually maintained by an individual with regular entries of commentary, descriptions of events, or other material such as graphics or video.

BPO: Business Process Outsourcing—the practice of outsourcing some or all of the business's back-office processes to an external company or service provider; common with call centres and IT support.

BPR: Business Process Re-engineering—re-engineering business processes to either reduce costs or improve the flow of a process for customers.

CapEx: Capital Expense

CES: Consumer Electronics Show

Churn: This refers to customers moving from a service provider within one specific product category to another, based on price, value or some other factor.

CLID: Caller Line Identification—a system that identifies a customer based on the phone number they use to call a service provider.

Cloud computing: An emerging computing technology that uses the Internet and central remote servers to maintain data and applications; players include DropBox, YouSendIt and Flickr.

CPM: Cost per impression; in online advertising, it relates to cost per (thousand) impressions

CRM: Customer Relationship Management; sometimes Credit Risk Management.

Cross-Selling: A method of targeting and selling new products to an existing customer.

Crowdsourcing: Tapping into the collective intelligence of the public at large to complete business-related tasks that a company would normally either perform itself or outsource to a third-party provider. It enables managers to expand the size of their talent pool while also gaining deeper insight into what customers really want.

CSR: Customer Service Representative—staff who work within the call centre to assist customers with enquiries.

CTI: Computer-Telephony Integration/Interface—a system that integrates telephone systems with computer networks.

CTR: Click-Through Rate

Digital Natives: Y-Gen and younger users of technology

DM: Direct Mail

Durbin Amendment: The Dodd-Frank Wall Street Reform and Consumer Protection Act of 2010, which reduced fee income for banks of credit and debit card swipes at the point of sale in the US.

ECN: Electronic Communications Network—an electronic network that facilitates trading between stock or commodities exchanges.

EMV: An international standard for smart credit cards that have a built-in CPU chip. Used with brand names such as Chip and PIN and IC Credit, the smartcard provides greater safety than a magnetic stripe because it can support sophisticated security methods and make decisions on its own.

ETFs: Exchange-Traded Funds

Facebook: A hugely popular online social network founded in 2004 for helping friends stay in touch and share information

FAQ: Frequently Asked Questions—questions asked frequently by customers and put on the company's website to expedite answers.

FMCG: Fast-Moving Consumer Goods—products that are sold quickly at relatively low costs.

Geolocation: The technique of identifying the geographical location of a person or device by means of digital information processed via the Internet.

Gilder's Law: Proposed by George Gilder, this law states that bandwidth grows at least three times faster than computer power.

GPR prepaid cards: General Purpose Reloadable prepaid cards

GPRS: General Packet Radio Switching—a packet-oriented mobile data service available to users of 2G and 3G cellular communication systems in Global Systems for Mobile Communications (GSM).

GSM: Global Systems for Mobile Communications—the primary standard for digital mobile phones, in use by 80 per cent of the global mobile market.

Haptic Touch: Technology that interfaces with the user through the sense of touch.

High-Counter: The typical teller station within a branch for conducting over-the-counter transactions.

HNWI: High-Net-Worth Individual—the most attractive client segment for retail banks; HNWIs typically invest US$150,000–US$1 million in investment type products.

IC: Integrated Circuit

IDV: Identity Verification

IM: Instant Messaging—a protocol for communicating between two parties using text-based chat through IP-based clients.

IN: Innovation Newspaper

iOS: Apple's mobile operating system for its iPhone, iPod touch, iPad, Apple TV and similar devices.

IP: Internet Protocol—the primary protocol for transmitting data or information over the Internet.

ISP: Internet Service Provider—a company that provides Internet access to customers.

IVR: Interactive Voice Response (systems)—the automated telephone support systems you hear when you call a 1-800 help line or customer support number, which uses menus and responses via touch-tone and/or voice response for navigation.

IxD: Interaction Design—a customer-led design methodology for improving the interaction between customers and systems.

KPI: Key Performance Indicators—metrics (or measures) used within corporations to measure the performance of one department against another in respect of things such as revenue, sales lead conversion, costs, customer support, etc.

KYC: Know Your Customer—an internal compliance regulation to ensure accurate identification and validation of a customer and understanding of his transactional behaviour

LAN: Local Area Network—a computer network covering a small physical area, such as a home, office, or small group of buildings.

LCD: Liquid Crystal Display

LED: Light Emitting Diode

LOLA: A Siri-like technology (see Siri below) through the Internet and via voice.

Low-Counter: Typically a desk station within a branch where the relationship manager can sit with customers and potential clients and advise them on available products and services.

Lo-Fi Prototype: A simple method of prototyping products, interfaces or applications and testing with target customers or users.

LIBOR: London Interbank Offered Rate

LinkedIn: An online social network for business professionals.

Metcalfe's Law: Attributed to Robert Metcalfe, this law states that the value of a telecommunications network is proportional to the square of the number of connected users of the system (n^2).

MFI: Microfinance Institution—an alternate form of bank found in developing countries which provides microcredit lending.

MIRC: Magnetic Ink Character Recognition

Mobile Portal: A website designed specifically for mobile phone interfaces and mini-browsers.

Mobile Money: Bank-like services delivered over a mobile device to enable payments between two parties; successful providers include M-Pesa, Edy, G-CASH, MTN Money, T-money, Edy, Suica.

Mobile Wallet: An electronic account, dominated in a currency, held on a mobile phone that can be used to store and transfer value.

Moore's Law: Named after Gordon Moore, this law basically states that the number of transistors on a chip doubles every 24 months.

NFC: Near Field Communication—a short-range high-frequency wireless communication technology which enables the exchange of data between devices over about a 10-centimetre distance

OCR: Optical Character Recognition

OpEx: Operating Expense

OLED: Organic Light-Emitting Diode (also Organic Electro-luminescent Device OELD)—an LED whose electroluminescent layer is composed of a film of organic compounds.

OTC: Over the Counter—refers to physical transactions or trades done on behalf of a customer by a trader or customer representative who has access to a specific closed financial system or network.

PayPal: A leading P2P payment provider; others include Square, i-Zettle, ClearXchange, Dwolla, PingIt, PopMoney, QuickPay, Vermo, ZashPay.

PCI compliant: Complying with Payment Card Industry data security standards.

PFM: Personal Financial Management

PPC: Pay-per-Click; a method of paying for appearing in search engine results by bidding and paying for specific keywords; you then pay at the successful bid rate every time a user/visitor clicks on your link.

P2P: Peer-to-Peer or Person-to-Person—a method of passing information or data via IP-based communication methods between two individuals connected to the Internet via computer or mobile devices

Pod: Modular customer engagement station

POS: Point of Sale—the location where a retail transaction occurs; a POS terminal refers more generally to the hardware and software used at checkout stations.

Prosumer: A portmanteau word formed by contracting either the word "professional" or "producer" with the word "consumer"; in respect of this publication, it identifies the role of the modern consumer of content who is also a producer of content on, for example, YouTube, Facebook and Twitter.

PSTN: Public Switched Telephone Network—the traditional copper-wire and exchange based landline telephone system.

QD-OLED: Quatum Dot Organic LED

RFID: Radio Frequency Identification—a short-range radio communication methodology that uses "tags" or small integrated circuits connected to an antenna that when passed within the range of a magnetic reader is able to send a signal.

RM: Relationship Manager—a dedicated customer service manager assigned to look after specific customers, usually high-net-worth ones

ROMI: Return on Marketing Investment

SDK: Software Development Kit—a package provided by a mainstream software or operating system provider to the developer community to assist them with application construction.

SEO: Search Engine Optimisation—the science of optimising websites so that they appear in the top results for search engine enquiries.

SIM Card: Subscriber Identity Module (SIM)—securely stores the service-subscriber key (IMSI) used to identify an individual subscriber on a mobile phone.

Siri: Siri on iPhone 4S lets you use your voice to send messages, make calls, set reminders, and more.

Skype: A technology allowing web chat.

SMS: Short Message Service—a system of communicating by short messages over the mobile telephone network.

Snail Mail: The term used by proponents of digital technologies to describe traditional mail and the postal system.

Spam: Unsolicited bulk email sent out simultaneously to thousands of thousands of email addresses to promote products or services.

Stored-Value Card: Monetary value stored on a card not in an externally recorded account; examples are the Octopus, Oyster and Suica systems used to replace public transport ticketing.

STP: Straight-Through Processing—the implementation of a system that requires no human intervention for the approval or processing of a customer application or transaction

T-DMB: TV via Digital Multimedia Broadcasting

TiVo: A brand and model of digital video recorder available in the US, UK, New Zealand, Canada, Mexico, Australia and Taiwan.

Tablets: A general-purpose computer contained in a single panel, with a touch screen as the input device.

Touch point: Any channel or mechanism by which a consumer has day-to-day interaction with a retail service company, such as a bank, in order to transact or conduct business

TVC: The industry abbreviation for television commercials.

Twitter: A social media website that supports microblogging between participants in the network; sort of like an SMS broadcast system for the web.

UCD: User-Centred Design

Up-Selling: A system of selling an additional service of a higher margin or total revenue within the same product or asset class to a customer, typically upgrading from one class of product to another.

URL: Uniform Resource Locator—an "address" or identifier that is used to locate and retrieve documents hosted on the World Wide Web.

UT: Usability Testing—the science of testing how users interact with a system, product or interface through observation.

VBC: Video Banking Centre (Citibank, circa 1996)—an interactive, 24-hour personal banking centre providing access to personal banking experts through integrated voice, video and data connection.

Virtual Currency: Currencies such as Linden dollars, QQ coins, Project Entropia Dollars (PED), etc. that exist in the virtual world and can be exchanged for real currency by users.

VoIP: Voice Over Internet Protocol—an Internet-based protocol that allows users to use voice communication such as over a telephone system

VSC: Virtual Support Centre—a call centre virtually supported by customer service representatives who typically operate from home (i.e. homesourcing).

WAP: Wireless Access Protocol—the original protocol for simple Internet browsing or simple menu interactions via 2G (digital) mobile phones.

Web 2.0: Web applications that facilitate interactive information sharing, interoperability, user-centred design and collaboration on the World Wide Web.

Widget: A generic type of software application that is usually portable and works across different operating systems and devices.

WiMax: Worldwide Interoperability for Microwave Access—a telecommunications technology that enables wireless transmission of data from point-to-multipoint links to portable and fully mobile Internet access.

XML: eXtensible Markup Language—a set of rules for encoding documents electronically.

Yelp: A website that lets users review businesses ranging from plumbers to pet shops and which introduced a check-in service for mobile phones in 2010.

References

Australian Broadcasting Commission. "Community banks silence sceptics". Retrieved from The 7:30 Report (18 August 2002). http://www.abc.net.au/7.30/content/2002/s679904.htm

Berghman, L., & P. Matthyssens, P. and K. Vandenbempt. "Building competencies for new customer value creation: An exploratory study". Industrial Marketing Management, Vol. 35, No. 8 (2006), pp. 961-73.

Cavell, D. J. The Branch is Bank: Global Case Studies in 21st Century Banking Success. London, United Kingdom: VRL Financial News (2008).

Colurcio, M., & C. Mele. La generazione delle idee. La gestione dei percorsi di innovazione. Giappichelli, Torino (2008).

Dan Milmo, J. T. "Treasury tells shareholders to block bank bonuses". The Guardian, 9 January 2010.

Federal Reserve Bank of Philadelphia. "An Examination of Mobile Banking and Mobile Payments: Building Adoption as Experience Goods." Philadelphia: Federal Reserve Bank (2008).

FinExtra. "Philippines mobile phone-based microfinance bank set for launch" (13 October 2009). From Finextra.com: http://www.finextra.com/fullstory.asp?id=20598

First Data/Tower Group. "The Risks and Opportunities in a Mobile Commerce Economy." First Data/Tower Group (2008).

Fitzpatrick, D. "BofA Seeks to Repay a Portion of Bailout" (online ed.). The Wall Street Journal, 1 September 2009.

Gilb, T. "Usability is good business". In T. Gilb, Principles of Software Engineering Management (20th ed., Vol. 1, p. 464). Ormerudsveien, Kolbotn, Norway: Addison-Wesley Longman (1988).

Internet Advertising Bureau. IAB Internet Advertising Revenue Report. New York, NY, USA: PricewaterhouseCoopers, New Media Group (2009).

Lomas, N. "Barclaycard and Orange unwrap contactless credit card" (7 January 2010). From Silicon.com: http://www.silicon.com/technology/mobile/2010/01/07/barclaycard-and-orange-unwrap-contactless-credit-card-39744115/

Lunden, I. "Murdoch Paper Blocks UK Aggregator Before Paywall Goes Up" (8 January 2010). From Paidcontent.org: http://www.creditcards.com/credit-card-news/credit-cards-of-the-distant-future-1273.php

Markowitz, J. "Illinois little guy takes on big stink at Goldman". *Pittsburgh Tribune-Review*, 10 January 2010.

Mbugua, J. "Big Banks in Plot to Kill M-Pesa". *Nairobi Star*, 23 December 2008.

McDonald, J. "What will credit cards look like in 25, 50 or 100 years?" (17 February, 2009) From CreditCards.com: http://www.creditcards.com/credit-card-news/credit-cards-of-the-distant-future-1273.php

Melouney, Carmel . "BlackBerry users becoming addicted to gadget". *Sunday Telegraph*, 11 May 2008. Retrieved from http://www.news.com.au/technology/story/0,25642,23676081-5014108,00.html

Parliament of New South Wales. Bank Branch Closures. Full Day Hansard Transcript (15 October, 1998). Sydney, NSW, Australia: Parliament of New South Wales.

Pisani, Joseph. C. "Workplace BlackBerry Use May Spur Lawsuits" (9 July 2008). Retrieved from CNBC: http://www.cnbc.com/id/25586129

Quinn, J. "Record bonus pot at JP Morgan". *Telegraph* (UK), 9 January 2010.

Reserve Bank of Australia. "Bank Fees in Australia". Melbourne, Australia: Reserve Bank of Australia (1999–2009).

Sang-Hun, C. "In South Korea, All of Life is Mobile". *International Herald Tribune* (Technology), 25 May, 2009, p. 1.

Sophos Security. "50% of employees blocked from accessing Facebook at work, Sophos survey reveals" (21 August 2007). From Sophos.com: http://www.sophos.com/pressoffice/news/articles/2007/08/block-facebook.html

Szuc, G. G. The Usability Kit. 397. Melbourne, Vic, Australia: Sitepoint (November 2006).

UK Payments Organization. "Statistical release – 30 November 2009". London, United Kingdom: APACS (2009).

User Strategy Ltd. Global Internet Strategy and Online Survey. Standard Chartered. Hong Kong: User Strategy, (2007)

User Strategy Ltd. (2003). Wealth Management Usability and Interaction Study. HSBC, Electronic Channel Development. Hong Kong: User Strategy Ltd., (2007).

UserCentric.com. "Early Adopter iPhone User Study Identifies Baseline Issues with iPhone Interface" (12 July, 2007). Retrieved March 2009 from UserCentric.com: http://www.usercentric.com/news/2007/07/12/early-adopter-iphone-user-study-identifies-baseline-issues-iphone-interface

World Bank Organization. Migration and Development Brief (11). Washington, DC, USA: World Bank (2009).

Wurster, P. E. *Blown to Bits: How the New Economics of Information Transforms Strategy.* Harvard Business School Press, (2000).

References and Case Studies concerning HSBC Asia Pacific and HSBC Hong Kong provided with the permission of HSBC Banking Group (HK) Ltd.

All references to Reserve Bank Australia Bulletins and data with the permission of Reserve Bank Australia.

iPhone™ and the App Store™ are trademarks of Apple, Inc. iPod touch® and iTunes® are trademarks of Apple, Inc., registered in the US and other countries.

Other References
electronic trading. In *Encyclopaedia Britannica.* Retrieved 16 July 2008, from Encyclopaedia Britannica Online: http://www.britannica.com/EBchecked/topic/183888/electronic-trading

Wikipedia